THE
NAMES
OF
GOD

THE NAMES OF GOD

GEORGE W. KNIGHT

BARBOUR
PUBLISHING

Published by Barbour Publishing, Inc., P.O. Box 719, Uhrichsville, Ohio 44683, www.barbourbooks.com

Our mission is to publish and distribute inspirational products offering exceptional value and biblical encouragement to the masses.

 Member of the
Evangelical Christian
Publishers Association

Printed in the United States of America.

PART 1 Names of God the Father

CONTENTS

PART 2 Names of God the Son

CONTENTS

CONTENTS

PART 3 Names of God the Holy Spirit

A Book of Names

A friend recently asked me what project I was working on. When I told him I was writing a book on the divine names in the Bible—those of the Father, the Son, and the Holy Spirit—he said, "That's great, but I wonder how you will ever fill up a book with just those three names."

Like my friend, many people are surprised to learn that there are many names assigned to God the Father, God the Son, and God the Holy Spirit in the Bible. I have covered only the major ones here in this book—and the number still comes to more than 250. The three Persons of the Trinity are so exalted in Their glory that it takes multiple names to describe who They are and the work They perform in the world.

Writing this book opened my eyes to a new and exciting way to study God's Word. I had studied the Bible in all the traditional ways—by focusing with intensity on each book, by exploring major subjects and themes, and by examining the lives of Bible personalities. But I had not spent as much time concentrating on the divine names contained in scripture. When I did, it changed some of my preconceived ideas, enriched my theological understanding, and gave me a new appreciation for the awesome God we serve. My prayer is that this book will guide you to the same experience.

I also discovered that many of the divine names in the Bible have been immortalized in the great old hymns of the church. Often when I was musing over a name, the words of a hymn that incorporated that name would come to mind. For example, Martin Luther's "A Mighty Fortress Is Our God" fits the prophet Jeremiah's description of God as our Fortress (see Jeremiah 16:19 and *Fortress* in part 1, Names of God the Father).This connection between names and hymns was so natural that I decided to use words from some of these hymns as sidebars alongside the corresponding names throughout the book. This added feature may bring back some fond memories of the great Christian hymns we used to sing more often than we do today.

The book falls naturally into three sections: names of God the Father, God the Son, and God the Holy Spirit. The names in each section are arranged alphabetically. At the back of the book, you will find a handy scripture index, arranged from Genesis through Revelation, that will help you find the Bible passages where these names occur.

In compiling the names for this book, I used the familiar King James Version of the Bible. But alternate names from four modern translations—the Holman Christian Standard Bible, the New American Standard Bible, the New International Version, and the New Revised Standard Version—are also included and cross-referenced to the KJV names.

You may be surprised at how these modern translations follow the KJV rendering in many places. But your understanding will be enriched by their different translations of other names. For example, the KJV's *Daysman* as a name for Jesus is rendered as *Umpire* by the NASB and the NRSV, and as *Someone to Arbitrate* by the NIV. Thus, the idea suggested by this name is that Jesus serves like a referee or impartial judge who speaks to God the Father on our behalf.

My thanks to Paul Muckley of Barbour Publishing for challenging me to write this book. The discipline it required made me a better person. It stretched my mental faculties further than I thought they could go. And it deepened my commitment to our Savior Jesus Christ, who was exalted by God the Father and "given. . .a name which is above every name" (Philippians 2:9).

George W. Knight
Nashville

PART 1

Names of God the Father

The Bible declares that God is a unique, one-of-a-kind being. No idea, object, or person is comparable to Him. His various names show that He is at work in the world and in the lives of Christians.

As the Creator, God brought the world into being. Before anything existed, He was. He is all-powerful, stronger than any force in the universe. He never changes, and He is present everywhere at one and the same time. Because there is no place where God is not, He knows everything about us. It is impossible for humans to hide their thoughts and actions from Him.

God has certain moral attributes that define His character. He is holy, righteous, loving, and wise. All these truths about Him are illustrated by the following seventy-three names assigned to Him in the Bible.

ABBA, FATHER

And he said, **Abba, Father**, all things are possible unto thee; take away this cup from me: nevertheless not what I will, but what thou wilt.
MARK 14:36

This is the name by which Jesus the Son addressed God the Father in His agonizing prayer in the Garden of Gethsemane. *Abba* is an Aramaic word of affection for "father," similar in meaning to *Papa* in English.

The Jews generally avoided such affectionate terms for God. They thought of Him as an exalted and larger-than-life being who demanded respect. He was to be spoken of in hushed reverence, rather than addressed as if He were a member of the family.

A child's love of their father can mirror Christians' love for God the Father.

But it was appropriate for Jesus to address the Father as "Abba." As God's Son, Jesus knew Him more intimately than anyone has ever known God. Jesus Himself declared, "As the Father knoweth me, even so know I the Father" (John 10:15).

Through Jesus' death on the cross, He made it possible for us to know God as a loving, forgiving Father. The apostle Paul declares, "Because ye are sons, God hath sent forth the Spirit of his Son into your hearts, crying, Abba, Father" (Galatians 4:6).

ALMIGHTY GOD

God had already promised Abraham that He would make his descendants a great nation and give them a land of their own (see Genesis 12:1–3; 13:15–17). But Abraham had no son through whom this promise could be fulfilled. The Lord, by identifying Himself as the Almighty God in this verse, declared to Abraham that He had the power to make this happen.

And when Abram was ninety years old and nine, the LORD appeared to Abram, and said unto him, I am the **Almighty God**; walk before me, and be thou perfect [NIV: blameless].
GENESIS 17:1

The Hebrew words behind this compound name also express the idea of plenty. Some interpreters suggest that they may be rendered as "the All-Sufficient One" or "the All-Bountiful One." God not only has the power to bless His people, but He will also do so abundantly. The apostle Paul put it like this: God is "able to do exceeding abundantly above all that we ask or think" (Ephesians 3:20).

Other titles of God that express the same idea as Almighty God are Lord Almighty (2 Corinthians 6:18), Lord God Almighty (Revelation 15:3), Lord God Omnipotent (Revelation 19:6), Mighty God (Jeremiah 32:18), Mighty One of Israel (Isaiah 1:24), Mighty One of Jacob (Isaiah 49:26), and Most Mighty (Psalm 45:3).

ANCIENT OF DAYS

This name of God is used only by the prophet Daniel (see Daniel 7:13, 22). He had a vision of four world empires that rose to great power and prominence, only to eventually fall and crumble into insignificance.

In contrast to the short shelf life of these world powers is One who has always existed and always will. Daniel's use of the imagery of old age to describe God suggests His eternalness. Unlike humans and worldly affairs, the Ancient of Days is not limited by time. Everything around us changes, but He remains the same. The only real security we have in this world is to place our trust in the Ancient of Days.

King of Old, a title used by the psalmist (see Psalm 74:12), expresses basically the same idea about God as Ancient of Days.

> I beheld till the thrones were cast down, and the **Ancient of days** did sit, whose garment was white as snow, and the hair of his head like the pure wool: his throne was like the fiery flame, and his wheels as burning fire.
> DANIEL 7:9
> [NRSV: **Ancient One**]

Praise for the Ancient of Days

In his hymn "Immortal, Invisible," Walter Chalmers Smith expresses exuberant praise for the Lord as the Ancient of Days.

Immortal, invisible, God only wise,
In light inaccessible hid from our eyes,
Most blessed, most glorious, the Ancient of Days,
Almighty, victorious, Thy great name we praise.

BEAUTIFUL CROWN. See *Crown of Glory/ Diadem of Beauty*.

BEAUTIFUL WREATH. See *Crown of Glory/ Diadem of Beauty*.

BUCKLER

As for God, his way is perfect: the word of the LORD is tried: he is a **buckler** to all those that trust in him.
PSALM 18:30
[NASB, NIV, NRSV: **shield**]

A buckler was a small shield that warriors wore on their arms. It was a defensive weapon that protected them from the thrusts of swords and spears in hand-to-hand combat. To the psalmist, the Lord was like a buckler because He shielded him from the harsh words and savage attacks of his enemies.

According to the writer of Proverbs, God is also "a buckler to them that walk uprightly" (Proverbs 2:7). God promises protection for His people if we trust in Him and follow His commands.

Assyrian bronze shield from the eighth century BC. It was easy for people in Bible times to understand God as a "buckler" or shield since they were used to seeing them worn by the armies of the day.

Wherefore we receiving a kingdom which cannot be moved, let us have grace, whereby we may serve God acceptably with reverence and godly fear: For our God is a **consuming fire**.
HEBREWS 12:28–29

CONSUMING FIRE

God is often associated with fire in the Bible. Sometimes fire symbolizes His guidance and protection. For example, He spoke to Moses from a burning bush (see Exodus 3:2). He guided the Israelites through the wilderness at night by a pillar of fire (see Exodus 13:21).

But this verse from the book of Hebrews shows that fire is also a symbol of God's wrath. To those who are disrespectful or disobedient, He is a searing flame of judgment. Every person must decide for himself whether the Lord will be a guiding light or a consuming fire in his life.

CREATOR

The prophet Isaiah was amazed that the people of Judah had rejected the one true God and were worshipping false gods instead. The Creator God had brought the universe into being by the power of His word (Hebrews 11:3). These pagan idols were weak and puny by comparison.

From the first chapter of the Bible, we learn several important truths about God's creation of the world and its inhabitants. (1) He created the world from nothing; He is the ultimate cause of all that exists. (2) The Creation was accomplished in orderly fashion, in six successive days. This means that God has placed order and design into the universe. (3) Man is the crown of God's creation. (4) The Lord has given us the responsibility to take care of His world.

As Isaiah reminded the people of his nation, only the one-and-only Creator God is worthy of our loyalty and worship.

> Hast thou not known? hast thou not heard, that. . . the **Creator** of the ends of the earth fainteth not, neither is weary? there is no searching of his understanding [NIV: his understanding no one can fathom].
> ISAIAH 40:28

The expanse of all creation reveals the power of our Creator.

> I am the LORD,
> your Holy One,
> the **creator of
> Israel**, your King.
> ISAIAH 43:15
> [NIV: **Israel's
> Creator**]

CREATOR OF ISRAEL

Through the prophet Isaiah, the Lord made it clear why the nation of Israel existed. They had been created by God Himself to serve as His agents of redemption to the rest of the world. This had been revealed centuries before Isaiah's time when the Lord told Abraham, "I will make of thee a great nation. . .and in thee shall all families of the earth be blessed" (Genesis 12:2–3).

But over and over again, the Israelites forgot the reason for their existence. They tended to think they deserved God's special blessing because of their cultural traditions and moral superiority. They had to be reminded constantly of the purpose of the One who was the Creator of Israel.

God, through His Son Jesus Christ, is still in the business of creating a special kingdom of people for Himself. It's known as the church. But our purpose is not to celebrate our favored status as believers. We should be about the task of helping others come to know Jesus as Lord and Savior.

Other "Israel" Names of the Creator of Israel

- God of Israel (Matthew 15:31)
- Holy One of Israel (Psalm 78:41)
- Hope of Israel (Jeremiah 14:7–8)
- Judge of Israel (Micah 5:1)
- Light of Israel (Isaiah 10:17)
- Lord God of Israel (1 Kings 8:23)
- Redeemer of Israel (Isaiah 49:7)
- Rock of Israel (2 Samuel 23:3)
- Stone of Israel (Genesis 49:24)
- Strength of Israel (1 Samuel 15:29)

CROWN OF GLORY/DIADEM OF BEAUTY

Isaiah 28 contains a prediction that Israel's sin will cause it to be overrun by an enemy nation. But God has a special "residue," or remnant, of people who will avoid His judgment because of their faithfulness to Him. God will be a Crown of Glory to these obedient ones. They will share in His character—His holiness, righteousness, and justice.

God will also reward this obedient remnant by giving

them a *Diadem of Beauty*. A diadem was a band around the head of a king that symbolized his royal authority. We as Christians wear a diadem of sorts—our salvation. This shows to the world that we belong to the Lord and that He has commissioned us to serve as His witnesses in the world.

This copper crown, over 5,000 years old, was discovered near the Dead Sea. It represented religious or royal authority in its day.

In that day shall the LORD of hosts be for a **crown of glory**, and for a **diadem of beauty**, unto the residue [NASB, NIV: remnant] of his people.
ISAIAH 28:5
[NASB: **beautiful crown/glorious diadem**; NIV: **glorious crown/ beautiful wreath**; NRSV: **garland of glory/diadem of beauty**]

DELIVERER

Deliverer is a name for God that was used often by David, as he does in this psalm. Perhaps it was one of his favorite divine names (see Psalms 18:2; 40:17; 2 Samuel 22:2) because he had experienced God as Deliverer many times throughout his life.

For example, David escaped several attempts by King Saul to kill him (see 1 Samuel 18:10–11; 19:11–12; 23:24–28). Before facing Goliath, the Philistine giant, this shepherd boy who later became the king of Israel declared, "The LORD that delivered me out of the paw of the lion, and out of the paw of the bear, he will deliver me out of the hand of this

But I am poor and needy: make haste unto me [NIV: come quickly to me], O God: thou art my help and my **deliverer**; O LORD, make no tarrying [NIV: do not delay].
PSALM 70:5

Philistine" (1 Samuel 17:37). David prevailed over the giant because of his faith in the divine Deliverer.

God may not choose to deliver us from every danger in this life. But He has provided ultimate deliverance from sin and death through the death of His Son for all who believe.

DIADEM OF BEAUTY. See *Crown of Glory/ Diadem of Beauty.*

DWELLING PLACE

This psalm may be the oldest in the entire book of Psalms, because it is attributed to Moses (see title above this psalm), who led the Israelites during their years of wandering in the wilderness. This was a time, before they settled in Canaan, when they did not have permanent houses. They lived in tents, which they moved from place to place (see Numbers 9:17; Joshua 3:14).

In spite of their spartan living arrangements, they still thought of God as their ultimate Dwelling Place. His presence followed them wherever they moved, and His faithfulness continued from one generation to the next.

God is still a Dwelling Place for His people. Whether we live in a mobile home or a mansion, we find in Him all the joys and comforts of home.

Lord, thou hast been our **dwelling place** in [NIV: throughout] all generations.
PSALM 90:1

Modern-day Bedouins' nomadic lifestyle recalls the experience of the Israelites in the wilderness.

EL-ROI. See *God Who Sees.*

ETERNAL GOD. See *Everlasting God.*

EVERLASTING GOD

Abraham had moved from place to place for several years in the land of Canaan, the territory that God had promised to his descendants (see Genesis 12:1–5). Finally, he decided to make a site known as Beersheba the center of the territory where he would graze his flocks and herds. There he dug a well and planted a grove of trees to mark the site as his settling-down place.

At Beersheba, it was appropriate that Abraham call on

> And Abraham planted a grove in Beersheba, and called there on the name of the LORD, the **everlasting God**.
>
> GENESIS 21:33
> [NIV: **Eternal God**]

A grove of tamarisk trees in modern-day Beersheba—perhaps like Abraham saw when settling this area of the Negev.

the name of the Everlasting God, the One without beginning and end, who would never cease to be. He would guide Abraham into the future and fulfill His promise that Abraham's offspring would eventually populate this entire region.

God kept His promise, but it took a while. It was more than five centuries after Abraham's time before the Israelites conquered this land and made it their own. We should remember that the Everlasting God does not watch the clock like we humans do.

EVERLASTING KING. See *King Eternal, Immortal, Invisible.*

FATHER

> But now, O LORD, thou art our **father**; we are the clay, and thou our potter; and we all are the work of thy hand.
> ISAIAH 64:8

In this verse, the prophet Isaiah declares that God has a role in shaping His people, just as earthly fathers participate in the creative process of bringing children into the world.

This is one of the few places in the Old Testament where God is referred to as *Father* (see also Deuteronomy 32:6; Psalm 89:26; Isaiah 63:16; Malachi 2:10). By contrast, *Father* as a name for God occurs often in the New Testament, particularly on the lips of Jesus (e.g., Matthew 26:39; Luke 23:34; John 17:1).

People of Old Testament times generally did not think of God in fatherly terms. To them, He was an all-powerful being who stood above and beyond the relationships and events of everyday life. It took Jesus to show us that God is a loving Father: "For God so loved the world, that he gave his only begotten Son, that whosoever believeth in him should not perish, but have everlasting life" (John 3:16).

FATHER OF COMPASSION. See *Father of Mercies*.

FATHER OF GLORY

> That the God of our Lord Jesus Christ, the **Father of glory**, may give unto you the spirit of wisdom and revelation in the knowledge of him.
> EPHESIANS 1:17

Ephesians 1 is the only place in the Bible where God is called the Father of Glory. The apostle Paul used this name in his assurance to the believers at Ephesus that he was praying to the Father on their behalf.

The word *glory* appears many times throughout the Bible, usually in reference to God's splendor, moral beauty, and perfection. At times, His glory was revealed visibly, as

Beautiful sunsets such as this one over the mountains of Edom reveal the splendor of God's creation.

in the tabernacle and temple after they were built (see Exodus 40:34; 1 Kings 8:11). The prophet Isaiah declares of the Lord, "The whole earth is full of his glory" (Isaiah 6:3). Or, to put it another way, the beauty and majesty of the physical world gives evidence of God's presence in His creation.

God the Father is also referred to in the Old Testament as the Crown of Glory (see Isaiah 28:5). In his long speech before his persecutors, Stephen in New Testament times also referred to Him as the God of Glory (see Acts 7:2).

Other Manifestations of God's Glory

- To Moses, on Mount Sinai, when God revealed His plan for the tabernacle (Exodus 24:16–17)
- To the world at the coming of the Messiah (Isaiah 40:4–5; 60:1)
- To the prophet Ezekiel, as he ministered among Jewish exiles in Babylon (Ezekiel 3:22–23)
- To the shepherds at the announcement of the birth of Jesus (Luke 2:9)

FATHER OF LIGHTS

With this name of God, James probably had in mind the creation account in the book of Genesis. On the fourth day, God created the sun, moon, and stars and "set them in the firmament of the heaven to give light upon the earth" (Genesis 1:17).

The people of many ancient cultures thought of the heavenly bodies as gods. But James declared that they were created things, brought into being by the one true God of the universe. Only the Father of Lights is worthy of worship.

This God who created the light-giving bodies of the heavens is also dependable and trustworthy. As the NIV translates it, God "does not change like shifting shadows." His presence is an unwavering light that guides His people throughout this life and beyond.

> Every good gift and every perfect gift is from above, and cometh down from the **Father of lights**, with whom is no variableness, neither shadow of turning [NIV: who does not change like shifting shadows].
> JAMES 1:17
> [NIV: **Father of the heavenly lights**]

FATHER OF MERCIES

Father of Mercies is another of the apostle Paul's names for God that appears in only one verse in the Bible (see also Father of Glory). In this case, he used *Father of Mercies* in his prayer for the believers in the church he founded at Corinth.

God is the Father of Mercies because He has mercy on

His people. If He withheld His mercy and grace, and gave us exactly what we deserved, we would be destitute and lost, hopelessly trapped by our sin and rebellion. But His love and patience won't let us go. He keeps calling us back into His presence by extending His mercy and forgiveness.

Because God is the originator—or Father—of Mercies, He expects His people to show this attribute of His character to others. Jesus declared, "Be ye therefore merciful, as your Father also is merciful" (Luke 6:36).

> Blessed be God, even the Father of our Lord Jesus Christ, the **Father of mercies**, and the God of all comfort.
> 2 CORINTHIANS 1:3
> [NIV: **Father of compassion**]

FATHER OF OUR LORD JESUS CHRIST

This name of God used by the apostle Paul draws attention to the miraculous birth of Jesus the Son. Jesus did not have a human father, but was miraculously conceived in the womb of Mary by God the Father, acting through the Holy Spirit (see Luke 1:34–35).

> We give thanks to God and the **Father of our Lord Jesus Christ**, praying always for you.
> COLOSSIANS 1:3

Jesus was sent by God to fulfill the Father's work of redemption in the world. When He was only twelve years old, Jesus stated that this was His divine mission (see Luke 2:48–49). His declaration from the cross, "It is finished" (John 19:30), shows that He accomplished the purpose for which He was sent—our salvation.

God Shows He Is Pleased with His Son

- "And there came a voice from heaven, saying, Thou art my beloved Son, in whom I am well pleased" (Mark 1:11).
- "And the Holy Ghost descended in a bodily shape like a dove upon him, and a voice came from heaven, which said, Thou art my beloved Son; in thee I am well pleased" (Luke 3:22).
- "For it pleased the Father that in him should all fulness dwell" (Colossians 1:19).
- "For he received from God the Father honour and glory, when there came such a voice to him from the excellent glory, This is my beloved Son, in whom I am well pleased" (2 Peter 1:17).

FATHER OF OUR SPIRITS. See *Father of Spirits.*

FATHER OF SPIRITS

This is one of those places in the Bible where the addition of one word makes all the difference in its meaning. Rather than "Father of spirits," the NIV renders this name of God as

"Father of Our Spirits." This rendering makes it clear that the writer of Hebrews was contrasting physical fathers ("fathers of our flesh") with God as our Father in a spiritual sense.

Earthly fathers discipline their children and teach them right from wrong and respect for others. God, our spiritual Father, teaches us to obey Him as the ultimate authority, to follow His commands, and to present our lives as living sacrifices for His honor and glory. The next verse in the NIV puts it like this: "Our fathers disciplined us for a little while as they thought best; but God disciplines us for our good, that we may share in his holiness" (Hebrews 12:10 NIV).

> We have had fathers of our flesh [NIV: human fathers] which corrected us, and we gave them reverence [NIV: respected them]: shall we not much rather be in subjection unto [NIV: submit to] the **Father of spirits**, and live?
> HEBREWS 12:9
> [NIV: **Father of our spirits**]

FATHER OF HEAVENLY LIGHTS. See *Father of Lights.*

FIRE. See *Consuming Fire; Wall of Fire.*

FORTRESS

A fortress was any heavily guarded or fortified place that provided protection from enemy attacks. In Bible times, a defensive wall around a city, with its reinforced towers and gates, was considered the ultimate fortress.

In this verse, Jeremiah portrays the Lord as his Fortress. The prophet's unpopular message that Judah would fall to its enemies subjected him to ridicule, imprisonment, and

> O LORD, my strength and my **fortress**, and my refuge in the day of affliction [NIV: distress].
> JEREMIAH 16:19
> [NASB, NRSV: **stronghold**]

The fortress ruins of Arad in southern Israel provide us with a visual image of what the prophet might have thought of when he wrote that the Lord was his fortress (Jeremiah 16:19).

charges of treason. At the beginning of Jeremiah's ministry, God promised that He would make him "a defenced city, and an iron pillar, and brasen walls against the whole land" (Jeremiah 1:18). The Lord had made good on His promise.

Like Jeremiah, all of us need a fortress at times. This advice from Peter can help us hang in there when troubles seem to fall from the sky like the spring rain: "Cast all your anxiety on him because he cares for you" (1 Peter 5:7 NIV).

Martin Luther's Fortress

The hymn "A Mighty Fortress Is Our God" was written by Martin Luther during the turbulent years of the Protestant Reformation in the 1500s. His faith in God in spite of the threats against his life have inspired generations of Christians.

> A mighty fortress is our God,
> A bulwark never failing;
> Our helper He, amid the flood
> Of mortal ills prevailing.
> Let goods and kindred go,
> This mortal life also;
> The body they may kill:
> God's truth abideth still,
> His kingdom is forever.

For my people have committed two evils; they have forsaken me the **fountain of living waters**, and hewed them out cisterns [NIV: dug their own cisterns], broken cisterns, that can hold no water.
JEREMIAH 2:13
[NIV: **spring of living water**]

FOUNTAIN OF LIVING WATERS

This name of God appears in Jeremiah's prophecy in connection with the Lord's condemnation of the people of Judah for their idolatry (see also Jeremiah 17:13). God found it hard to believe that they had rejected the waters of a flowing spring (that is, worship of the one true God) and instead chose to drink stagnant water from a broken cistern (by worshipping the untrustworthy and powerless gods of surrounding pagan nations).

This situation is not unique to Jeremiah's time. When we allow anything besides God to take first place in our lives, it's like drinking contaminated water from a muddy pond. God wants only the best for us. He gives water in abundance from "the fountain of the water of life" to all who will come and drink (Revelation 21:6).

The flowing waters at En Gedi near the Dead Sea. The Lord provides the waters of life even in wilderness areas.

GARLAND OF GLORY. See *Crown of Glory/Diadem of Beauty.*

GLORIOUS CROWN. See *Crown of Glory/Diadem of Beauty.*

GLORIOUS DIADEM. See *Crown of Glory/Diadem of Beauty.*

GOD MOST HIGH. See *Most High God.*

GOD MY SAVIOUR. See *God of My Salvation.*

GOD OF ABRAHAM, ISAAC, AND JACOB

God used this name for Himself when He called Moses to lead the Israelites out of slavery in Egypt. The Lord assured Moses that He had promised the land of Canaan to Abraham and his descendants many years before. He had not changed; He was the same God who would finally lead the Israelites to

The LORD God of your fathers, the **God of Abraham,** the God of **Isaac,** and the God of **Jacob,** hath sent me unto you: this is my name for ever, and this is my memorial unto all generations.
EXODUS 3:15

take this land and make it their own.

This promise had originally been made to Abraham, then renewed with Abraham's son Isaac, and then renewed again with Isaac's son Jacob. In Moses' time, this promise had been all but forgotten. The Israelites had been in Egypt for more than four hundred years, suffering as slaves for part of that time (see Exodus 12:40).

The message of this divine name is that God keeps His promises. Their fulfillment may take a while, but God will make good on what He says He will do for His people.

GOD OF ALL COMFORT

The context of this verse makes it clear that when the apostle Paul spoke of the Lord as the God of All Comfort, he was thinking of the sufferings that believers endure. We as Christians are often ridiculed by the world for our beliefs and the stands we take. But our persecution should not lead us to despair. God's comforting presence will enable us to remain joyful and optimistic in spite of our hurt (see James 1:2).

Because we know and feel God's comfort, we are expected to channel this comfort to others. Paul declares in the next verse of this passage that we should "comfort them which are in any trouble, by the comfort wherewith we ourselves are comforted of God" (2 Corinthians 1:4).

> Blessed be God, even the Father of our Lord Jesus Christ, the Father of mercies, and the **God of all comfort**.
> 2 CORINTHIANS 1:3
> [NRSV: **God of all consolation**]

GOD OF ALL CONSOLATION. See *God of All Comfort.*

GOD OF GLORY. See *Father of Glory.*

GOD OF GODS

King Nebuchadnezzar of Babylon had a disturbing dream about a huge statue. None of his pagan priests or magicians could interpret the dream. But the Hebrew prophet Daniel told him what the dream meant, after declaring that it would be revealed to him by the one true God.

The pagan king was so impressed by this interpretation of his dream that he declared Daniel's God to be the God of gods—or the God above all the other deities in the kingdom of Babylon. This was a shocking admission, because the Babylonians had a god for every need and purpose—war, fertility, science, literature, etc. This type of worship was typical

> The king answered unto Daniel, and said, Of a truth [NIV: Surely] it is, that your God is a **God of gods**, and a Lord of kings, and a revealer of secrets [NIV: mysteries], seeing thou couldest reveal this secret [NIV: mystery].
> DANIEL 2:47

of all the pagan nations during Bible times.

As Christians, we know that God is capable of mighty acts. But sometimes He amazes even unbelievers with His awesome deeds.

GOD OF HEAVEN

This verse describes Nehemiah's reaction when he heard disturbing news about the Jewish exiles who had returned to their homeland. The Persian king had allowed the people to return to rebuild the city of Jerusalem. But the work was at a standstill, and the Jews were being persecuted by their enemies.

Nehemiah's name for God in this verse—God of Heaven—appears several times in his book (see Nehemiah 1:5; 2:4, 20) as well as in the book of Ezra (see Ezra 5:12; 6:9–10; 7:21, 23). These two books describe the bleak conditions of God's people after the Exile. They had lived for almost seventy years as captives of the pagan nations of Babylon and Persia. They had to start life all over again when they were finally allowed to return to their homeland.

Perhaps the Israelites had a hard time seeing God at work in their midst during these turbulent times. But Ezra and Nehemiah assured them that God was still in His heaven and had not forsaken His people.

When you feel lonely and forgotten, try addressing a prayer to the God of Heaven—the One who has an unobstructed view of everything that is happening on the earth. This should assure you that He is watching over you.

> And it came to pass, when I heard these words, that I sat down and wept, and mourned certain days, and fasted, and prayed before the **God of heaven**.
> NEHEMIAH 1:4

This historical record known as the Cyrus cylinder describes the decree of the Persian king, Cyrus (539 BC), who granted the Jewish exiles permission to return to their homeland.

GOD OF ISRAEL. See *Creator of Israel.*

GOD OF JACOB. See *Mighty One of Jacob.*

GOD OF MY SALVATION

This passage from the little-known prophet Habakkuk is one of the most beautiful in the Bible. It is filled with agricultural imagery from the prophet's time, including crop failures and the loss of livestock. But Habakkuk's faith allowed him to see beyond the troubles of the moment to the deeper reality that the God of Salvation was in charge. He would not let him down.

Rephrased in modern terms, Habakkuk's sentiments might read something like this: "Although the grocery money is gone, energy prices are going through the ceiling, my mortgage payment just jumped by four hundred dollars a month, and I don't know where the next meal is coming from, I will rejoice in the Lord and continue to trust in the God of My Salvation."

> Although the fig tree shall not blossom, neither shall fruit be in the vines; the labour of the olive shall fail, and the fields shall yield no meat; the flock shall be cut off from the fold, and there shall be no herd in the stalls: Yet I will rejoice in the Lord, I will joy in the **God of my salvation**.
> HABAKKUK 3:17–18
> [NIV: **God my Savior**]

Our Faithful God

God's faithfulness to His people is celebrated in the hymn "Great Is Thy Faithfulness," written by Thomas O. Chisholm.

Great is Thy faithfulness, O God my Father;
There is no shadow of turning with thee;
Thou changest not, Thy compassions, they fail not;
As thou hast been, Thou forever wilt be.
Great is Thy faithfulness! Great is Thy faithfulness!
Morning by morning new mercies I see;
All I have needed Thy hand hath provided;
Great is Thy faithfulness, Lord, unto me!

GOD OF PEACE

The author of the epistle to the Hebrews brought his book to a close with a request for the blessings of the God of Peace to rest upon His people. This is one of the most beautiful benedictions in the Bible.

Some people think of peace as the absence of conflict. But peace according to the New Testament is the inner tranquillity of those who have placed their trust in Jesus Christ and have been reconciled to God because their sins have been forgiven.

The Lord is the God of Peace because He sent His own Son to make it possible for us to experience this sense of well-being. This is how the apostle Paul expresses it: "Therefore being justified by faith, we have peace with God through our Lord Jesus Christ" (Romans 5:1).

GOD OF THE WHOLE EARTH

This name of God from the prophet Isaiah emphasizes His unlimited jurisdiction. There is no place on earth where His authority is limited. This idea is just the opposite of the view of most pagan nations of Bible times. They believed their gods were local or regional in scope. These deities existed to serve their needs and protect them from their enemies, so their authority as gods did not extend beyond national borders.

This is why Naaman, a Syrian military commander, wanted to carry dirt from Israel back to his country after he was healed by the prophet Elisha in Israelite territory (see 2 Kings 5:17). He thought this miracle-working God was a regional god whose power he could transfer to his own people.

The Lord's presence doesn't have to be carried back and forth from one country to another. He already exists in every place—the supreme God over all the world. The psalmist declares, "The earth is the LORD's, and the fulness thereof; the world, and they that dwell therein" (Psalm 24:1).

A "household" idol from modern-day Iraq, dating back to at least 1600 BC.

Now the **God of peace**, that brought again from the dead our Lord Jesus. . . through the blood of the everlasting covenant, make you perfect in every good work [NIV: equip you with everything good] to do his will, working in you that which is wellpleasing in his sight, through Jesus Christ; to whom be glory for ever and ever. Amen.
HEBREWS 13:20–21

For thy Maker is thine husband; the LORD of hosts is his name; and thy Redeemer the Holy One of Israel; The **God of the whole earth** shall he be called.
ISAIAH 54:5

Other Earth-Related Names of God the Father
- Judge of All the Earth (Genesis 18:25)
- King over All the Earth (Psalm 47:2)
- Lord of All the Earth (Joshua 3:13)
- Lord of the Whole Earth (Micah 4:13)
- Most High over All the Earth (Psalm 83:18)
- Possessor of Heaven and Earth (Genesis 14:19)

GOD THE FATHER. See *Abba, Father; Father*.

GOD WHO SEES

And she called the name of the LORD that spake unto her, **Thou God seest me**: for she said, Have I also here looked after him [NIV: I have now seen the One] that seeth me?
GENESIS 16:13
[NRSV: **El-roi**]

Sarah's servant, Hagar, called God by this name when the angel of the Lord appeared to her in the wilderness. After conceiving a child by Abraham, she had been driven away by Sarah, Abraham's wife. The Lord assured Hagar that He was aware of her plight, and He would bless her and others through the life of her unborn child.

After Hagar gave birth to a son, she named him Ishmael, meaning "God hears." Hagar's experience shows us that the Lord is not a distant and detached God who refuses to get involved in our lives. He sees our needs, hears our prayers, and comes to our aid in our times of trouble.

Hagar encountered the Lord somewhere in the wilderness of Paran, pictured here. Despite such a vast expanse, the Lord sees us wherever we are.

GOVERNOR

The word *governor* appears often in the Bible as a designation for a ruler over a nation or a section of a nation. For example, Joseph was made a governor in Egypt (see Genesis 42:6), and Nehemiah held a similar position for a time in the nation of Judah (see Nehemiah 12:26).

But Psalm 22 is the only place in the Old Testament where this title is applied to God. Earthly rulers sometimes abuse their authority, but the Lord rules over the nations and

His people with righteousness and justice (see Nehemiah 9:32–33; Exodus 9:27).

In the New Testament, Jesus is also described as a Governor (Matthew 2:6). He is the perfect ruler who governs the spiritual kingdom to which all believers belong—the church.

GUIDE EVEN TO THE END. See *Guide unto Death.*

GUIDE FOREVER. See *Guide unto Death.*

GUIDE UNTO DEATH

The unknown author of this psalm made the same declaration that David did when he wrote the Twenty-third Psalm. God will abide with us and continue to lead us, even through the experience of death itself. As David expresses it, "Yea, though I walk through the valley of the shadow of death, I will fear no evil: for thou art with me" (Psalm 23:4).

The prophet Jeremiah spoke of God as "the guide of my youth" (Jeremiah 3:4). It is comforting to know that whether our life is just beginning or coming to an end, we can trust God as our never-failing Guide.

HIDING PLACE

This name of God appears in a psalm that is attributed to David. During his early years, David had to flee for his life because the jealous King Saul was trying to kill him. Once, he hid in a cave; he later wrote about this experience in one of his psalms (see 1 Samuel 22:1; Psalm 142).

> For the kingdom is the LORD's: and he is the **governor** among the nations.
> PSALM 22:28

> For this God is our God for ever and ever: he will be our **guide** even **unto death**.
> PSALM 48:14
> [NRSV: **guide forever**; NIV: **guide even to the end**]

> Thou art my **hiding place**; thou shalt preserve [NIV: protect] me from trouble; thou shalt compass me about [NIV: surround me] with songs of deliverance.
> PSALM 32:7

David found hiding places from King Saul in the caves near En Gedi. David understood that while the terrain provided a physical hiding place, the Lord was the One who really kept him hidden from danger.

The problem with a physical hiding place is that it can't last forever. David eventually had to come out of his cave for food and water. But he found the Lord to be his ultimate Hiding Place. There's no safer place to be than under the protective hand of a loving, benevolent God.

HIGH TOWER. See *Strong Tower*.

HOLY ONE

I am the LORD, your **Holy One**, the creator of Israel, your King.
ISAIAH 43:15

This name of God, spoken by the Lord Himself, shows one of His most distinctive attributes—His holiness. The Hebrew word behind "holy" expresses the idea of separation. Thus God is separated from or exalted above all earthly things. We as humans are limited in our abilities and are subject to sin and death. But God is totally different and separate in His nature. He is perfect in His moral excellence.

The holiness of God is one of the major themes of the prophet Isaiah. At the beginning of his ministry, Isaiah had a vision of God in the temple. He was sitting on His throne, and winged seraphim (angelic messengers) were singing His praises: "Holy, holy, holy, is the LORD of hosts: the whole earth is full of his glory" (Isaiah 6:3).

This vision of the Holy One made Isaiah aware of his sin and unworthiness. But God seared his lips with a hot coal carried by one of the seraphim. This symbolized God's purging of the prophet's sin (see Isaiah 6:5). God's holiness and our sin are just as pronounced as they were in Isaiah's time; His forgiveness is still our only hope.

In addition to calling God the Holy One, Isaiah also refers to Him several times as the Holy One of Israel (see Isaiah 1:4; 12:6; 60:9) and the Holy One of Jacob (see Isaiah 29:23).

Holy to the Third Degree

The repetition of the word holy in Isaiah 6:3 is reflected in the hymn "Holy, Holy, Holy," by Reginald Heber. The threefold repetition emphasizes this attribute of God's character.

Holy, holy, holy! tho' the darkness hide Thee,
Tho' the eye of sinful man Thy glory may not see;
Only Thou art holy; there is none beside Thee;
Perfect in power, in love, and purity.

HOLY ONE OF ISRAEL. See *Creator of Israel*; *Holy One*.

HOLY ONE OF JACOB. See *Holy One*; *Mighty One of Jacob*.

HOPE OF ISRAEL. See *Creator of Israel*.

HORN OF MY SALVATION

David wrote this psalm to express his praise to God for saving him from "all his enemies, and from the hand of Saul" (Psalm 18 NIV). In David's time, the horn of an animal was a symbol of strength. To lift one's horn in arrogance like an ox or a goat was to show pride and power (see Psalm 75:4–5). Thus, God had been a Horn of Salvation on David's behalf by delivering him from those who were trying to kill him.

This imagery from the Old Testament was picked up in the New Testament and applied to Jesus in a spiritual sense. Zacharias, the father of John the Baptist, declared that God, through His Son, had "raised up an horn of salvation for us in the house of his servant David" (Luke 1:69).

The LORD is my rock, and my fortress, and my deliverer; my God, my strength, in whom I will trust; my buckler, and the **horn of my salvation**, and my high tower.
PSALM 18:2

The majestic horns of the Ibex could have been an inspiration to David as he wrote Psalm 18.

HUSBAND

This name of God appears in connection with the prophet Jeremiah's description of the new covenant that God will make with His people. He had led them out of Egypt and through the wilderness like a loving husband cares for his family. But He would provide even more abundantly for His own by sending the Messiah, who would save them from their sins.

The role of a husband involves more than providing for the physical needs of his family. He should also be an encourager, a listener, an emotional support, and a protector for his wife and children. God as a loving Husband provides all of these things in abundance for His people.

Behold, the days come, saith the LORD, that I will make a new covenant with the house of Israel, and with the house of Judah: Not according to the covenant that I made with their fathers in the day that I took them by the hand to bring them out of the land of Egypt; which my covenant they brake [NIV: broke], although I was an **husband** unto them, saith the LORD.
JEREMIAH 31:31–32

I AM THAT I AM

And God said unto Moses, **I AM THAT I AM**: and he said, Thus shalt thou say unto the children of Israel [NIV: Israelites], I AM hath sent me unto you.
EXODUS 3:14
[NASB, NIV, NRSV: **I AM WHO I AM**]

When God appeared to Moses in a burning bush, Moses wanted to know who was sending him back to Egypt to lead the Israelites out of slavery. He may have been puzzled by the Lord's reply that I Am That I Am was behind this plan.

This name for God is a form of the verb "to be" in the Hebrew language. It expresses His self-existence and the unchangeableness of His character. He transcends the past, the present, and the future. We might express the meaning of this name like this: He has always been, He is, and He will always be.

This is the only place in the Bible where this name appears. But *Jehovah* or *Yahweh*, generally rendered as *Lord*, is a closely related name that also comes from the Hebrew form of "to be." This name appears hundreds of times throughout the Old Testament. In most translations of the Bible, it appears with a large capital *L* and smaller capital letters like this: LORD.

The great I Am never changes; he will never leave us or forsake us. The hymn writer Henry F. Lyte expressed this truth in the form of a prayer:

Change and decay in all around I see:
O Thou who changest not, abide with me!

Jebel Caterina—one of many mountains in the Sinai region thought to be associated with Mount Horeb. The Lord revealed Himself to Moses as "I AM" at Mount Horeb in this region of the Sinai Mountains.

I AM WHO I AM. See *I Am That I Am.*

ISRAEL'S CREATOR. See *Creator of Israel.*

JAH

Jah (pronounced *Yah*) is a shortened form of the Hebrew title *Jehovah* (see below), which is rendered as "Lord" in most English translations of the Bible. This is the only place where *Jah* appears in the King James Version of the Bible.

The word also appears as part of several compound biblical names. For example, the name Abijah means "whose father is Jehovah." The word *alleluiah* [NIV: *hallelujah*] means "praise the Lord" (see Revelation 19:1).

> Sing unto God, sing praises to his name: extol him that rideth upon the heavens [NIV: rides on the clouds] by his name **JAH**, and rejoice before him.
> PSALM 68:4
> [NASB, NIV, NRSV: **the LORD**]

JEHOVAH

With these words, the Lord reassured Moses that He would stand with him and give him the strength and power to lead the Israelites out of Egyptian slavery. He had already given Moses this promise at the burning bush (see Exodus 3:2, 12), but Moses needed encouragement after Pharaoh rejected his first request to release the Israelites.

God declared to Moses that He was prepared to perform miracles for His people that they had never seen before. As Jehovah, He was the infinite and self-existent God who caused everything to happen and to whom all things must eventually be traced. He would not fail in His determination to bring freedom to His people.

When God makes a promise, it's as good as done.

See also *I Am That I Am.*

> And I appeared unto Abraham, unto Isaac, and unto Jacob, by the name of God Almighty, but by my name **JEHOVAH** was I not known to them.
> EXODUS 6:3
> [NASB, NIV, NRSV: **the LORD**]

Guidance from Jehovah

In his hymn "Guide Me, O Thou Great Jehovah," Peter Williams asked God to provide for him, just as He had cared for the Israelites in the wilderness.

Guide me, O Thou great Jehovah,
Pilgrim through this barren land;
I am weak, but Thou art mighty;
Hold me with Thy powerful hand.

JEHOVAH-JIREH

And Abraham called
the name of that place
Jehovah-jireh:
as it is said to this
day, In the mount
[NIV: mountain] of the
LORD it shall be seen.
GENESIS 22:14
[NASB, NIV, NRSV: **The
LORD Will Provide**]

Abraham called God by this name and assigned it to the site where God had told him to sacrifice his son, Isaac, as a burnt offering to the Lord. This was God's way of testing Abraham's faith and obedience.

When Abraham raised a knife to take Isaac's life, God stopped him. Then Abraham noticed a ram that had been trapped in a nearby thicket. He offered this ram as a sacrifice instead of Isaac. It was clear to him that God had provided the ram for this purpose—thus the name The Lord Will Provide, as rendered by modern translations.

God still delights in providing for His people. Whatever our needs, He will meet them through His love and grace.

Byzantine relief from Asia Minor depicting Abraham's willingness to sacrifice his son Isaac. This artistic representation helped people remember how the Lord provided a substitute ram for Abraham.

JEHOVAH-NISSI

And Moses built
an altar, and called
the name of it
Jehovah-nissi.
EXODUS 17:15
[NASB, NIV, NRSV: **The
LORD is my Banner**]

Moses gave this name to an altar that he built in the wilderness near Rephidim. The altar memorialized an Israelite victory over the Amalekites because of God's miraculous intervention on their behalf. Most modern translations render these two Hebrew words as The LORD Is My Banner.

In Bible times, armies fought under a banner or battle flag that identified their tribe or nation. *Jehovah-nissi* was Moses' way of saying that the Israelites in the wilderness did not need such a flag. The Lord was the banner under which they fought, and He had given the victory.

In a messianic passage in the book of Isaiah, the prophet looks forward to the coming of the Messiah, whom he describes as an *Ensign*, or battle flag (see Isaiah 11:10).

JEHOVAH-SHALOM

God gave Gideon the task of delivering His people from Midianite raiders who were destroying their crops and stealing their livestock. He assured Gideon of His presence and guidance by burning up a sacrificial offering that Gideon had placed on an altar.

This display frightened Gideon. But God showed him that His intentions were peaceful and that Gideon had nothing to fear. With this assurance, Gideon gave God a special name—translated as The Lord Is Peace by modern translations—and also applied this name to the altar he had built.

"Peace to you and your house" was a common greeting of Bible times, just as we greet people today with "Good morning" or "How are you?" With this divine name, Gideon expressed his confidence that God intended to bless him and to strengthen him for the task to which he had been called.

God extends this same promise to His people today. The psalmist declares, "The Lord will give strength unto his people; the Lord will bless his people with peace" (Psalm 29:11).

> And the Lord said unto him, Peace be unto thee; fear not: thou shalt not die. Then Gideon built an altar there unto the Lord, and called it **Jehovah-shalom**. Judges 6:23–24 [NASB, NIV, NRSV: **The Lord Is Peace**]

JUDGE

The clear teaching of this verse is that some people are worthy of positions of leadership and authority while others are not. God as Judge has the ability to tell the difference and to elevate one and demote the other.

Right and wrong, good and evil, often get so intermingled in this world that even the most discerning people can't tell the difference. But God is the ultimate dispenser of justice. He has the insight to separate the true from the false. He can be trusted to sort things out, reward the deserving, and punish the pretenders.

The Bible is filled with accounts of God's actions as Judge. For example, King Ahab of Israel and his wicked queen, Jezebel, cheated, lied, and enlisted false witnesses to have Naboth killed so they could take his vineyard (see 1 Kings 21:1–16). No earthly judge or civil court had the

> But God is the **judge**: he putteth down one [NIV: brings one down], and setteth up [NIV: exalts] another. Psalm 75:7

resolve or courage to bring this powerful couple to trial. But God had the last word in the matter.

King Ahab was killed by a stray arrow from an enemy soldier (see 1 Kings 22:34–40). Jezebel was tossed to her death from a window when Jehu took over the kingship (2 Kings 9:30–37). These events didn't happen immediately, but God's justice eventually prevailed—and it always does.

JUDGE OF ALL. See *Judge of All the Earth.*

JUDGE OF ALL THE EARTH

This name of God was spoken by Abraham when he talked with the Lord about His decision to destroy the city of Sodom because of its wickedness. Abraham believed that God was just in all His actions. Surely the Judge of All the Earth would not destroy the righteous people of Sodom along with the wicked.

God did follow through on His plan to destroy the city. But He sent an angel to warn the only righteous people in Sodom—Lot and his family—to flee before His judgment fell (see Genesis 19:1, 15–17). This proved that the Lord is fair and equitable in His work in the world as the righteous dispenser of justice.

Two related titles of God that express this same idea are Judge of the Earth (see Psalm 94:2) and Judge of All (see Hebrews 12:23).

That be far from thee to do after this manner [NIV: Far be it from you to do such a thing], to slay the righteous with the wicked. . . . Shall not the **Judge of all the earth** do right?
GENESIS 18:25

Remains of the city wall of Bab edh-Dhra, thought to be the ancient city of Sodom. The scant remains of where this sinful city once stood are a reminder of God as Judge over all evil on the earth.

JUDGE OF ISRAEL. See *Creator of Israel.*

JUDGE OF THE EARTH. See *Judge of All the Earth.*

JUST ONE. See *Most Upright.*

KEEPER

This is the only place in the Bible where God is referred to as our Keeper. This name refers to His protection, provision, and watchfulness. The NIV translates the phrase as "The LORD watches over you."

No matter where we are or what we are doing, God has His watchful eye on us. This is both comforting and disturbing. As the writer of Proverbs said, "The eyes of the LORD are in every place, beholding the evil and the good" (Proverbs 15:3).

The LORD is thy **keeper**: the LORD is thy shade upon thy right hand.
PSALM 121:5

KING

Samuel spoke these words to the leaders of Israel when they requested that he appoint a central political figure to rule over them. It was clear to Samuel that they were choosing poorly—turning away from God as their ruler and King to place their confidence in an earthly king.

The Lord is spoken of as King many times throughout the Bible. Kings of ancient times had unlimited authority. They were answerable to no one, and their word was considered the law of the land. When they died, their sons had the right to succeed them. Thus their influence and power were passed on from generation to generation.

But above all these political kings stands the ultimate King, the ruler of the universe. He alone is worthy of our worship and unquestioning obedience.

And when ye saw that Nahash the king of the children of Ammon came against you, ye said unto me, Nay; but a king shall reign over us: when the LORD your God was your **king**.
1 SAMUEL 12:12

Bow Down Before the King

- "The LORD is King for ever and ever" (Psalm 10:16).
- "For the LORD. . .is a great King over all the earth" (Psalm 47:2).
- "Make a joyful noise before the LORD, the King" (Psalm 98:6).
- "Let the children of Zion be joyful in their King" (Psalm 149:2).
- "Then said I, Woe is me! for I am undone; because I am a man of unclean lips, and I dwell in the midst of a people of unclean lips: for mine eyes have seen the King, the LORD of hosts" (Isaiah 6:5).

KING ETERNAL, IMMORTAL, INVISIBLE

Now unto the **King eternal, immortal, invisible**, the only wise God, be honour and glory for ever and ever. Amen.
1 TIMOTHY 1:17
[NRSV: **King of the ages, immortal, invisible**]

This benediction from the apostle Paul in his first epistle to Timothy is the only place in the Bible where God is called by this name. The adjectives *eternal*, *immortal*, and *invisible* express three of His characteristics, or attributes.

God is eternal because He has always existed and He always will. Unlike man, who is mortal, God is not subject to sickness and death. And He is invisible, because He is a spiritual being who exists everywhere at the same time (see John 4:24).

The prophet Jeremiah also referred to God as the Everlasting King (Jeremiah 10:10). Both he and Paul were familiar with earthly kings who ruled for a few years and then were succeeded by other members of the royal family. Even the long reign of fifty-five years achieved by King Manasseh of Judah (see 2 Kings 21:1) is like the blink of an eye when compared to God's eternal kingship over the nations of the world.

KING OF GLORY

Lift up your heads, O ye gates; and be ye lift [NIV: lifted] up, ye everlasting doors; and the **King of glory** shall come in. Who is this **King of glory?** The LORD strong and mighty, the LORD mighty in battle. Lift up your heads, O ye gates; even lift them up, ye everlasting doors; and the **King of glory** shall come in. Who is this **King of glory?** The LORD of hosts, he is the **King of glory**.
PSALM 24:7–10

This is the only place in the Bible where God is called the King of Glory, and the name appears five times in these four verses. The title of the psalm ascribes authorship to David.

The exuberant joy of Psalm 24 leads some interpreters to speculate that it may have been sung when the ark of the covenant was moved to the city of Jerusalem in David's time. On this occasion, David "danced before the LORD" as trumpets sounded and the people shouted with joy (2 Samuel 6:14–15).

Two choirs, singing responsively, may have accompanied the ark. One choir sang, "Who is this King of glory?" And the other choir responded by identifying Him as Yahweh, the strong and mighty God of the Israelites.

As the King of Glory, God is worthy of our praise. The psalmist declares, "Not unto us, O LORD, not unto us, but unto thy name give glory" (Psalm 115:1).

KING OF OLD. See *Ancient of Days.*

KING OF JACOB. See *Mighty One of Jacob.*

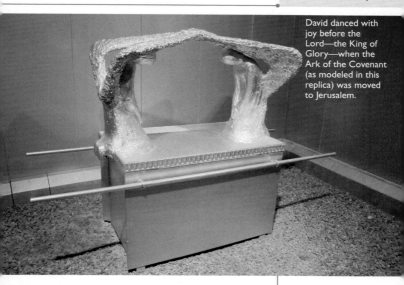

David danced with joy before the Lord—the King of Glory—when the Ark of the Covenant (as modeled in this replica) was moved to Jerusalem.

KING OF THE AGES, IMMORTAL, INVISIBLE. See *King Eternal, Immortal, Invisible.*

KING OVER ALL THE EARTH. See *God of the Whole Earth.*

LAWGIVER

God revealed His Ten Commandments to Moses (see Exodus 20:1–17), a moral code to guide the behavior of His people. These laws are a good example of God's role as Lawgiver. God is sovereign over His creation, and He is the source of truth, righteousness, and holiness. He has the right to make the laws and set the standards by which people should live.

Many people have a strictly negative view of God's laws. They think of them only in binding and restrictive terms. But these laws are actually given for our benefit. Following God the Lawgiver's directives and commands is the key to joy and contentment in this life. The psalmist focuses on this positive side of God's laws when he declares, "You are good, and what you do is good; teach me your decrees" (Psalm 119:68 NIV).

For the LORD is our judge, the LORD is our **lawgiver**, the LORD is our king; he will save us.
ISAIAH 33:22
[NRSV: **ruler**]

The LORD is my **light** and my salvation; whom shall I fear? the LORD is the strength of my life; of whom shall I be afraid?
PSALM 27:1

LIGHT

When God created the world, the first thing He brought into being was light (see Genesis 1:3–5). His glory or presence is often compared to the light (see Psalm 104:1–2). He led His people in the wilderness during the Exodus with the light from a pillar of fire (see Exodus 13:21). Perhaps the psalmist had all these things in mind when he referred to the Lord as his Light.

As the Light, God is still a guide for His people. He gives us wisdom and insight to help us make good decisions. In our moments of darkness and discouragement, He gives us hope. He lights up our lives constantly with His love and grace.

God's written Word, the Bible, also shows that Light is an appropriate name for Him. He inspired it by divine revelation many centuries ago. Then He worked throughout history to preserve it and pass it down to our generation. His eternal Word still shines like a beacon in a dark and sinful world. As Christians, we can declare with the psalmist, "Thy word is a lamp unto my feet, and a light unto my path" (Psalm 119:105).

The psalmist also refers to God as the Sun (Psalm 84:11), comparing Him to the brightest light in the universe.

Guided by the Lord's Light

- "Come ye, and let us walk in the light of the LORD" (Isaiah 2:5).
- "The sun shall be no more thy light by day. . .but the LORD shall be unto thee an everlasting light" (Isaiah 60:19).
- "When I sit in darkness, the LORD shall be a light unto me" (Micah 7:8).

And the **light of Israel** shall be for a fire, and his Holy One for a flame: and it shall burn and devour his thorns and his briers in one day.
ISAIAH 10:17

LIGHT OF ISRAEL

This name of God was used by the prophet Isaiah in connection with his prophecy about the nation of Assyria. The Assyrians overran the nation of Israel (the northern kingdom) about 722 BC. Isaiah predicted that Assyria would eventually be punished by the Lord for their mistreatment of His people. God—the Light of Israel—would become a blazing fire that would consume this pagan nation. This prophecy was fulfilled about a century after Isaiah's time, when Assyria fell to the Babylonians.

These images of light and fire show two different sides of

God's nature. It is always better to experience the light of His love than the fire of His wrath.

LIVING GOD

King Darius of Persia called the Lord by this name when he came to see if Daniel had survived the night he spent among the lions. Even a pagan king recognized that it would take the Living God to deliver Daniel from this den of ferocious animals, which had been turned into an execution chamber.

God is referred to as the Living God several times throughout the Bible (see Joshua 3:10; 1 Samuel 17:26; Jeremiah 10:10; Hebrews 10:31). This title contrasts the one true God—the One who actually exists—with pagan idols that are lifeless counterfeits.

Unlike pagan deities, the Living God is capable of acting on behalf of His people. Just as He saved Daniel from the lions, He hears our prayers and stands beside us in our time of need.

And the king spake and said. . .O Daniel, servant of the **living God**, is thy God, whom thou servest continually, able to deliver thee from the lions?
DANIEL 6:20

This lion statue, near the ruins of ancient Babylon, is a reminder of Daniel, the lion's den, and king Darius's proclamation of "The Living God."

LIVING WATERS. See *Fountain of Living Waters.*

LORD. See *I Am That I Am.*

LORD ALMIGHTY. See *Almighty God; Lord of Hosts.*

LORD GOD ALMIGHTY. See *Almighty God; Lord of Hosts.*

LORD GOD OF ISRAEL

Blessed be the **Lord God of Israel**; for he hath visited and redeemed his people.
LUKE 1:68

Zacharias, the father of John the Baptist, used this name for God when he broke out in praise at the news that the Messiah would soon be born. Just as the Lord had blessed His people in the past, He was now getting ready to fulfill His promise to send a great Deliverer.

But the Messiah was more than a gift to Israel alone. Through Him the entire world would be blessed. We as Christians proclaim this truth every year at Christmas when we sing this familiar hymn by Isaac Watts:

Joy to the world! The Lord is come;
Let earth receive her King;
Let every heart prepare Him room,
And heaven and nature sing.

LORD GOD OMNIPOTENT. See *Almighty God.*

LORD IS MY BANNER. See *Jehovah-nissi.*

LORD IS PEACE. See *Jehovah-shalom.*

LORD OF ALL THE EARTH. See *God of the Whole Earth.*

LORD OF HOSTS

Yea, many people and strong nations shall come to seek the **Lord of hosts** in Jerusalem, and to pray before the LORD.
ZECHARIAH 8:22
[NIV: **Lord Almighty**]

Zechariah 8 could be called the "Lord of Hosts" chapter of the Bible, because this divine name appears eighteen times in the chapter. Actually, this name is one of the more popular in the entire Bible. It appears about 250 times, particularly in the prophets and the Psalms.

The compound Hebrew word behind this name is *Yahweh-sabaoth*, "Lord of Hosts." *Sabaoth* means "armies" or "hosts." Thus, one meaning of the name is that God is superior to any human army, no matter its number. The Lord often led His people to victory over a superior military force (see, for example, Judges 7:12–25).

Another possible meaning of Lord of Hosts is that God exercises control over all the hosts of heaven—or the heavenly bodies—including the sun, moon, and stars. The psalmist declares, "Praise ye him, all his hosts. Praise ye him, sun and moon: praise him, all ye stars of light" (Psalm 148:2–3).

In the King James Version, the title *Lord of Sabaoth* appears twice (see Romans 9:29; James 5:4). These are rendered as "Lord of Hosts" by modern translations.

LORD OF SABAOTH. See *Lord of Hosts.*

LORD OF THE WHOLE EARTH. See *God of the Whole Earth.*

LORD OUR RIGHTEOUSNESS

These words of the Lord were delivered to His people through the prophet Jeremiah. God would punish His people for their sin and idolatry by allowing the Babylonians to overrun the nation of Judah. But He would preserve a remnant of His people, who would remain faithful to Him. He would bless them, allow them to return to their homeland, and give them a special name—the Lord Our Righteousness.

This name of God emphasizes two of the more important truths of the Bible: (1) God demands righteousness of His people, and (2) we are not able to meet this demand on

> In his days Judah shall be saved, and Israel shall dwell safely: and this is his name whereby he shall be called, THE **LORD OUR RIGHTEOUSNESS**.
> JEREMIAH 23:6

Depending on the Lord Our Righteousness
- "Hear me when I call, O God of my righteousness" (Psalm 4:1).
- "The LORD. . .shall judge the world with righteousness, and the people with his truth" (Psalm 96:13).
- "I the LORD speak righteousness, I declare things that are right" (Isaiah 45:19).
- "This is the heritage of the servants of the LORD, and their righteousness is of me, saith the LORD" (Isaiah 54:17).

our own. We must look to Him as the Lord Our Righteousness to provide for us what we cannot attain no matter how hard we try.

The ultimate fulfillment of this verse did not occur until several centuries after Jeremiah's time. God sent His own Son into the world to pay the price for our sin, so that we could become justified, or righteous, in His sight. This is strictly a gift of His grace, not something we deserve because we measure up to His demands. The apostle Paul expresses it like this: "For he [God] hath made him [Jesus] to be sin for us, who knew no sin; that we might be made the righteousness of God in him" (2 Corinthians 5:21).

LORD WHO HEALS

This is the only place in the Bible where God is called the Lord Who Heals. The Lord used this name to describe Himself after He healed the bitter waters at Marah in the wilderness, making it safe for the Israelites to drink.

The healing power of God is often demonstrated in the Old Testament. For example, He healed Miriam of her leprosy (see Numbers 12:10–16). He healed King Hezekiah of Judah of a mysterious illness (see 2 Kings 20:1–10). He healed people in the wilderness after they were bitten by poisonous snakes (see Numbers 21:5–9).

God is also portrayed in the Old Testament as the healer of the ultimate sickness—sin. The psalmist prays, "LORD, be merciful unto me: heal my soul; for I have sinned against thee" (Psalm 41:4).

> And [God] said, If thou wilt diligently hearken [NIV: listen carefully] to the voice of the LORD thy God. . .I will put none of these diseases upon thee, which I have brought upon the Egyptians: for I am the **LORD that healeth** thee.
> EXODUS 15:26
> [NASB: **LORD your healer**]

This well, from the area with the bitter waters of Marah, is associated with the Springs of Moses where the Lord healed the "bitter waters."

LORD WHO MAKES YOU HOLY. See *Lord Who Sanctifies.*

LORD WHO SANCTIFIES

God reminded the Israelites, through Moses, that the Sabbath was a special day that had been set apart, or sanctified, by Him (see Genesis 2:3). His people were to honor this day by resting from their labors and praising Him through acts of worship.

Just as God set apart the seventh day of the week as a memorial to Himself, so He also sanctified the Israelites as a nation devoted to Him. As the Lord

Who Sanctifies, He has the right to demand loyalty and commitment from His people. When He sets us apart for His special use, He also empowers us with the strength and ability to serve as His witnesses in the world.

LORD WILL PROVIDE. See *Jehovah-jireh.*

LORD YOUR HEALER. See *Lord Who Heals.*

MAJESTY IN THE HEAVENS. See *Majesty on High.*

Speak thou also unto the children of Israel, saying, Verily my sabbaths ye shall keep: for it is a sign between me and you throughout your generations; that ye may know that I am the **LORD that doth sanctify you**.
EXODUS 31:13
[NIV: **LORD who makes you holy**]

Fresco of Jesus in His "Majesty on High." Church of the Ascension, Mount of Olives.

MAJESTY ON HIGH

This powerful verse from the book of Hebrews refers to Jesus' ascension into heaven. After His resurrection, He spent forty days among His followers. Then He was "taken up" into heaven and "a cloud received him out of their sight" (Acts 1:9). Now in heaven, He is seated at the right hand of God His Father (see Ephesians 1:20; Colossians 3:1; 1 Peter 3:22)—or, as the writer of Hebrews puts it, next to the Majesty on High.

Who being the brightness of his glory. . .when he had by himself purged our sins, sat down on the right hand of the **Majesty on high**.
HEBREWS 1:3
[NIV: **Majesty in heaven**]

This name of God is a poetic way of referring to His power and glory. He is incomparable in His excellence, magnificence, and splendor. This name appears only here in the Bible. The book of Hebrews also speaks of God as the Majesty in the heavens (Hebrews 8:1).

God's Majesty in the Psalms

- "The voice of the LORD is powerful; the voice of the LORD is full of majesty" (Psalm 29:4).
- "Honour and majesty are before him: strength and beauty are in his sanctuary" (Psalm 96:6).
- "O LORD my God, thou art very great; thou art clothed with honour and majesty" (Psalm 104:1).
- "To make known to the sons of men his mighty acts, and the glorious majesty of his kingdom" (Psalm 145:12).

MAKER

Shall mortal man be more just [NIV: Can a mortal be more righteous] than God? shall a man be more pure than his **maker**?
JOB 4:17

This name of God was spoken by Eliphaz the Temanite, one of Job's three friends who came to counsel him in his affliction. Job had accused God of causing His suffering when he, Job, had done nothing wrong. To Eliphaz, a mere mortal such as Job had no right to question the actions of his Maker, the immortal One who did not have to explain His actions to anyone.

God's role as our Maker is similar to His acts as our Creator and Provider (see *Creator*). The psalmist declares, "Know ye that the LORD he is God: it is he that hath made us, and not we ourselves; we are his people, and the sheep of his pasture" (Psalm 100:3).

A craftsman chisels designs into wood. Though he is "making" a piece of art, he's using existing materials. Only God could "make" from nothing.

MIGHT. See *Song*.

MIGHTY GOD. See *Almighty God*.

MIGHTY ONE OF ISRAEL. See *Almighty God*.

MIGHTY ONE OF JACOB

This name of God appears only twice in the Bible, both times in the book of Isaiah (see also Isaiah 60:16). In these two verses, "Jacob" is a poetic way of referring to the nation of Israel. The descendants of Jacob's twelve sons developed into the twelve tribes of Israel. Jacob himself was also known as "Israel," a name given to him by the Lord after his struggle with God at Peniel (see Genesis 32:28; 35:10).

Three similar names for God that appear in the Old Testament are God of Jacob (2 Samuel 23:1; Psalm 75:9), Holy One of Jacob (Isaiah 29:23), and King of Jacob (Isaiah 41:21).

> And all flesh [NIV: all mankind] shall know that I the LORD am thy Saviour and thy Redeemer, the **mighty One of Jacob**.
> ISAIAH 49:26

MOST HIGH

This name of God appears in a psalm that David wrote after he was delivered from King Saul and others who were trying to kill him (see 2 Samuel 22:1; 1 Samuel 20:1; Psalm 18). David compares God's ability to save to the power that is unleashed during a severe thunderstorm. The rolling thunder is like God's voice from heaven.

The book of Psalms refers frequently to God as the Most High (see Psalms 9:2; 73:11; 107:11). The prophet Daniel also used this name (see Daniel 4:24; 7:18). In his long speech in the New Testament, just before his death, the martyr Stephen declares that "the most High dwelleth not in temples made with hands" (Acts 7:48).

There is nothing in this world greater than the Most High. He deserves our deepest loyalty and most fervent praise.

> The LORD thundered from heaven, and the **Most High** resounded.
> 2 SAMUEL 22:14 NIV

Our Vision of the Most High

An ancient Irish hymn titled "Be Thou My Vision" declares that God as the Most High should be the inspiration of our lives.

Be thou my vision, O Lord of my heart;
Naught be all else to me, save that Thou art:
Thou my best thought, by day or by night,
Walking or sleeping, Thy presence my light.

And Melchizedek king of Salem brought forth bread and wine: and he was the priest of the **most high God**. And he blessed him, and said, Blessed be Abram of the **most high God**, possessor of heaven and earth.

GENESIS 14:18–19

[NIV: **God Most High**]

MOST HIGH GOD

Both Abraham and Melchizedek worshipped and served the same God—the Most High God—the One in whose name Melchizedek blessed Abraham. This God had given Abraham victory over a coalition of Canaanite kings (Genesis 14:1–24). To express his thanks to God, Abraham gave Melchizedek a tithe of all his goods.

"Most High God" is a name for the one true God. He is superior to all the false gods that were worshipped by the pagan peoples of Abraham's time. They had a god for every need and purpose—a god of war, fertility, love, rain, science, literature, truth, etc. But Melchizedek and Abraham worshipped only one God. He was the supreme God of creation, who stood above all these "lesser gods" in power and authority.

A lot has changed since the days of Melchizedek and Abraham. But the temptation to worship the "lesser gods" of the world rather than the one true God of the universe has not. Money, fame, and power are the new gods of our age. But the first of God's Ten Commandments still stands: "Thou shalt have no other gods before me" (Exodus 20:3).

MOST HIGH OVER ALL THE EARTH.

See *God of the Whole Earth.*

MOST MIGHTY.

See *Almighty God.*

This Babylonian idol, dating as far back as 2000 BC, was believed to be responsible for omens. Ancient people often had gods for limited purposes—as opposed to the "Most High God" who has authority over everything.

MOST UPRIGHT

This is the only place in the Bible where this name of God appears. Isaiah's point is that even the most righteous and upright people are as nothing in comparison to the holiness of God.

Even Christians who try to walk the path of righteousness are capable of slipping into sin at any time. But God is not capable of error or wrongdoing. He is the Most Upright, the one consistent standard by which all human behavior is judged. Isaiah considers this dramatic contrast between the Lord's righteousness and our sin, then declares, "All our righteousnesses are as filthy rags. . .and our iniquities, like the wind, have taken us away" (Isaiah 64:6).

But that is not the end of the story. In spite of our unworthiness, God comes to our rescue through the sacrificial death of His Son: "For by grace are ye saved through faith; and that not of yourselves: it is the gift of God: not of works, lest any man should boast" (Ephesians 2:8–9).

> The way of the just is uprightness: thou, **most upright**, dost weigh the path of the just [NIV: make the way of the righteous smooth].
> ISAIAH 26:7
> [NASB, NIV: **Upright One**; NRSV: **Just One**]

PORTION

The word *portion* appears often in the Bible in connection with inheritance rights. For example, each of the twelve tribes of Israel received a portion of the land of Canaan as an inheritance that the Lord had promised (see Joshua 19:9). By law, the firstborn son in a family received a double portion of his father's estate as an inheritance (see Deuteronomy 21:17). In Jesus' parable of the prodigal son, the youngest son asks his father for his portion, or share, of the estate ahead of time (see Luke 15:12).

The psalmist probably had this inheritance imagery in mind when he called God his Portion. The Lord was his spiritual heritage, passed down to him by godly people of past generations. Unlike an earthly inheritance that can be squandered, this is an inheritance that will last forever.

But comparing God to a legacy from the past has its limits. Truths about God can be passed on from generation to generation, but personal faith cannot. Parents can and should teach their offspring about God, but it is up to each child to accept this heritage through his own personal choice.

Two other names of God the Father that describe Him as a portion are Portion in the Land of the Living (Psalm 142:5) and Portion of Mine Inheritance (Psalm 16:5).

> Thou art my **portion**, O LORD: I have said that I would keep thy words.
> PSALM 119:57

PORTION IN THE LAND OF THE LIVING. See *Portion.*

PORTION OF MINE INHERITANCE. See *Portion.*

POSSESSOR OF HEAVEN AND EARTH. See *God of the Whole Earth.*

POTTER

But now, O LORD, thou art our father; we are the clay, and thou our **potter**; and we all are the work of thy hand.
ISAIAH 64:8

The prophet Isaiah longed for the wayward people of Judah to subject themselves to God. If they became pliable clay in the Lord's hands, they would be shaped into beautiful vessels who would glorify His name.

God as the master Potter is a graphic image that appears often throughout the Bible. For example, while the prophet Jeremiah looked on, a potter ruined a vase he was working on and had to start over again with the same lump of clay. Jeremiah compared the nation of Judah to this pottery reshaping process. Shape up, he declared, or you will be reshaped by the Lord's discipline.

The hymn writer George C. Stebbins expresses this truth in a positive way:

Have thine own way, Lord! Have thine own way!
Thou art the Potter, I am the clay.
Mold me and make me after thy will,
While I am waiting, yielded and still.

REDEEMER

This name of God is a reflection of the Old Testament concept of the kinsman redeemer. In the close-knit families and clans of Bible times, the nearest relative of a family member in trouble was expected to come to that person's rescue.

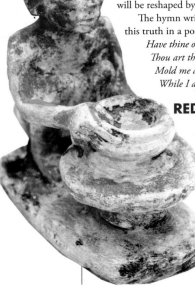

Ancient Egyptian clay figurine of a potter working his potter's wheel.

For example, if a person lost his property as a debtor, his kinsman redeemer was responsible for buying back the property and restoring it to his family member. This is exactly what happened in the book of Ruth. Boaz, a kinsman of Naomi's deceased husband, Elimelech, bought back the property Elimelech had lost and restored it to Naomi (see Ruth 4:1–11).

The prophet Isaiah declares that God is the ultimate Redeemer who will come to the rescue of His people. We can rest assured that no trouble we experience is so deep that it is beyond His reach. Job had this assurance. From out of his suffering, he declared, "I know that my redeemer liveth, and that he shall stand at the latter day upon the earth" (Job 19:25).

In another passage in his book, the prophet Isaiah also refers to the Lord as "the Redeemer of Israel" (Isaiah 49:7).

> In a little wrath [NIV: a surge of anger] I hid my face from thee for a moment; but with everlasting kindness will I have mercy on thee, saith the LORD thy **Redeemer**.
> ISAIAH 54:8

REDEEMER OF ISRAEL. See *Redeemer*.

REFUGE

Moses called God by this name as the Israelites were getting ready to enter the Promised Land. He reminded the people to follow the Lord as they populated the land, because He alone was a dependable source of refuge and protection.

After they settled in Canaan, the Israelites designated

> The eternal God is thy **refuge**, and underneath are the everlasting arms.
> DEUTERONOMY 33:27
> [NASB: **dwelling place**]

Remains of ancient Shechem (Tell Balata). Shechem was one of the six cities of refuge described in the books of Numbers and Joshua.

certain population centers as cities of refuge (see Numbers 35:6–7; Joshua 20:7–9). An Israelite who killed another person accidentally could flee to one of these cities to escape the dead man's family who were seeking revenge. The killer's safety was guaranteed by the elders of the city while the circumstances surrounding the homicide were under investigation.

With God as our refuge, we have nothing to fear from those who seek to do us harm. Even in death, there is no safer place to be than in the arms of the everlasting God.

Another name of God that expresses basically the same idea as Refuge is Shelter (Psalm 61:3). See also *Dwelling Place.*

Safe in the Arms of the Lord

The phrase everlasting arms in Deuteronomy 33:27 has been immortalized in the hymn "Leaning on the Everlasting Arms," by Elisha A. Hoffman. Generations of Christians have been inspired by this grand old hymn.

What a fellowship, what a joy divine,
Leaning on the everlasting arms;
What a blessedness, what a peace is mine,
Leaning on the everlasting arms.
Leaning, leaning,
Safe and secure from all alarms;
Leaning, leaning,
Leaning on the everlasting arms.

ROCK

There is none holy as the LORD: for there is none beside thee: neither is there any **rock** like our God.
1 SAMUEL 2:2

This verse is part of Hannah's prayer of dedication when she brought her son, Samuel, to Eli the priest. God had answered her prayer for a son, and she followed through on her promise to devote him to the Lord. She had found the Lord to be the Rock, the strong and dependable One who answers the prayers of His people.

The word *rock*, when used of God, refers not to a small stone but to a massive outcropping, such as that on a mountainside. These huge formations are common throughout the land of Israel. These types of rocks remain fixed in place from one generation to the next, just as God is the eternal, unmovable One who is not subject to the ravages of time.

Other names of God the Father that describe Him as the Rock or the Stone are Rock of Israel (2 Samuel 23:3), Rock of My Refuge (Psalm 94:22), Rock of My Salvation (2 Samuel 22:47), and Rock of My Strength (Psalm 62:7).

Rock façade at Caesarea Philippi associated with Jesus' proclamation that the kingdom of evil would not overpower those belonging to God's Kingdom (Matthew 16:13–18).

ROCK OF ISRAEL. See *Rock*.

ROCK OF MY REFUGE. See *Rock*.

ROCK OF MY SALVATION. See *Rock*.

ROCK OF MY STRENGTH. See *Rock*.

SALVATION. See *God of My Salvation*; *Horn of Salvation*.

SAVIOUR

And there is no God else beside me [NIV: no God apart from me]; a just God and a **Saviour**; there is none beside me [NIV: none but me].
ISAIAH 45:21

These words from the Lord were delivered to the Israelites through the prophet Isaiah. God reminded the people that He, as their Savior, was the only true God. He demanded their loyalty and obedience.

The word *savior* refers to one who rescues or delivers others from danger. When used of God in the Old Testament, it usually refers to physical deliverance. The supreme example of this was God's rescue of the Israelites from Egyptian slavery through the Exodus. Acting as a Savior, or Deliverer, He sent plagues against the Egyptians until Pharaoh gave in and let God's people leave the country.

Not until the New Testament does God's role as Savior reach its full flower. He sent His Son Jesus as a spiritual Savior to deliver us from our bondage to sin.

Giza pyramids and Sphinx. When the Lord rescued the Israelites from the mighty hand of Pharaoh during the time of Moses, the pyramids in Egypt were no longer in use.

SHADE

This unusual name for God was probably inspired by the hot, dry climate of the land of Israel. To the psalmist, God was his figurative Shade under whom he could rest from the oppressive heat during the hottest part of the day.

In this verse, he also describes God as his cooling-off

place "upon [his] right hand." The right hand was considered the place of favor and honor. Thus, to experience the Lord as his Shade on the right was to be doubly refreshed and blessed.

Are you overworked, overheated, frustrated, confused, or confounded? Maybe it's time you took a refreshing break by sitting down under the ultimate Shade.

> The LORD is thy keeper: the LORD is thy **shade** upon thy right hand.
> PSALM 121:5

Like Elijah, who slept under a broom tree, people today still seek relief from the heat in the hot, dry climate of Israel.

SHELTER. See *Refuge.*

SHEPHERD

This name of God is one of the favorites of Bible students, perhaps because it occurs in one of the more familiar passages in God's Word—the Twenty-third Psalm. This psalm has been called the "Shepherd Psalm" because of its beautiful description of the Lord as the Shepherd of His people.

David wrote this psalm in his latter years, as he reflected on the Lord and how He had led him throughout his life. Like a shepherd who leads his sheep to green pastures and peaceful streams for food and water, the Lord had supplied David's needs. From David's humble beginnings as a shepherd boy, to the throne of Israel, God had walked with him and blessed him with more than he deserved. David was confident that God would continue to sustain him, even as he walked "through the valley of the shadow of death" (Psalm 23:4).

Like David, we all need the divine Shepherd, who will guide us throughout this life and beyond. What a blessing it is to count ourselves as "the sheep of his pasture" (Psalm 100:3).

Another name of God that uses shepherd imagery is Shepherd of Israel (Psalm 80:1)

> The LORD is my **shepherd**; I shall not want [NIV: I shall not be in want].
> PSALM 23:1

A shepherd caring for his sheep. Such an image would have been common to people of Bible times.

SHEPHERD OF ISRAEL. See *Shepherd*.

SHIELD

For thou, LORD, wilt bless the righteous; with favour wilt thou compass [NIV: surround] him as with a **shield**.
PSALM 5:12

This verse is from one of the psalms of David, in which he prays for protection from his enemies. He uses military terminology to characterize God as his Shield who will surround him and absorb the blows of those who are on the attack.

The Hebrew word behind *shield* in this verse refers to the large, full-body shield that warriors crouched behind. This protected them from arrows being shot by archers from a distance. Another type of shield was the buckler, which was worn on the arm to protect soldiers in hand-to-hand combat (see *Buckler*).

As our Shield, God provides maximum protection. He literally surrounds us with His watchful care.

SONG

The twelfth chapter of Isaiah is one of the shortest in his book. But it is unapologetically joyful as the prophet thinks about the Lord whom he serves. In addition to this verse, which describes God as his Song, every one of its verses expresses this theme of praise and celebration (see sidebar).

God's people have a lot to sing about. He has provided for our salvation through His Son. He sustains us every day with His love and grace. He has promised us eternal life with Him in heaven after we depart this earthly life. He, as our Song, deserves to be praised with our songs of joy.

Behold, God is my salvation; I will trust, and not be afraid: for the LORD JEHOVAH is my strength and my **song**; he also is become my salvation.
ISAIAH 12:2
[NRSV: **might**]

Egyptian statuette of a person playing the lyre.

Other Verses of Isaiah 12

- "O LORD, I will praise thee" (verse 1)
- "With joy shall ye draw water out of the wells of salvation" (verse 3)
- "Praise the LORD" (verse 4)
- "Sing unto the LORD" (verse 5)
- "Cry out and shout" (verse 6)

SPRING OF LIVING WATER. See *Fountain of Living Waters.*

STONE OF ISRAEL. See *Creator of Israel.*

STRENGTH

This verse is part of the passage of scripture known as the Song of Moses (Exodus 15:1–19). Moses led the Israelites to sing this song of praise to the Lord after He rescued them from the pursuing army of Pharaoh at the Red Sea.

The people had witnessed the awesome power of the Lord as He divided the waters of the sea to give them safe passage. Even before this event, the Lord had plagued the Egyptians again and again until Pharaoh allowed the Israelites to leave the country. No wonder Moses referred to this wonder-working God as his Strength.

The LORD is my **strength** and song, and he is become my salvation. . .my father's God, and I will exalt him.
EXODUS 15:2

There is no shortage of power in the God we serve. And He invites us to partake of His strength in our times of need.

Claiming the Promises of God's Strength

- "But they that wait upon the LORD shall renew their strength; they shall mount up with wings as eagles; they shall run, and not be weary; and they shall walk, and not faint" (Isaiah 40:31).
- "The LORD God is my strength, and he will make my feet like hinds' feet, and he will make me to walk upon mine high places" (Habakkuk 3:19).
- "God is our refuge and strength, a very present help in trouble" (Psalm 46:1).

STRENGTH OF ISRAEL. See *Creator of Israel.*

STRONGHOLD. See *Fortress.*

STRONG TOWER

The name of the LORD is a **strong tower**: the righteous runneth into it, and is safe.
PROVERBS 18:10

In ancient cities, towers were massive stone structures built above the defensive perimeter walls. From these elevated positions, defenders could shoot arrows or hurl stones on the enemy forces outside. These towers also served as a final line of defense if the invading army should succeed in breaking through the walls or battering down the city gates.

Towers from an Israelite fortress at Arad may have inspired the proverb writer's description of God as a "strong tower."

The author of this proverb compares the Lord to one of these defensive towers. His righteous followers can seek safety and security in Him as the Strong Tower.

This imagery also appears in the Psalms, where God is referred to as a High Tower (see Psalms 18:2; 144:2).

SUN. See *Light*.

TOWER. See *Strong Tower*.

UPRIGHT ONE. See *Most Upright*.

WALL OF FIRE

This name of God appears only here in the Bible. The prophet Zechariah uses it to describe God's protection of the city of Jerusalem after the Exile. The city's defensive walls had been destroyed by the Babylonians several decades before. This meant that the Jewish exiles who returned to Jerusalem were in a precarious position. But God promised to protect them by becoming a Wall of Fire around the city.

Fire is often associated in the Bible with God's presence and protection. For example, He used a pillar of fire at night to guide His people on their journey through the wilderness (see Exodus 13:21). The prophet Zechariah was assuring the citizens of Jerusalem that they could depend on the Lord's protective presence at this dangerous point in their lives.

> For I, saith the LORD, will be unto her a **wall of fire** round about, and will be the glory in the midst of her.
> ZECHARIAH 2:5

The Wall of Fire Still Burns

"The Lily of the Valley," an old hymn by Charles W. Fry, assures us that God continues to guide and protect His people.

> He will never, never leave me, nor yet forsake me here,
> While I live by faith and do His blessed will;
> A wall of fire about me, I've nothing now to fear,
> With His manna He my hungry soul shall fill.

YAHWEH. See *I Am That I Am*.

PART 2
Names of God the Son

The following 151 names by which Jesus is known show the revolutionary nature of His life and ministry.

He was the Messiah, the One whom God had promised to send to restore the fortunes of His people. But He was more than the earthly ruler that the people expected. He was the divine Son of God, who came into the world as a man to die as an atonement for human sin.

Jesus' work did not end with His crucifixion, resurrection, and ascension into heaven. He continues to intercede for Christians at the right hand of God the Father. And He has promised that we will reign with Him eternally upon His triumphant return.

ADAM. See *Last Adam.*

ADVOCATE

This is the only place in the Bible where Jesus is called by this name. It expresses the idea that He stands before God on our behalf. He serves as our "defense attorney," to represent us before the Father in heaven when Satan, the accuser, charges us with sin. Jesus' argument on our behalf is solid because it is based on His own atoning work—His death on the cross for our sins.

Any attorney will tell you that his client must be totally honest with him about the charges that have brought him into court. Unless the attorney, as the accused's legal representative, knows everything about the circumstances of the case, he cannot represent his client adequately before the judge and the jury.

In the same way, we as Christians must be honest with our Lord, Jesus, when sin creeps into our lives, if we expect Him to serve as our Advocate before God. Full disclosure, or confession, is essential. As the apostle John expresses it in another place in his first epistle, "If we confess our sins, he [Jesus] is faithful and just to forgive us our sins, and to cleanse us from all unrighteousness" (1 John 1:9).

My little children, these things write I unto you, that ye sin not. And if any man sin, we have an **advocate** with the Father, Jesus Christ the righteous.
1 JOHN 2:1
[NIV: **one who speaks to the Father in our defense**]

A defense attorney speaks on behalf of his client, in a nineteenth-century illustration, "The Advocate," by Honoré Daumier.

ALIVE FOR EVER AND EVER. See *Alive for Evermore.*

ALIVE FOR EVERMORE

These words are among the first that Jesus spoke to the apostle John when He revealed Himself to John on the Isle of Patmos. This revelation occurred about fifty or sixty years after Jesus' death and resurrection. He assured John that He was not only alive but that He was Alive for Evermore.

During His brief ministry of about three years, Jesus predicted His death and resurrection on more than one occasion (see Matthew 16:21–28; Mark 10:32–34; Luke 9:43–45). But even His disciples had a hard time believing this would happen.

Even after Jesus appeared to them in His resurrection body, they had doubts. To show that He had flesh and bones and that they were not seeing a ghost or a vision, He asked them to touch His hands and feet. He even ate a piece of fish and a honeycomb, as they looked on, to prove that He had a physical body just like they did (see Luke 24:37–43).

Because Jesus experienced a physical resurrection and is Alive for Evermore, we as Christians have His assurance that death is not the end of life but a glorious new beginning. "I am the resurrection, and the life," He declared. "Whosoever liveth and believeth in me shall never die" (John 11:25–26).

> I am he that liveth, and was dead; and, behold, I am **alive for evermore**, Amen; and have the keys of hell and of death.
> REVELATION 1:18
> [NIV: **Alive for ever and ever**]

ALL, AND IN ALL

Jesus was born into a divided world. Jews looked down on Gentiles. Greeks considered themselves superior in education and culture to the Jews. But the apostle Paul declares in this famous passage that the coming of Jesus changed all that. He is the All in All—the great unifier—who brings all people together at the foot of the cross.

To those who know Jesus, worldly distinctions and social status are no longer important. The only thing that really matters is Christ. He is the sum and substance of life—the absolute and the center of our existence. Because He gave His all to purchase our salvation, our purpose in life is to bring honor and glory to Him.

> Where there is neither Greek nor Jew, circumcision nor uncircumcision, Barbarian, Scythian, bond nor free: but Christ is **all, and in all**.
> COLOSSIANS 3:11

"Jesus Paid It All," a hymn written by Elvina M. Hall, expresses the all-
sufficiency of Christ in the salvation He provides for all believers.

I hear the Savior say,
"Thy strength indeed is small,
Child of weakness, watch and pray,
Find in me thine all in all."
Jesus paid it all,
All to Him I owe;
Sin had left a crimson stain,
He washed it white as snow.

ALMIGHTY

Jesus is referred to as the Almighty only in the book of Revelation (see Revelation 4:8; 16:7; 19:15). This name is also
applied to God in both the Old and New Testaments (see
Ruth 1:20; 2 Corinthians 6:18; see also *Almighty God* in part
1, Names of God the Father).

I am Alpha and
Omega, the beginning
and the ending, saith
the Lord, which is,
and which was, and
which is to come, the
Almighty.
REVELATION 1:8

Revelation portrays the final victory of Jesus Christ over
the forces of evil. As the Almighty, He is to "rule all nations
with a rod of iron" (Revelation 12:5). He is also the source
of the believer's new life with God the Father in the heavenly
Jerusalem (see Revelation 21:22; 22:1).

God as the Almighty has delegated all authority and
power to His Son, who is also known as the Almighty. Using
His unlimited power, Jesus will bring the world to its conclusion in accordance with God's purpose.

In his famous prophecy about the coming Messiah, Isaiah declares that Jesus will be called the Mighty God (Isaiah
9:6). He also referred to Him as the Mighty One of Israel
(Isaiah 30:29) and the Mighty One of Jacob (Isaiah 60:16).

Praise for the Almighty

The hymn "Praise to the Lord, the Almighty," by Joachim Neander,
invites all people to worship the all-powerful Lord. Both God the Father
and God the Son deserve our highest praise.

Praise to the Lord, the Almighty, the King of creation!
O my soul, praise Him, for He is thy health and salvation!
All ye who hear,
Now to His temple draw near;
Praise Him in glad adoration!

ALPHA AND OMEGA

I am **Alpha and Omega**, the beginning and the end, the first and the last.
REVELATION 22:13

This is one of four places in the book of Revelation where Jesus is called by this name (see Revelation 1:8, 11; 21:6). In all four places, Jesus uses this name of Himself.

Alpha and omega are the first and last letters of the Greek alphabet—the language in which most of the New Testament was written. Thus, this name is a poetic way of declaring that Jesus is the beginning and the end of all things. We might put it this way in modern terms: "Jesus is the A and Z of life, and everything in between."

No letter stands before alpha, and no letter follows omega. This shows that Jesus defines truth and reality. All other gods that people worship are counterfeit deities. Jesus encompasses everything and rejects all limitations.

Other names for Jesus that mean essentially the same thing as Alpha and Omega are Beginning and the Ending (Revelation 1:8) and First and the Last (Revelation 1:17; 2:8; 22:13).

AMEN

And unto the angel of the church of the Laodiceans write; These things saith the **Amen**, the faithful and true witness, the beginning of the creation of God.
REVELATION 3:14

This verse was spoken by Jesus as He prepared to deliver a special message to the church at Laodicea. By designating Himself as the Amen, He claimed to be speaking a truthful, authoritative word for this church.

The word *amen* has a rich biblical history. In the Old Testament, it was used to confirm an oath or consent to an agreement. For example, Nehemiah called on the people of his time not to cheat and defraud one another. The people responded with "amen" to pledge their agreement with Nehemiah's proposal (Nehemiah 5:13).

Jesus often used the word *verily* in His teachings to show that He was about to speak God's words of truth (see Matthew 16:28). This Greek word is rendered as "I tell you the truth" (NIV) or "I assure you" (HCSB) by modern translations. The early church used *amen* to declare "let it be so" or "let it be true" at the close of prayers (see 2 Timothy 4:18), just as we do today.

Because Jesus is the great Amen, we can trust His words and His leadership. He is the sum and substance of Truth (see John 14:6). He will never say or do anything that will cause us to stumble or go astray. He has promised that if we follow Him, we will know the truth, "and the truth shall make you free" (John 8:32).

ANGEL OF HIS PRESENCE

This verse from the prophet Isaiah describes God's patience with His people. Although they sinned and rebelled against Him again and again, He never left them, and He provided the Angel of His Presence as their Savior and Redeemer.

Although angels are mentioned often throughout the Bible, this is the only place where the phrase Angel of His Presence occurs. This is probably a reference to Jesus Christ in His pre-earthly existence. There is no doubt that Jesus existed with God in His pre-incarnate state, long before He was born into the world (see John 1:1–3). So He certainly could have served as God's agent of redemption with His people in the days before His earthly ministry.

This name of Jesus may explain the references to the mysterious Angel of the Lord in the Old Testament. This special agent was sent by God to communicate His message and to assure selected individuals of His presence. This messenger was clearly not the typical angel, but neither was He God the Father. The best explanation is that this special messenger—the Angel of His Presence—was Jesus Christ.

> In all their affliction he was afflicted, and the **angel of his presence** saved them: in his love and in his pity [NIV: mercy] he redeemed them; and he bare them [NIV: lifted them up], and carried them all the days of old.
> ISAIAH 63:9

People to Whom the Angel of the Lord Appeared

- Hagar (Genesis 16:7–11)
- Abraham (Genesis 22:11–12)
- Jacob (Genesis 31:11)
- Moses (Exodus 3:1–2)
- Joshua (Joshua 5:14)
- Gideon (Judges 6:11–12)
- Samson's parents (Judges 13:1–18)
- The prophet Zechariah (Zechariah 1:7–12)

ANOINTED

Psalm 2 is a messianic psalm that predicts the coming of the Messiah. Rebellion against the Lord by the nations of the world is futile, the psalmist declares, because the Lord has appointed Christ, His Anointed, as the King of the earth.

The kings of the earth set themselves [NIV: take their stand], and the rulers take counsel together, against the LORD, and against his **anointed**, saying, Let us break their bands asunder, and cast away their cords [NIV: fetters] from us.
PSALM 2:2–3
[NIV: **Anointed One**]

This name of Jesus ties into the anointing custom of the Old Testament. Priests and kings were anointed by having oil poured on their heads (see Leviticus 8:10–12; 1 Samuel 16:13). This ritual showed that a person had been especially chosen or set apart to perform the responsibilities of his office.

As God's Anointed, Jesus Christ was set apart for His role as the divine Mediator and Redeemer. Through Him we find forgiveness for our sins and the abundant life that God intends for His people. He in turn has anointed us as Christians for the task of declaring His message of hope in a desperate world. The apostle Paul puts it like this: "We are therefore Christ's ambassadors, as though God were making his appeal through us. We implore you in Christ's behalf: Be reconciled to God" (2 Corinthians 5:20 NIV).

Mosaic from the Church of Lazarus at Bethany depicting Jesus being anointed by Mary just prior to His crucifixion.

ANOINTED ONE. See *Anointed.*

APOSTLE

Jesus selected twelve disciples, or apostles (see Mark 3:14; 6:30), to learn from Him and to carry on His work after He was gone. But here in Hebrews 3, He Himself is called the

Apostle. This is the only place in the Bible where this name of Jesus occurs.

The basic meaning of the word *apostle* is a person sent on a special mission with delegated authority and power. Jesus sent out the twelve disciples to teach and heal, and He gave them the ability to succeed in this mission (see Mark 6:7–13). They continued this teaching and healing ministry even after Jesus' resurrection and ascension to the Father (Acts 2:38–43).

But Jesus was the ultimate Apostle. Under the authority of His Father, He came into the world on a mission of love and grace. This mission wasn't a cushy assignment. He was opposed by the religious establishment of His time. Some people who saw His miracles tried to turn Him into a military deliverer. Even His own "sent ones," the apostles, were slow to understand who He was and what He was about.

But as the author of Hebrews expresses it in these verses, Jesus was "faithful to him that appointed him." He did not falter in the mission on which He was sent. From the cross, He triumphantly declared, "It is finished" (John 19:30). His provision for our salvation was a done deal, but the Good News about His death and resurrection—the gospel—rolls on across the ages.

> Wherefore, holy brethren, partakers of the heavenly calling, consider [NIV: fix your thoughts on] the **Apostle** and High Priest of our profession, Christ Jesus; who was faithful to him that appointed him.
> HEBREWS 3:1–2

The Beat Goes On

In her hymn "I Love to Tell the Story," Katherine Hankey reminds us that Jesus' work as the Apostle goes on through His followers as we tell others about His love and grace.

I love to tell the story of unseen things above,
Of Jesus and His glory, of Jesus and His love:
I love to tell the story because I know 'tis true;
It satisfies my longing as nothing else can do.
I love to tell the story, 'twill be my theme in glory
To tell the old, old story of Jesus and His love.

ATONING SACRIFICE FOR OUR SINS.

See *Propitiation for Our Sins.*

AUTHOR AND FINISHER OF OUR FAITH

Jesus is called *author* in two verses in the King James Version (Hebrews 12:2 [see next page] and Hebrews 5:9: "And being made perfect, he became the *author of eternal salvation* unto all them that obey him" [emphasis added]). In two modern translations, He is also called the Author of Salvation (see Hebrews 2:10, NASB, NIV). An author is someone who creates. Jesus is the author of our faith, or our salvation, in that He has provided us with the only flawless example of what the life of faith is like. The NRSV expresses this idea by calling Him the *pioneer* of our faith. He blazed the trail for all others who seek to follow His example.

But Jesus not only started the journey of faith, He also brought it to completion as the "finisher" (NRSV: perfecter) of faith. He did not stop until He had guaranteed our final redemption, making it possible for us to enjoy eternal life with Him in heaven.

> Looking unto Jesus the **author and finisher of our faith**; who for the joy that was set before him endured the cross, despising the shame, and is set down at the right hand of the throne of God.
> HEBREWS 12:2
> [NASB, NIV: **author and perfecter of our faith**; NRSV: **pioneer and perfecter of our faith**]

AUTHOR OF SALVATION. See *Captain of Salvation.*

BABE

This verse from Luke brings to mind the Christmas plays that are presented every year at Christmastime. We see shepherds in bathrobes with towels around their heads. Mary and Joseph kneel beside a rough feeding trough that some member of the church has hammered together. Inside the trough is a doll—or a baby if a newborn is available and the parents can be persuaded to lend him for the occasion—representing the baby Jesus. Even though we have seen it all before, we still get a little misty-eyed when we stand at the conclusion of the play and sing "Joy to the World."

> And they [shepherds] came with haste, and found Mary, and Joseph, and the **babe** lying in a manger.
> LUKE 2:16
> [NIV: **baby**; NRSV: **child**]

The wonder of Christmas is that Jesus came into the world like any newborn of the ancient world. He was a helpless baby, who cried when He was hungry and uncomfortable. He had to be fed, burped, and changed. He probably got His days and nights mixed up like any baby, causing Mary and Joseph to wonder if they would ever again get a good night's sleep.

It's natural for us to wonder why God would choose this way to send His

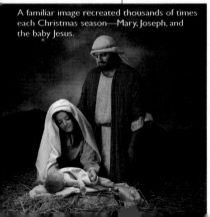

A familiar image recreated thousands of times each Christmas season—Mary, Joseph, and the baby Jesus.

Son into the world. He could have arrived as a king to the blast of trumpets. He could have dazzled the crowds by riding into town as a triumphant general at the head of a massive army. But perhaps God wanted His Son to experience the helplessness of a little baby so He could sympathize with us in our sin and weakness. Going through the stages of life like all people do, He could participate fully in the humanity of those He came to serve.

The writer of the book of Hebrews expresses it like this: "For we do not have a high priest who is unable to sympathize with our weaknesses, but we have one who has been tempted in every way, just as we are—yet was without sin" (Hebrews 4:15 NIV).

BABY. See *Babe.*

BANNER FOR THE NATIONS. See *Ensign for the Nations.*

BEGINNING AND THE ENDING.
See *Alpha and Omega.*

BEGINNING OF THE CREATION OF GOD

The affirmation of this verse is that Jesus has always been. Before He was born into the world in human form, He existed with God the Father. The Nicene Creed, a famous statement of faith formulated by the church in AD 325, puts it like this: "I believe in one Lord, Jesus Christ. . .born of the Father before all ages." Thus, He is called the Beginning of the Creation of God.

Not only has Jesus existed eternally; but the Bible also affirms that He participated with God in the creation of the universe. On the sixth day of creation, the Lord declared, "Let us make man in *our* image, after *our* likeness" (Genesis 1:26, emphasis added). The plural *our* probably refers to God in His three trinitarian modes of existence: God the Father, God the Son, and God the Holy Spirit.

Two key passages from the New Testament also teach that Jesus Christ was involved in the creation of the universe (see sidebar, next page).

And unto the angel of the church of the Laodiceans write; These things saith the Amen, the faithful and true witness, the **beginning of the creation of God**. REVELATION 3:14 [NIV: **ruler of God's creation**; NRSV: **origin of God's creation**]

Jesus as Creator Before the Beginning

"In the beginning was the Word, and the Word was with God, and the Word was God. The same was in the beginning with God. All things were made by him; and without him was not any thing made that was made" (John 1:1–3).

"For by him were all things created, that are in heaven, and that are in earth. . . . And he is before all things, and by him all things consist" (Colossians 1:16–17).

BEGOTTEN. See *Only Begotten Son*.

BELOVED SON

This verse describes in graphic terms what happened when Jesus was baptized by John the Baptist at the beginning of His public ministry. The heavens opened, the Holy Spirit settled on Jesus, and God identified Him clearly as His Beloved Son, who brought Him joy. God was pleased with Jesus because He had waited patiently on God's timing. Now He was ready to begin the work for which He had been sent into the world.

God repeated these words near the end of Jesus' public ministry following His transfiguration (see Matthew 17:1–5). God's words on this occasion showed He was pleased with what His Beloved Son had done. Only Jesus'

A section of the Jordan River, believed by some to be where Jesus was baptized.

death and resurrection to follow could top the divine work He had already accomplished.

Because Jesus was God's Beloved Son, we as Christians are also known as God's beloved (see Romans 1:7; Ephesians 1:6). We hold a special place in Jesus' heart, because we have been cleansed by His blood and are committed to the work of His everlasting kingdom.

BISHOP OF YOUR SOULS

Only here in the Bible is Jesus called by this name. The word *bishop*, in its New Testament usage, refers to a person who oversees, supervises, or watches over the welfare of others. Thus the translation of this name as "Guardian" or "Overseer" by modern translations.

Notice the mention of "sheep" and "Shepherd" in connection with this name in 1 Peter 2:25. Sheep were helpless animals who often wandered away from the flock. They needed a shepherd—a guardian or overseer—to watch over them and keep them out of danger. The shepherd, or bishop, is a good image for leaders, particularly church leaders. The terms *bishop* and *elder* are often used interchangeably in the Bible to designate those who are responsible for leading God's flock, the church (see Acts 14:23; 1 Timothy 3:1).

It's good to know that we, as wandering sheep, have someone to watch over us. The Bishop of Our Souls is on the job, and He will keep us safe.

BLESSED AND ONLY POTENTATE

In this verse from Paul's first epistle to Timothy, he heaps up three names of God the Son in a row, each showing His unlimited power. The titles King of kings and Lord of lords appear elsewhere in the Bible (see Revelation 17:14; 19:16), but this is the only place where Jesus is called the Blessed and Only Potentate.

The word *potentate* comes from the Latin word *potent*, which means "power." A potentate was a king, monarch, or ruler with total power over his subjects. He shared his power with no one, and no earthly council could question his judgment or veto his decisions.

But Jesus is a Potentate of a different type—a spiritual ruler who will triumph over all the forces of evil when He judges the world at His second coming. He is the *Blessed*

And Jesus, when he was baptized, went up straightway out of the water: and, lo, the heavens were opened unto him, and he saw the Spirit of God descending like a dove, and lighting upon him: and lo a voice from heaven, saying, This is my **beloved Son**, in whom I am well pleased. MATTHEW 3:16–17 [NIV: **my Son, whom I love**; NRSV: **my Son, the Beloved**]

For ye were as sheep going astray; but are now returned unto the Shepherd and **Bishop of your souls**. 1 PETER 2:25 [NASB, NRSV: **Guardian of your souls**; NIV: **Overseer of your souls**]

Which in his times he shall shew, who is the **blessed and only Potentate**, the King of kings, and Lord of lords. 1 TIMOTHY 6:15 [NASB, NRSV: **blessed and only Sovereign**; NIV: **blessed and only Ruler**]

Potentate: Chosen and blessed by God, He has been given ultimate power and authority. He is the *Only* Potentate: the sole ruler who has the right to reign over the new creation that God will bring into being in the end time.

BLESSED AND ONLY SOVEREIGN. See *Blessed and Only Potentate.*

BLESSED AND ONLY RULER. See *Blessed and Only Potentate.*

BOY JESUS. See *Child Jesus.*

BRANCH OF RIGHTEOUSNESS

The prophet Jeremiah predicted that God's judgment would fall on the nation of Judah because of their sin and rebellion against the Lord. But in this verse, he looked beyond that time of destruction to the day when God would send the Messiah, who would be known as the Branch of Righteousness, and who would rule over God's people with love and mercy.

> In those days, and at that time, will I cause the **Branch of righteousness** to grow up unto David [NIV: **sprout from David's line**]; and he shall execute judgment and righteousness in the land.
> JEREMIAH 33:15
> [NIV, NRSV: **righteous Branch**; NASB: **righteous Branch of David**]

The Messiah would be like a new shoot or limb that sprang from a dead tree trunk. God had promised King David centuries before Jeremiah's time that a descendant of David's would always rule over His people (see 2 Samuel 7:12–16). This promise was fulfilled in Jesus Christ. He was the new Davidic king, in a spiritual sense, who came to redeem the world from its bondage to sin and the powers of darkness.

In a prophecy about the coming Messiah, the prophet Jeremiah also refers to Jesus as the Righteous Branch (Jeremiah 23:5).

Other Prophecies About the Branch

"In that day shall the branch of the LORD be beautiful and glorious, and the fruit of the earth shall be excellent and comely for them that are escaped of Israel" (Isaiah 4:2).

"I will raise unto David a righteous Branch, and a King shall reign and prosper, and shall execute judgment and justice in the earth" (Jeremiah 23:5).

"I will bring forth my servant the BRANCH" (Zechariah 3:8).

BREAD

John 6 might be called the "bread chapter" of the New Testament. It begins with Jesus' miracle of multiplying five small loaves of bread and two fish to feed a large crowd of hungry people (see John 6:2–13). It continues across seventy-one verses as Jesus talks with the crowds and the religious leaders about the spiritual bread that He came to provide for the world.

In this long chapter, Jesus uses four different names for Himself that involve the imagery of bread: Bread from Heaven (verse 32), Bread of God (verse 33), Bread of Life (verse 35), and Living Bread (verse 51).

Jesus probably used these names for Himself because bread made from wheat or barley was the staple food of His day. The common people could identify with this comparison. Bread was also closely identified with some of the major events from Israel's history. When the Israelites left Egypt in the Exodus, they baked their bread without leaven, because they didn't have time to wait for the bread to rise (see Exodus 12:30–34). They commemorated this event in future years with a religious festival known as the Feast of Unleavened Bread (see Exodus 13:3–10). The Lord also kept His people alive in the wilderness after the Exodus by providing manna, a bread substitute, for them to eat (see Numbers 11:6–9).

Just as God provided food in the wilderness, He also provides spiritual sustenance for His people. Jesus is the Bread from Heaven that was sent by God Himself. As the Living Bread and the Bread of Life, Jesus provides eternal life for

My Father giveth you the **true bread from heaven**.
JOHN 6:32

For the **bread of God** is he which cometh down from heaven, and giveth life unto the world.
JOHN 6:33

I am the **bread of life**: he that cometh to me shall never hunger.
JOHN 6:35

I am the **living bread** which came down from heaven. . . and the bread that I will give is my flesh, which I will give for the life of the world.
JOHN 6:51

Bread from Thebes in Egypt, dating as far back as 1550 BC.

those who claim Him as their Lord and Savior. "This is that bread which came down from heaven," Jesus declared. "Not as your fathers did eat manna, and are dead: he that eateth of this bread shall live for ever" (John 6:58).

In her hymn "Break Thou the Bread of Life," Mary A. Lathbury expresses the deep desire of all Christians for fellowship with Christ, the Living Bread.

Break thou the bread of life, dear Lord, to me,
As thou didst break the loaves beside the sea;
Beyond the sacred page I seek thee, Lord;
My spirit pants for Thee, O living Word.

BREAD FROM HEAVEN. See *Bread.*

BREAD OF GOD. See *Bread.*

BREAD OF LIFE. See *Bread.*

BRIDEGROOM

And Jesus said unto them, Can the children of the bridechamber [NIV: guests of the bridegroom] mourn, as long as the **bridegroom** is with them? but the days will come, when the **bridegroom** shall be taken from them, and then shall they fast.
MATTHEW 9:15

Jesus responded with these words when the followers of John the Baptist asked why He and His disciples did not participate in the ritual of fasting. His answer picked up imagery from a Jewish wedding, with Jesus referring to Himself as the Bridegroom and His disciples as the wedding guests ("children of the bridechamber").

It was not appropriate, Jesus said, for His disciples to fast or mourn while He as the Bridegroom was physically present with them. They should save their fasting for the time when He would be taken up to heaven by God the Father after His death and resurrection.

We are accustomed to thinking of Jesus as the King, Redeemer, or Savior. But Bridegroom? This name strikes us as a little strange. What did He mean when He applied this name to Himself?

One possibility is that He used this name to identify closely with God the Father, who referred to Himself as the Husband of His people (see *Husband* in part 1, Names of God the Father). Jesus as the Bridegroom will provide for His followers, just as any bridegroom assumes responsibility for taking care of his wife and children.

Another possibility is that Jesus was looking ahead to the birth of the church, which is spoken of symbolically as His bride (see Revelation 21:9). The apostle Paul points out that, just as "the husband is head of the wife," so "Christ is the head of the church" (Ephesians 5:23). Jesus loved the church so much that He laid down His life for it (see Ephesians 5:25). Every single member of His kingdom has experienced this sacrificial love.

Maybe Bridegroom is not such a strange name for Jesus, after all.

BRIGHT AND MORNING STAR

This is one of the last names of God the Son mentioned in the Bible, since it appears in the final chapter of the last book of the Bible. How appropriate that Jesus should call Himself the Bright and Morning Star, a name associated with a heavenly body and its light.

The people of ancient times did not know as much about stars, planets, and heavenly bodies as we know today. To them, the last star to disappear in the eastern sky as the sun began to rise was known as the morning star. Scholars and astronomers of modern times have identified this "star" as the planet Venus, Earth's closest neighbor. Because of its closeness, Venus is the third brightest object in the sky, outshone only by the sun and the moon.

When the light from all the other stars disappears in the early morning, Venus twinkles on, signaling the beginning of

I Jesus have sent mine angel to testify unto you these things in the churches. I am the root and the offspring of David, and the **bright and morning star**.
REVELATION 22:16

Venus, the "morning star," shines along with the crescent moon.

a new day. The birth of Jesus also marked the beginning of a new day. This truth should bring joy to our hearts. What better way to greet the dawning of each new day than to breathe a prayer of thanks to God for sending His Bright and Morning Star into the world.

Another name of God the Son that means basically the same thing as Bright and Morning Star is Day Star (2 Peter 1:19).

BRIGHTNESS OF GOD'S GLORY

The Old Testament contains many references to God's glory, referring to His excellence and majesty (see *Father of Glory* in part 1, Names of God the Father). But the writer of Hebrews in this verse says, in effect, "You don't know divine glory until you experience the glory that appears in Jesus Christ." He is the Brightness of God's Glory. In Him, the glory of God appeared as it had never appeared before.

> Who being the **brightness of his glory**, and the express image of his person, and upholding all things by the word of his power [NIV: sustaining all things by his powerful word], when he had by himself purged our sins, sat down on the right hand of the Majesty on high.
> HEBREWS 1:3
> [NASB: **Radiance of His glory**; NIV: **Radiance of God's glory**; NRSV: **reflection of God's glory**]

As God's Son, Jesus shared in the Father's glory, or His divine nature. He was born into the world by supernatural conception in Mary's womb (see Luke 1:34–35). His teachings and His miracles were performed under God's authority, causing people to exclaim, "We have never seen anything like this!" (Mark 2:12 NIV). His glorious resurrection demonstrated His power over the forces of evil and death.

But the greatest demonstration of Jesus' glory is reserved for the future. In the end time, at His return, the apostle Paul declares, "every knee should bow. . .and every tongue confess that Jesus Christ is Lord, to the glory of God the Father" (Philippians 2:10–11 NIV).

Another name of God the Son that expresses basically the same idea as Brightness of God's Glory is Lord of Glory (James 2:1).

Jesus and His Glory

"And the Word was made flesh, and dwelt among us, (and we beheld his glory)" (John 1:14).

"Father, I will that they also, whom thou has given me [Jesus' disciples], be with me where I am; that they may behold my glory" (John 17:24).

"God. . .hath shined in our hearts, to give the light of the knowledge of the glory of God in the face of Jesus Christ" (2 Corinthians 4:6).

CAPSTONE. See *Head of the Corner.*

CAPTAIN OF SALVATION

This is the only place in the Bible where Jesus is called the Captain of Salvation. The Greek word behind *captain* in this verse is rendered as "author" in Hebrews 12:2 (see *Author and Finisher of Our Faith* above). Other meanings of this word are "prince" and "leader" (see NRSV).

In what sense is Jesus the Captain or Leader of Salvation? For one thing, this verse from Hebrews goes on to say that He was made "perfect in sufferings." A genuine leader does not ask his followers to do something that he is not willing to do himself. He sets the example for those whom he leads. This is what Jesus did when He died on the cross for us. We as Christians will never suffer more by following Him than He did to make it possible for us to be cleansed of our sins.

A leader also guides, encourages, inspires, and motivates the people in his charge. We can rest assured that we are in good hands when we follow our Captain of Salvation.

> For it became him, for whom are all things, and by whom are all things, in bringing many sons unto glory, to make the **captain of their salvation** perfect through sufferings.
> HEBREWS 2:10
> [NASB, NIV: **author of their salvation**; NRSV: **pioneer of their salvation**]

Following the Lord's Leadership

God the Father and His Son, Jesus Christ, are trustworthy leaders who will lead us in the right paths. This sentiment was expressed beautifully by Joseph H. Gilmore in his hymn "He Leadeth Me! O Blessed Tho't!"

He leadeth me! O blessed tho't!
O words with heav'nly comfort fraught!
Whate'er I do, where'er I be,
Still 'tis God's hand that leadeth me!
He leadeth me, He leadeth me,
By His own hand He leadeth me:
His faithful foll'wer I would be,
For by His hand He leadeth me.

CAPTAIN OF THE HOST OF THE LORD

This is the name by which the mysterious messenger of the Lord identified Himself to Joshua as the Israelites prepared to enter Canaan. The best explanation of this verse is that the messenger was the Angel of the Lord, also called the Angel of His Presence in Isaiah 63:9 (see *Angel of His Presence* above).

In the third century of the modern era, the scholar

Origen identified this messenger as Jesus Christ in a pre-incarnate appearance. This approach to the passage has been followed by many modern Bible students. One strong argument for this interpretation is that Joshua bowed down and worshipped this Captain of the Host of the Lord. This indicates that He was a divine being of high stature, not just a messenger of a lower angelic order.

This name of God the Son uses military imagery. The NIV and NRSV render it as "Commander of the Army of the Lord." After Moses died, Joshua became the new leader of Israel. He faced the daunting task of leading Israel against the Canaanites and claiming the land of promise for God's people. The appearance of the Captain of the Host of the Lord assured Joshua that he would be successful in this campaign. This would happen not because of their military might, but because God would go before them into battle.

CARPENTER

During His ministry, Jesus paid a visit to His hometown of Nazareth. This verse describes the skeptical response to His teachings by the people who had known Him for many years. To them, He was nothing but "the carpenter," a skilled tradesman who had grown up in their midst and who was nothing special.

This is the only place in the Bible where this name is applied to Jesus. The people of His hometown used it in a derogatory way, but it is actually a name of honor and dignity. Jesus probably learned this skill from His earthly father, Joseph. He must have worked at this trade for at least fifteen or twenty years before He began His public ministry at about thirty years of age (see Luke 3:23).

The word *carpenter* in our society applies generally to a skilled workman who constructs buildings. But in New Testament times, this occupation was more likely what we know today as woodworking. Jesus probably worked with Joseph in a woodworking shop, making and repairing furniture and tools for the citizens of Nazareth.

As the Carpenter of Nazareth, who worked with His hands, Jesus dignified labor and identified with the common people of His day. He spoke in language they could understand, driving home His teachings with parables drawn from everyday life. No wonder "the common people heard him gladly" (Mark 12:37).

In Matthew's Gospel, the skeptical people of Nazareth refer to Jesus not as "the carpenter" but as "the carpenter's son" (Matthew 13:55).

CARPENTER'S SON. See *Carpenter.*

CHIEF CORNERSTONE

With these words, the apostle Paul assured the believers in the church at Ephesus that they were recipients of God's grace. Their faith in Christ had brought them into God's kingdom, because He was the Chief Cornerstone on which this kingdom was built.

Jesus as the Cornerstone of our faith is one of the most important images of God the Son in the Bible. It is rooted in a famous messianic passage that was written several centuries before Jesus was born. In Psalm 118:22, the psalmist declares, "The stone which the builders refused is become the head stone of the corner."

Jesus identified with this messianic passage during the final days of His ministry. He knew that He would be rejected as the Messiah and executed by the religious leaders

Now therefore ye are no more strangers and foreigners, but fellowcitizens with the saints [NIV: God's people], and of the household of God. And are built upon the foundation of the apostles and prophets, Jesus Christ himself being the **chief corner stone**. EPHESIANS 2:19–20 [NIV, NRSV: **cornerstone**)

George Washington lays the cornerstone of the U.S. Capitol in a painting by DeLand.

of His nation. So he told them: "Did ye never read in the scriptures, The stone which the builders rejected, the same is become the head of the corner: this is the Lord's doing, and it is marvellous in our eyes? Therefore. . .the kingdom of God shall be taken from you, and given to a nation bringing forth the fruits thereof" (Matthew 21:42–43).

Jesus was referring to the non-Jewish or Gentile nations that would accept Him as Lord and Savior. This is exactly what happened as the gospel was proclaimed throughout the Roman world after Jesus' death and resurrection. The leader of this movement was a Jewish zealot and persecutor of the church—the apostle Paul—who was gloriously converted to Christianity and transformed into the "apostle to the Gentiles" (see Acts 9:15).

In the stone buildings of Bible times, a cornerstone was used to hold two opposing rows of stones together at the point where they came together. Jesus as the Chief Cornerstone is the force on which our faith is based. Though He may be rejected by the non-believing world, He is our hope in this life and the life to come.

In a famous prophecy about the coming Messiah, Isaiah also refers to Jesus as the Precious Corner Stone and the Tried Stone (Isaiah 28:16).

CHIEF SHEPHERD. See *Good Shepherd.*

CHILD. See *Babe.*

CHILD JESUS

This verse is part of the only account we have in the Gospels about the childhood of Jesus. According to Luke 2:41–52, when Jesus was twelve, He made a trip to Jerusalem with His parents to observe the Passover Feast. Joseph and Mary were traveling with a group back to Nazareth when they discovered that the boy Jesus was missing. He had "tarried behind" in Jerusalem.

Joseph and Mary returned quickly to the Holy City, where they discovered Jesus in the temple among the Jewish teachers and scholars, listening to them expound on the scriptures and asking them questions. Everyone was amazed at His religious insights at such a young age.

And when they had fulfilled the days [NIV: After the Feast was over], as they returned, the **child Jesus** tarried [NIV: stayed] behind in Jerusalem; and Joseph and his mother knew not of it.
LUKE 2:43
[NASB, NIV, NRSV: **boy Jesus**]

This account tells us that, even as a child, Jesus was aware of His special mission as the Son of God. When His mother scolded Him for staying behind in Jerusalem and causing her and Joseph such anxiety, He replied, "Why were you searching for me? . . . Didn't you know I had to be in my Father's house?" (Luke 2:49 NIV).

This account in Luke goes on to report that Jesus returned to Nazareth with His earthly parents, and He "increased in wisdom and stature, and in favour with God and man" (Luke 2:52). In other words, He grew up like any typical Jewish boy of the first century. As the Child Jesus, He went through all the normal stages of life—from birth, to infancy, to childhood, to adulthood. He is a Savior who can identify with us in all our human experiences.

In Peter's remarks to the Jewish Sanhedrin after healing a lame man near the temple, he referred to Jesus as the Holy Child Jesus (Acts 4:27, 30).

CHOSEN BEFORE THE CREATION OF THE WORLD. See *Foreordained before the Foundation of the World.*

CHOSEN OF GOD

Chosen of God is the name that the religious leaders and the scoffing crowd assigned to Jesus as He was dying on the cross. The irony is that the name that they used in ridicule was a perfect description of Jesus and the mission from His Father that had brought Him into the world.

For generations, the Jewish people had looked for a Messiah sent from God, who would serve as a Deliverer for His people. Jesus was that Chosen One, but He was not the type of champion they expected. He came not as a military conqueror, but as a spiritual Savior who died to deliver people from their sin. His work as the Chosen One of God continues to this day, as He calls people to take up their crosses and follow Him (see Matthew 16:24).

And the people stood beholding [NIV: watching]. And the rulers also with them derided [NIV: sneered at] him, saying, He saved others; let him save himself, if he be Christ, the **chosen of God**.
LUKE 23:35
[NASB, NIV, NRSV: **Chosen One**]

Others Chosen of God

Jesus was deemed the Chosen of God in a special sense. But He followed in the tradition of many people in the Bible who were said to be chosen of God. These include

- Descendants of Jacob, or the Israelites (1 Chronicles 16:13)
- King Solomon (1 Chronicles 29:1)
- Moses (Psalm 106:23)
- Zerubbabel (Haggai 2:23)
- The apostle Paul (Acts 9:15)
- All Christians (Ephesians 1:4; 1 Peter 2:9)

CHOSEN ONE. See *Chosen of God*; *Elect*.

CHRIST

And Simon Peter answered and said, Thou art the **Christ**, the Son of the living God. MATTHEW 16:16 [NRSV: **Messiah**]

These two verses are part of the account of Peter's recognition and confession of Jesus as the Messiah in the Gospel of Matthew (see Matthew 16:13–20).

Notice the use of the article the ("the Christ") in both verses. The English word *Christ* comes from the Greek word *christos*, which means "anointed." Thus, Peter was declaring that Jesus was the Anointed One, a special agent who had been sent into the world under divine appointment by God Himself. He was the Son of God, the Messiah, the great Deliverer for whom the Jewish people had been looking for many years.

Then charged he his disciples that they should tell no man that he was Jesus the **Christ**. MATTHEW 16:20 [NRSV: **Messiah**]

Jesus commended Peter for his recognition of Him as God's Anointed One. But why did He want His identity as the Messiah to be kept a secret?

He probably charged His disciples to keep quiet about His messiahship because the Jewish people expected their Messiah to be a military and political champion. They thought He would rally the people, raise an army, deliver their nation from Roman tyranny, and restore Israel to its glory days.

Jesus could not live up to these expectations, because He was a Messiah in a spiritual sense. He had been sent to teach about the kingdom of God, to heal the sick, and to deliver the people from their sin. He would eventually reveal Himself as the Son of God (see Luke 22:70–71), but only after He had completed the spiritual mission on which He had been sent.

Jesus is called *Christ* (the Messiah or the Anointed One) hundreds of times throughout the New Testament. Often this name or title is grouped with other names. For example, *Jesus Christ* actually means "Jesus the Anointed One" or "Jesus the Messiah." *Christ of God* (see Luke 9:20) means "the Anointed One of God." *Christ Jesus* appears often in the epistles, especially in those written by the apostle Paul (see Romans 3:24; 1 Corinthians 1:2). This reversal of the two names places emphasis on the messiahship of God's Son.

Because Jesus was the Anointed One of God, we as His followers are also commissioned to continue His work in the world. The apostle Paul declares, "Now he which stablisheth us with you in Christ, and hath anointed us, is God" (2 Corinthians 1:21).

A Name to Carry Proudly

The name or title Christ is carried by all Christians—those who belong to Jesus Christ. This name—Christians—appears only three times in the New Testament. According to the book of Acts, it was first applied to the believers in the church at Antioch (see Acts 11:26). An unbeliever, King Agrippa, used it when he told the apostle Paul, "Almost thou persuadest me to be a Christian" (Acts 26:28). And the apostle Peter encouraged the persecuted Christians to whom he wrote with these words: "Yet if any man suffer as a Christian, let him not be ashamed; but let him glorify God on this behalf" (1 Peter 4:16).

CHRIST CRUCIFIED

This is the only place in the Bible where this name of God the Son appears. Since the name or title *Christ* means "the Anointed One" or "the Messiah" (see *Christ* above), the literal meaning of this name is "the Messiah Crucified."

In Jewish tradition, the coming Messiah was to be a powerful leader who would defeat all their enemies and rule over a restored Israel in splendor and glory. That this Messiah would die on a Roman cross like a common criminal was something they found totally unacceptable—a "stumblingblock" that prevented them from accepting Jesus as the Messiah.

A crucified Savior who died in our place to set us free from bondage to sin is still a foreign concept to many people.

But we preach **Christ crucified**, unto the Jews a stumblingblock, and unto the Greeks foolishness.
1 CORINTHIANS 1:23

Like the rich young ruler, they want to know "what good thing" (Matthew 19:16) they must do in order to be assured of eternal life. But there is nothing we can do that will buy us God's favor. We must accept by faith the provision for our salvation that God has already made through the death of His Son.

The apostle Paul puts it like this: "For by grace are ye saved through faith; and that not of yourselves: it is the gift of God: not of works, lest any man should boast" (Ephesians 2:8–9).

Jesus' death on the cross may be one of the most painted and sculpted events of human history.

CHRIST JESUS. See *Christ*.

CHRIST JESUS OUR LORD

This is one of the more inspiring passages in all the writings of the apostle Paul. Generations of Christians have claimed its promise that no force on earth or heaven is strong enough to break the grip of God's love on their lives.

This passage is also unusual because Paul strings together three separate names or titles of God the Son—*Christ*, *Jesus*, and *Lord*—to express this truth in such a powerful way. *Christ* means "the Anointed One" or "the Messiah" (see *Christ* above). *Jesus* was His personal name, which means "God Is Salvation" (Luke 1:31; 2:21). *Lord* expresses His unlimited dominion and power, a characteristic that Jesus shares with God His Father.

With Paul, we can declare that Christ Jesus Our Lord walks with us through every experience of life, and His love will never let us go.

Other variations on this name are Lord and Saviour Jesus Christ (2 Peter 3:18), Lord Christ (Colossians 3:24), and Lord Jesus Christ our Saviour (Titus 1:4).

CHRIST OF GOD. See *Christ*.

COMMANDER OF THE ARMY OF THE LORD. See *Captain of the Host of the Lord*.

CONSOLATION OF ISRAEL

A few weeks after Jesus was born, Joseph and Mary took Him to the temple in Jerusalem to dedicate Him to the Lord. A man named Simeon was moved by the Holy Spirit to come to the temple while they were there. He immediately recognized the young Jesus as the Messiah who had been sent as the Consolation of Israel.

The word *consolation* means "comfort" or "relief." God had promised in the Old Testament that He would send His Messiah to His people someday. Simeon was convinced that he would not die before he had seen this promise fulfilled (see Luke 2:26). God apparently showed him by divine revelation that the baby Jesus was the Promised One for whom the nation of Israel had been waiting.

> For I am persuaded, that neither death, nor life, nor angels, nor principalities, nor powers, nor things present, nor things to come, nor height, nor depth, nor any other creature, shall be able to separate us from the love of God, which is in **Christ Jesus our Lord**.
> ROMANS 8:38–39

> And, behold, there was a man in Jerusalem, whose name was Simeon; and the same man was just [NIV: righteous] and devout, waiting for the **consolation of Israel**: and the Holy Ghost was upon him.
> LUKE 2:25

But this good news had a dark side. Simeon told Mary and Joseph that many people would accept their Son as the Messiah, but many would not (see Luke 2:34). He also revealed to Mary that "a sword shall pierce through thy own soul also" (Luke 2:35)—a prediction of Jesus' future crucifixion.

Today, as then, Jesus' birth was a good news/bad news scenario—good news for those who accepted His messiahship, and bad news for those who refused to believe He had been sent by God the Father. Our task as Christians is to help others find the consolation that Jesus can bring into their lives.

Simeon's Prayer When He Saw the Infant Jesus

"Lord, now lettest thou thy servant depart in peace, according to thy word: For mine eyes have seen thy salvation, which thou hast prepared before the face of all people; a light to lighten the Gentiles, and the glory of thy people Israel" (Luke 2:29–32).

CORNERSTONE. See *Chief Cornerstone; Head of the Corner.*

COUNSELLOR

This verse is probably the most familiar messianic prophecy in the book of Isaiah. It is especially quoted at Christmastime when we gather with other believers to celebrate the birth of Jesus.

Most modern translations drop the comma between *Wonderful* and *Counselor* and render this name as Wonderful Counselor. But no matter how many words are included in the name, Counselor is one of the most significant titles of God the Son in the Bible.

The word *counsel* refers to guidance, advice, or instruction. The Bible is filled with models of good counsel and bad counsel and counselors who fall into both categories.

For example, on the good side, Daniel provided wise counsel to Arioch, an aide to King Nebuchadnezzar of Babylon, when the king issued an order to have all his wise men put to death (see Daniel 2:10–16). But on the foolish side, King Rehoboam of Judah rejected the wise counsel of the older leaders of the nation and listened to the foolish counsel of his young associates (see 1 Kings 12:8). This led to the rebellion of the northern tribes and the division of the united

For unto us a child is born, unto us a son is given: and the government shall be upon his shoulder: and his name shall be called Wonderful, **Counsellor**, The mighty God, The everlasting Father, The Prince of Peace.
ISAIAH 9:6
[NASB, NIV, NRSV: **Wonderful Counselor**]

kingdom of Solomon into two separate nations (see 1 Kings 12:16–19).

We can depend on Jesus, our wise Counselor, to always provide us with good instruction. He guides us with grace and righteousness. He will never give us bad advice that would cause us to go astray.

A counselor provides guidance to a troubled patient.

COVENANT OF THE PEOPLE

The forty-second chapter of Isaiah is one of the famous "servant songs" of his book. This Servant is Jesus, the Messiah, who will bring salvation to all people.

In 42:6, the prophet refers to the Messiah as a Covenant of the People. He will do more than establish a new covenant of God with the people. He *is* the new covenant. Through the Messiah, and His death and resurrection, God provides the means by which people can have unbroken fellowship with the Lord of the universe. Jesus is the only mediator between man and God that people need.

I the LORD have called thee in righteousness, and will hold thine hand, and will keep thee, and give thee for a **covenant of the people**, for a light of the Gentiles.
ISAIAH 42:6

Standing on the Solid Rock

"The Solid Rock," a hymn by Edward Mote, declares that the blood of Jesus seals the new covenant between God and His people.

His oath, His covenant, His blood
Support me in the whelming flood;
When all around my soul gives way,
He then is all my hope and stay.
On Christ, the solid Rock, I stand;
All other ground is sinking sand,
All other ground is sinking sand.

DAWN FROM ON HIGH. See *Dayspring from on High.*

DAYSMAN

Neither is there any **daysman** betwixt us, that might lay his hand upon us both.
JOB 9:33
[NASB, NRSV: **Umpire**;
NIV: **someone to arbitrate**]

This verse is part of Job's complaint that God was punishing him without cause. Job was convinced that he had done nothing to deserve his suffering. To make matters worse, God was all-powerful and Job was but a weak human being, who had no right to question God. So he longed for a Daysman—a referee, mediator, or impartial judge—who could speak to God on his behalf.

Job's desire for someone to represent him before God the Father was eventually fulfilled with the coming of Jesus Christ into the world. As the God-man, Jesus is fully human and fully divine. He communicates directly with the Father, because He is God's Son. But He identifies with us humans in our frailties, because He came to earth in human form. As Job expressed it, Jesus is able to "lay his hand upon us both"—God and man.

It's difficult for us to comprehend how Jesus could be both human and divine at the same time. But just because we don't understand it doesn't mean it isn't true. Here's how the apostle Paul expressed this great truth: "Let this mind be in you, which was also in Christ Jesus: who, being in the form of God, thought it not robbery to be equal with God:

Today, we would call a "daysman" an "umpire"—a term even the most casual baseball fan understands.

but made himself of no reputation, and took upon him the form of a servant, and was made in the likeness of men: and being found in fashion as a man, he humbled himself, and became obedient unto death, even the death of the cross" (Philippians 2:5–8).

DAYSPRING FROM ON HIGH

This verse is part of the passage in the Gospel of Luke known as the "Benedictus" (see Luke 1:68–79). This passage consists of a prayer uttered by Zacharias, father of John the Baptist, after John was born. An angel had revealed to Zacharias, even before John's birth, that his son would be the forerunner of the Messiah. In this prayer, Zacharias praises God for sending the Messiah, Jesus, whom he calls the Dayspring from on High.

The English word *dayspring* comes from a Greek word that means "a rising up." It is generally used to describe the rising of the sun in the morning and the appearance of stars in the night sky. Thus, Zacharias thought of Jesus the Messiah as a bright light that God was preparing to send into a dark world.

The phrase *on high* reveals the origin of this Daystar. Jesus did not come into the world on His own as a "Lone Ranger." He was on a mission of redemption from God the Father.

The prophet Malachi uses a similar name for Jesus in his prophecy about the coming Messiah. He calls Him the Sun of Righteousness who would "arise with healing in his wings" (Malachi 4:2).

DAY STAR. See *Bright and Morning Star.*

DELIVERER

In this verse, Paul refers to Psalm 14:7, a portion of a messianic psalm written many years before. This psalm is attributed to David, who declares that the salvation of God's people would come from Zion, or Jerusalem.

This is an unusual reference to the Messiah, because Jesus was born in Bethlehem, not Jerusalem. But Jesus was crucified and resurrected in Jerusalem. This is also the place where the church was born on the day of Pentecost (see Acts 2:1–41) following Jesus' ascension to God the Father. These facts are probably what Paul had in mind when he declared that Jesus as our Deliverer came out of Jerusalem.

Through the tender mercy of our God; whereby the **dayspring from on high** hath visited us.
LUKE 1:78
[NASB: **Sunrise from on high**; NIV: **rising sun**; NRSV: **dawn from on high**]

And so all Israel shall be saved: as it is written, There shall come out of Sion [NIV: Zion] the **Deliverer**, and shall turn away ungodliness from Jacob.
ROMANS 11:26

The great work that Jesus performs as our Deliverer is to rescue us from sin. He sets us free from the guilt that accompanies our sin and separates us from God (see Isaiah 59:2). He delivers us from the power of Satan, who tempts us constantly to fall back into sin (see Ephesians 6:11–13). And He will deliver us from a world filled with sin when He returns to claim us as His own (see Galatians 1:4).

God is also referred to in the Old Testament as our Deliverer (see *Deliverer* in part 1, Names of God the Father). His deliverance in that section of the Bible is expressed mainly in physical terms. But His work as our Deliverer in a spiritual sense continues through His Son.

DESCENDANT OF DAVID. See *Root and Offspring of David*.

DESIRE OF ALL NATIONS

The prophet Haggai spoke these words to the Jewish exiles who had returned to Jerusalem after their period of captivity in Babylonia and Persia. He challenged them to get busy at the task of rebuilding the Jewish temple that had been destroyed about eighty years before by the invading Babylonian army. The temple is apparently the "house" referred to in this verse.

But Haggai's words also look beyond his time to the distant future when Israel's Messiah would become the Desire of All Nations. At the Messiah's return in glory in the end time, all nations will pay Him homage and recognize his universal rule throughout the earth.

Jesus is not only the desire of Christians; He is the hope of the entire world. As the apostle Paul declares, "At the name of Jesus every knee should bow. . .and every tongue confess that Jesus Christ is Lord, to the glory of God the Father" (Philippians 2:10–11 NIV).

> And I will shake all nations, and the **desire of all nations** shall come: and I will fill this house with glory, saith the LORD of hosts.
> HAGGAI 2:7
> [NASB: **wealth of all nations**; NIV: **desired of all nations**; NRSV: **treasure of all nations**]

In his hymn "Jesus Shall Reign Where'er the Sun," Isaac Watts expresses his sentiments about the universal rule of Christ in the end time.

Jesus shall reign where'er the sun
Does his successive journeys run;
His kingdom stretch from shore to shore,
Till moons shall wax and wane no more.

DESTINED BEFORE THE FOUNDATION OF THE WORLD. See *Foreordained before the Foundation of the World.*

DOCTOR. See *Physician.*

DOOR

This is one of several "I Am" statements made by Jesus in the Gospel of John (see sidebar). A door is an opening or entryway into a building or a shelter. By affirming that He was the Door, Jesus made it clear that he was the only way to salvation and eternal life.

In His Sermon on the Mount, Jesus also addresses this topic by talking about two gates (Matthew 7:13–14). The broad gate, representing the way of the world, is so wide that people can drift through it without any conscious thought about what they are doing. But the narrow gate, representing Jesus and His teachings, requires commitment and sacrifice from those who want to enter this way and follow Him.

Maybe you have heard people say, "It doesn't matter what you believe as long as you're sincere," or "All religions are basically the same; they just take us to heaven by different paths."

Don't you believe it. Jesus declares, "I am the way, the truth, and the life: no man cometh unto the Father but by me" (John 14:6).

> I am the **door**: by me if any man enter in, he shall be saved, and shall go in and out, and find pasture.
> JOHN 10:9
> [NIV, NRSV: **gate**]

Other "I Am" Statements of Jesus
- "I am the bread of life" (John 6:35).
- "I am the light of the world" (John 8:12).
- "I am the door of the sheep" (John 10:7).
- "I am the good shepherd" (John 10:11, 14).
- "I am the resurrection, and the life" (John 11:25).
- "I am the true vine" (John 15:1).

DOOR OF THE SHEEP. See *Good Shepherd.*

ELECT

This is another verse from one of the "servant song" chapters in the book of Isaiah (see *Covenant of the People* above). In this verse, the prophet uses the name *Elect* to describe the relationship of Jesus to God the Father. God elected or chose to

Behold my servant, whom I uphold; mine **elect**, in whom my soul delighteth; I have put my spirit upon him: he shall bring forth judgment to the Gentiles.
ISAIAH 42:1
[NASB, NIV: **chosen one**; NRSV: **chosen**]

send His Son Jesus into the world on a mission of redemption.

The concept of *election* is one of the richer theological themes in the Bible. It refers simply to God's gracious calling of people to become part of His kingdom and participate in His work.

God elected the nation of Israel to become a special recipient of His grace, and to serve as a channel of His blessing to the rest of the world (see Genesis 12:1–3). When Israel failed at this task, God elected to send His own Son to serve as His agent of grace and salvation.

God is still in the election business. The church of Jesus Christ is the channel through which He continues His work. We as Christians are His elect, and we work under the authority of Jesus as the supreme Elect One. We are called to bear witness for Him in a dark and unbelieving world.

EMMANUEL. See *Immanuel/Emmanuel.*

END OF THE LAW

For Christ is the **end of the law** for righteousness to every one that believeth.
ROMANS 10:4

This is the only place in the Bible where Jesus is referred to by this name. The NIV clarifies the meaning of this verse by stating that He is the End of the Law, "so that there may be righteousness for everyone who believes." This name of Jesus has a double meaning.

First, Jesus is the End of the Law because He did everything required by the Old Testament law to become a righteous person. He lived a sinless life and obeyed all of God's commandments, although He was tempted to do wrong, like any human being (see Luke 4:1–13; Matthew 26:36–42; Hebrews 4:15).

Second, Jesus is the End of the Law because He brought an end to law-keeping as the way for people to find justification in God's sight. Belief in Jesus as Lord and Savior is the only way to deal with sin and eliminate the separation between God and mankind.

Some things outlive their usefulness and ought to be brought to an end or transformed into something better. Aren't you glad that Jesus as the End of the Law offers all believers a glorious new beginning?

Jesus, the Believer, and the Law

- "For sin shall not have dominion over you: for ye are not under the law, but under grace" (Romans 6:14).
- "We have believed in Jesus Christ, that we might be justified by the faith of Christ, and not by the works of the law" (Galatians 2:16).
- "For the law made nothing perfect, but the bringing in of a better hope did; by the which we draw nigh unto God" (Hebrews 7:19).

ENSIGN FOR THE NATIONS

The eleventh chapter of Isaiah is one of the more pronounced messianic passages in the prophet's book. In this verse from that chapter, Isaiah portrays the coming Messiah as an Ensign, or Banner, not only for the Jewish people (Israel and Judah) but for all nations of the world.

The prophet probably had in mind a battle flag under which warriors of Bible times fought (see *Jehovah-nissi* in part 1, Names of God the Father). An army was distinguished from its enemies, and from the fighting units of its allies, by the banner under which it marched. Their flag was visible to all members of the unit, and it served as a rallying point for the soldiers during the heat of battle.

As the Ensign for the Nations, Jesus calls on all Christians to fall in step behind Him and spread the Good News of the Gospel throughout the world. The Great Commission (see Matthew 28:19–20) is our call to action.

> And he shall set up an **ensign for the nations**, and shall assemble the outcasts of Israel, and gather together the dispersed of Judah from the four corners of the earth.
> ISAIAH 11:12
> [NASB: **standard for the nations**; NIV: **banner for the nations**; NRSV: **signal for the nations**]

This "ensign" identifies a British ship.

Marching Under the Royal Banner

The hymn "Onward, Christian Soldiers," by Sabine Baring-Gould, is a stirring call to arms for all who belong to the army of the Lord.

Onward, Christian soldiers, marching as to war,
With the cross of Jesus going on before!
Christ, the royal Master, leads against the foe;
Forward into battle, see His banners go!
Onward, Christian soldiers, marching as to war,
With the cross of Jesus going on before!

ETERNAL FATHER. See *Everlasting Father.*

ETERNAL LIFE

Jesus is described as the provider of eternal life in several places in the New Testament. For example:

- "The gift of God is eternal life through Jesus Christ our Lord" (Romans 6:23).
- "This is the promise that he hath promised us, even eternal life" (1 John 2:25).
- "Looking for the mercy of our Lord Jesus Christ unto eternal life" (Jude 1:21).

But 1 John 5:20 is the only verse in the Bible where Jesus Himself is given the name Eternal Life. The apostle John was probably thinking about the resurrection of Jesus, His ascension to the Father, and His declaration, "I am alive for evermore" (Revelation 1:18).

Jesus tasted death like all mortal human beings. But He was gloriously raised and restored to His place of honor with God the Father in heaven. As the perfect model of Eternal Life, Jesus promises that all who place their trust in Him will live forever. The apostle Paul puts it like this: "For as in Adam all die, even so in Christ shall all be made alive" (1 Corinthians 15:22).

EVERLASTING FATHER

We are accustomed to making the distinction between God and Jesus by referring to God as the Father and to Jesus as the Son. But in this famous messianic passage from Isaiah, the prophet seems to blur these neat lines by referring to Jesus as the Father—the Everlasting Father.

This name of Jesus focuses attention on the dilemma we face as Christians in trying to explain the Trinity, or God's existence in three different modes or essences—Father, Son, and Holy Spirit. Just where does the God mode stop and where do the Son and Spirit essences begin?

Some people explain the Trinity by using the analogy of water. We know that water is one substance, but it can exist in three different forms—liquid, ice, and vapor. In the same way, so this analogy goes, God exists in the three different modes known as the Trinity—one substance in three different forms.

And we know that the Son of God is come, and hath given us an understanding, that we may know him that is true, and we are in him that is true, even in his Son Jesus Christ. This is the true God, and **eternal life**.
1 JOHN 5:20

For unto us a child is born, unto us a son is given: and the government shall be upon his shoulder: and his name shall be called Wonderful, Counsellor, The mighty God, The **everlasting Father**, The Prince of Peace.
ISAIAH 9:6
[NASB: **Eternal Father**]

Rather than resorting to analogies like this, we are better off if we admit that there is no neat and easy way to explain the Trinity. This concept is filled with mystery that defies logical explanation. But this doesn't mean it isn't true.

So, was Jesus God's Son? Yes. Was Jesus also God, the Everlasting Father, as Isaiah declared? Yes. This doesn't make sense to our scientific, analytical minds, but faith in God's Word comes to our rescue. We believe that Jesus was separate from God but one with Him at the same time, because He Himself declared, "I and my Father are one" (John 10:30).

EVERLASTING LIGHT

In this verse, the prophet Isaiah looks ahead to the end time, when Christ will dwell with His people in heaven, or the New Jerusalem. There will be no need for the sun or moon in that time, because Jesus will serve as the Everlasting Light for His people.

The apostle John, in the book of Revelation, picks up on this prophecy, repeating Isaiah's declaration that no light would be needed in heaven except the light that Jesus will provide (see Revelation 21:23; 22:5).

It's difficult for earthbound human beings to realize that any light source could replace the sun. This hot, life-giving, luminous body has provided most of the light we have enjoyed throughout our lives. But scientists tell us that the sun is not immortal. They predict it will burn out in about five billion years.

Jesus, however, is the Everlasting Light. When the sun grows dark and disappears from the sky, Jesus' reign will continue, and we as Christians will be with him in this New Jerusalem.

EXACT IMPRINT OF GOD'S VERY BEING. See *Express Image of God.*

EXACT REPRESENTATION OF GOD'S BEING. See *Express Image of God.*

EXACT REPRESENTATION OF GOD'S NATURE. See *Express Image of God.*

The sun shall be no more thy light by day; neither for brightness shall the moon give light unto thee: but the LORD shall be unto thee an **everlasting light**, and thy God thy glory.
ISAIAH 60:19

EXPRESS IMAGE OF GOD

This name occurs at the beginning of the book of Hebrews, where the writer declares that Jesus is the climax of God's revelation of Himself to mankind (see Hebrews 1:1–3). In the past, God had communicated to His people through the prophets; but now He has "spoken unto us by His Son" (Hebrews 1:2).

The Greek word behind the phrase *express image* referred in New Testament times to engravings in wood, impressions in clay, or stamped images on coins. The imagery of this verse from Hebrews implies that Jesus was an exact duplicate of His Father in His attitudes, character, and actions. Physical features are not included in this resemblance, because God is a spiritual being (see John 4:24).

This name, the Express Image of God, tells us that Jesus perfectly represents God, His Father. If we want to know what God looks like, we should examine the life and ministry of His Son.

Have you ever heard someone say, "That boy is just like his father"? Sometimes this pronouncement can cause embarrassment for a father because of his son's bad behavior. But God was always pleased with the actions of His Son (see Luke 3:22).

Other names of God the Son that express the same meaning as this name are Image of God (2 Corinthians 4:4) and Image of the Invisible God (Colossians 1:15).

FAITHFUL

According to the dictionary, a person who is faithful displays "firm determination to stick to a cause or purpose." This definition is a perfect description of Jesus' earthly life and ministry. No wonder the apostle Paul applies the name Faithful to Him in this verse from his first epistle to the Thessalonians.

Throughout His brief earthly ministry, Jesus refused to be turned aside from His mission as the Messiah sent by the Father to bring people into His kingdom of grace. He resisted Satan's temptation at the beginning of His ministry to become a "bread Messiah" and dazzle the crowds with death-defying stunts (see Matthew 4:1–11). He also did not become the military conqueror or political hero that the Jewish people thought the Messiah should be. While on the cross, He did not try to save Himself, although He could have done

Who being the brightness of his glory, and the **express image** of his person, and upholding all things by the word of his power [NIV: sustaining all things by his powerful word], when he had by himself purged our sins, sat down on the right hand of the Majesty on high. HEBREWS 1:3 [NASB: **exact representation of His nature**; NIV: **exact representation of his being**; NRSV: **exact imprint of God's very being**]

Faithful is he that calleth you, who also will do it [NIV: The one who calls you is **faithful** and he will do it]. 1 THESSALONIANS 5:24

so. He chose instead to die for our sins (see Luke 23:35). He was faithful to His mission as the Suffering Servant to the very end.

Dogs are well-loved as faithful companions.

He who was faithful in His earthly existence continues to be the Faithful One to those who follow Him. We as Christians have His promise that we will enjoy eternal life with Him in heaven. As the apostle Paul declares, "He which hath begun a good work in you will perform it until the day of Jesus Christ" (Philippians 1:6).

Jesus Christ, the Faithful One

- "If we confess our sins, he is faithful and just to forgive us our sins, and to cleanse us from all unrighteousness" (1 John 1:9).
- "The Lord is faithful, and he will strengthen and protect you from the evil one" (2 Thessalonians 3:3 NIV).
- "God is faithful, by whom ye were called unto the fellowship of his Son Jesus Christ our Lord" (1 Corinthians 1:9).

FAITHFUL AND TRUE

In this verse near the end of the book of Revelation, the apostle John sees Jesus appear as the heavens are opened. The white horse on which He is seated symbolizes His triumph over all His enemies. As the Faithful and True, He is coming to earth in judgment against all forms of unrighteousness and injustice.

This verse contains images that are similar to the portrayal of God as the divine Judge in the Old Testament (see *Judge* in part 1, Names of God the Father). For example, in Psalm 96:13, the psalmist looks forward to the time when God will judge the earth. He will "judge the world with righteousness, and the people with his truth." Because God is the standard of truth, He has the right to set the standards by which the world will be judged.

In this verse from Revelation, God has delegated to His Son the authority to judge the world. Jesus is faithful to God's promise of judgment, and He is the True One who will judge by God's standard of ultimate truth.

As Christians, we recognize that truth does not always win out in an unjust and unrighteous world. But the final work of judgment belongs to God and His Son—the Faithful and True.

And I saw heaven opened, and behold a white horse; and he that sat upon him was called **Faithful and True**, and in righteousness he doth judge and make war.
REVELATION 19:11

FAITHFUL AND TRUE WITNESS

Witness is one of the words used again and again by the apostle John in his writings—the Gospel of John, his three epistles, and the book of Revelation. It occurs about seventy times in these five books. In this verse from Revelation, John applies this word to Jesus, calling Him the Faithful and True Witness.

A witness is a person who gives testimony to others about something he has seen, felt, or experienced. The best modern example of a witness is a person who is summoned by the justice system to present testimony in a legal proceeding, such as a trial. The task of a witness is to tell the court what he knows from personal experience that is relevant to the case under investigation.

The witness that Jesus bore about God grew out of His personal experience. He is the only person who has ever seen God the Father. Thus He knows God like no one has ever known Him. He came into the world

> And unto the angel of the church of the Laodiceans write; These things saith the Amen, the **faithful and true witness**, the beginning of the creation of God.
> REVELATION 3:14

Witnesses in court swear to speak the truth—and face penalties if found guilty of perjury, or lying under oath.

to show that His Father is a merciful God who relates to His people in love and grace. By dying on the cross, Jesus showed just how much God the Father and God the Son love us.

Those of us who have been transformed by God's love are also charged to give testimony about His love to others (see Luke 24:45–48). Jesus told His disciples, "This gospel of the kingdom shall be preached in all the world for a witness unto all nations" (Matthew 24:14). This witnessing work continues in our time through the church and individual Christians. If you know Jesus as Lord and Savior, you have no choice in the matter—you are automatically in the witnessing business.

FAITHFUL CREATOR

The apostle Peter wrote his first epistle to Christians who were undergoing persecution because of their commitment to Christ. Peter encouraged them to place their hope in their Faithful Creator, Jesus, and to "continue to do good" (NIV). This is the only place in the Bible where Jesus is called by this name.

Jesus as a participant in the physical creation with God the Father is described in other New Testament passages (see John 1:1–3; Colossians 1:16; see also *Beginning of the Creation of God* above). But the emphasis of this verse from 1 Peter is on Jesus' role as spiritual Creator. According to the apostle Paul, we become "new creatures" (2 Corinthians 5:17) when we accept Christ as Savior. As our Faithful Creator, Jesus not only gives us a new nature, but He also keeps us from falling back into sin and He leads us toward the goal of eternal life with Him in heaven.

All Christians can affirm with the apostle Paul, "The Lord will rescue me from every evil attack and will bring me safely to his heavenly kingdom" (2 Timothy 4:18 NIV).

FAITHFUL HIGH PRIEST. See *Great High Priest.*

FINISHER OF OUR FAITH. See *Author and Finisher of Our Faith.*

FIRST AND THE LAST. See *Alpha and Omega.*

FIRSTBEGOTTEN

The word *he* in this verse refers to God the Father, and *first-begotten* refers to His Son, Jesus Christ. But because Jesus has existed from eternity with the Father (see *Beginning of the Creation of God* above), how could Jesus be the firstborn or "firstbegotten into the world"?

Firstbegotten refers to Jesus' incarnation, or His appearance in human flesh. True, He has existed with the Father from the beginning; but there was a specific point in time when He was conceived by the Holy Spirit in Mary's womb and then born nine months later like any human infant (see Luke 1:35; 2:7). This is one sense in which the name Firstbegotten is applied to Jesus.

Wherefore let them that suffer according to the will of God commit the keeping of their souls to him in well doing, as unto a **faithful Creator**.
1 PETER 4:19

And again, when he bringeth in the **firstbegotten** into the world, he saith, And let all the angels of God worship him.
HEBREWS 1:6
[NASB, NIV, NRSV: **firstborn**]

The word also refers to rank or order. To say that Jesus is God's Firstbegotten is to declare that He ranks above all other earthly or divine beings, except God Himself. This verse from Hebrews makes the point that Jesus is higher than all of God's angels, because they are told to bow down and worship Him. Similar names of God the Son that express the idea of His preeminence and superiority are Firstborn (Psalm 89:27), Firstborn Among Many Brethren (Romans 8:29), and First-born of Every Creature (Colossians 1:15).

As God's Firstbegotten or Firstborn, Jesus is worthy of our honor and praise. The apostle Peter declares that all Christians should glorify Jesus Christ, "to whom be praise and dominion for ever and ever" (1 Peter 4:11).

Rights and Responsibilities of the Firstborn

Jesus as the Firstbegotten or Firstborn picks up on a key term that appears often throughout the Old Testament. The firstborn offspring of both humans and animals were considered special blessings of God, and they were to be devoted to Him (see Exodus 13:2). The firstborn son in a Jewish family inherited a larger share of the family property than the other sons, but he also assumed responsibility for taking care of the family after his father's death.

As the Firstborn, Jesus is exalted as head of the church, but He is also responsible for its welfare. Aren't you glad our well-being rests in such capable hands?

FIRST BEGOTTEN OF THE DEAD.
See *Firstborn from the Dead.*

FIRSTBORN. See *Firstbegotten.*

FIRSTBORN AMONG MANY BRETHREN. See *Firstbegotten.*

FIRSTBORN OF EVERY CREATURE.
See *Firstbegotten.*

FIRSTBORN FROM THE DEAD
The apostle Paul applies this name to Jesus in his description of Jesus as head of the church in his epistle to the Colossian Christians. *Firstborn from the Dead* expresses the same

essential meaning as the name *First Begotten of the Dead* in the book of Revelation (see Revelation 1:5).

This name obviously refers to Jesus' resurrection. But in what sense was He the Firstborn from the Dead? Jesus was not the first person in the Bible to be brought back to life following physical death. The prophet Elisha raised back to life the son of a family in Shunem (see 2 Kings 4:18–37). Jesus Himself raised three people from the dead: the daughter of Jairus (see Matthew 9:18–26), the son of a widow in the village of Nain (see Luke 7:11–15), and His friend Lazarus (see John 11:1–44).

But all of these resurrections were temporary stays of death. These resurrected people eventually died again. Jesus rose from the grave never to die again. He was the first person to overcome death and to appear in a glorified body (see Luke 24:36–39). He also rose as the head of a new creation, the church. As the Firstborn from the Dead, Jesus has the authority and power to provide bodily resurrection and eternal life for all who commit their lives to Him (see 1 Corinthians 15:12–26).

> And he is the head of the body, the church: who is the beginning, the **firstborn from the dead**; that in all things he might have the preeminence.
> COLOSSIANS 1:18

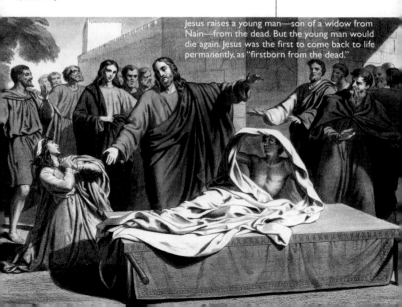

Jesus raises a young man—son of a widow from Nain—from the dead. But the young man would die again. Jesus was the first to come back to life permanently, as "firstborn from the dead."

FIRSTFRUITS

But now is Christ risen from the dead, and become the **firstfruits of them that slept**. 1 CORINTHIANS 15:20 [NIV: **firstfruits of those who have fallen asleep**; NRSV: **first fruits of those who have died**]

But every man in his own order: Christ the **firstfruits**; afterward they that are Christ's at his coming. 1 CORINTHIANS 15:23

These references to Jesus as the Firstfruits occur in the apostle Paul's famous passage about the resurrection of Jesus and His promise of a similar resurrection for all believers (see 1 Corinthians 15:12–57).

Some people in the church at Corinth apparently were teaching that the resurrection was spiritual, not physical, in nature, or that the resurrection of the dead had already happened. They may have even been denying the resurrection altogether, because Paul scolds them: "How say some among you that there is no resurrection of the dead?" (1 Corinthians 15:12).

Paul based his argument for Jesus' physical resurrection on the fact that He had been seen by His disciples as well as many other believers during the days after He rose from the dead (see 1 Corinthians 15:3–7). He was the Firstfruits of the resurrection, or the model that had blazed the trail for them.

The Jewish people thought of the firstfruits, or the first of

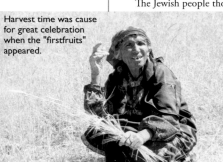

Harvest time was cause for great celebration when the "firstfruits" appeared.

their crops to be gathered, as God's harvest. These were presented as offerings to God on the day of the firstfruits—part of the festival known as Pentecost, which celebrated the harvest (see Numbers 28:26; 2 Chronicles 31:5).

To Paul, Jesus in His resurrection was the Firstfruits of a spiritual harvest known as eternal life. Believers in Jesus would be the rest of the harvest, which would be gathered in at the appointed time. Just as Jesus had been raised from the dead to reign with His Father in glory, so too the believers' bodies would be "raised incorruptible" (1 Corinthians 15:52) at Christ's second coming, and they would live with Him forever in heaven.

FIRSTFRUITS OF THOSE WHO HAVE DIED. See *Firstfruits*.

FLESH

This bold affirmation of the apostle John in his Gospel is the strongest declaration in the New Testament about the humanity of Jesus. And it carries the authority of an eyewitness.

John knew that Jesus existed in the flesh, because he had lived and worked with Him. As one of Jesus' disciples, John had walked with Him along the dusty roads of Palestine, watched His interaction with people, and learned from His teachings across a period of about three years. Certainly, John must have been impressed by Jesus' miracles and His claim to be the divine Son of God. But he was also convinced that Jesus was fully human.

In John's later years, his personal association with Jesus in the flesh was a valuable asset to the church. False teachers had begun to teach that Jesus did not exist in human form, and that He only seemed to be a man. John rejected this heresy with these strong words: "Every spirit that confesseth that Jesus Christ is come in the flesh is of God: and every spirit that confesseth not that Jesus Christ is come in the flesh is not of God: and this is that spirit of antichrist" (1 John 4:2–3).

We find it hard to understand how Jesus could be both divine and human in the same body. But this is the clear affirmation of the New Testament, and the church has upheld this doctrine for almost two thousand years, despite ridicule by the world. Even the apostle Paul admitted that it was a deep mystery, but he accepted it by faith. "And most certainly, the mystery of godliness is great," he said. "He was manifested in the flesh, justified in the Spirit, seen by angels, preached among the Gentiles, believed on in the world, taken up in glory" (1 Timothy 3:16 HCSB).

Other names of God the Son that emphasize the human side of Jesus' nature are God Manifest in the Flesh (1 Timothy 3:16), Man Approved of God (Acts 2:22), and Man Christ Jesus (1 Timothy 2:5).

> And the Word was made **flesh**, and dwelt among us, (and we beheld his glory, the glory as of the only begotten of the Father,) full of grace and truth.
> JOHN 1:14

Evidences from Mark's Gospel of Jesus' Existence in the Flesh

- His fatigue (Mark 4:38)
- His amazement (Mark 6:6)
- His disappointment (Mark 8:12)
- His displeasure (Mark 10:14)
- His anger (Mark 11:15–17)
- His sorrow (Mark 14:34)

FOREKNOWN BEFORE THE FOUNDATION OF THE WORLD. See *Foreordained before the Foundation of the World.*

FOREORDAINED BEFORE THE FOUNDATION OF THE WORLD

This verse from the apostle Peter's first epistle is the only place in the Bible where Jesus is called by this name. It echoes the words of Peter on the day of Pentecost, when three thousand people became believers in Christ (see Acts 2:41). In his sermon on that occasion, Peter told the crowd that Jesus had been sent into the world by "the determinate counsel and foreknowledge of God" (Acts 2:23).

The words *foreordained* and *foreknowledge* show that Jesus was especially chosen by God the Father for the redemptive mission on which He was sent. His coming to earth was no accident; it was part of God's plan. The phrase "before the foundation of the world" tells us that Jesus had existed with God the Father from the beginning (see John 1:1–3). Even before He created the world, God had designated His Son as the agent of salvation for all humankind.

This is difficult for us earthbound humans to understand. But aren't you glad that God didn't wait until we had perfect understanding before He sent Jesus to deliver us from the bondage of sin?

A name of Jesus similar in meaning to Foreordained before the Foundation of the World is Man Whom God Hath Ordained (Acts 17:31).

> Who verily was **foreordained before the foundation of the world**, but was manifest [NIV: revealed] in these last times for you.
> 1 PETER 1:20
> [NASB: **foreknown before the foundation of the world**; NIV: **chosen before the creation of the world**; NRSV: **destined before the foundation of the world**]

FORERUNNER

A forerunner is an advance agent, the lead person on a team. He goes ahead on a scouting mission to spot possible dangers and to prepare the way for others who will follow. Two good examples of forerunners in the Bible are the twelve spies sent by Moses to investigate the land of Canaan (see Numbers 13:1–3) and the forerunner of Jesus, John the Baptist (see Mark 1:1–8).

But the ultimate Forerunner, according to the author of Hebrews, was Jesus Christ. He came to prepare the way so we could become citizens of God's kingdom. Following His death and resurrection, He returned to His Father in heaven (see Acts 1:9). There, He has prepared a place for us. We as

> Whither the **forerunner** is for us entered, even Jesus, made an high priest for ever after the order of Melchisedec.
> HEBREWS 6:20

Christians have His word that we will live in heaven with Him forever. "If I go and prepare a place for you," He promised, "I will come again, and receive you unto myself, that where I am, there ye may be also" (John 14:3).

An advance scout serves as "forerunner" to his fellow soldiers.

FOUNDATION

In his first letter to the believers at Corinth, the apostle Paul dealt with divisions in the church (see 1 Corinthians 1:10–15). The people were following four different authority figures—Paul, Apollos, Cephas, and Christ. Paul made it clear in this verse (3:11) that the one Foundation on which they should be basing their faith was Jesus Christ.

For other **foundation** can no man lay than that is laid, which is Jesus Christ.
1 CORINTHIANS 3:11

The Ultimate Foundation

The old hymn "How Firm a Foundation" declares that Christians can rely on Jesus Christ and the promise of His abiding presence.

How firm a foundation, ye saints of the Lord,
Is laid for your faith in His excellent Word!
What more can He say than to you He hath said,
To you who for refuge to Jesus have fled?

Jesus Himself addressed this issue during His earthly ministry. In the parable of the two foundations, He described two men who built houses on two different sites (see Matthew 7:24–27). The house built on sand collapsed in the first storm that came up. The second house held firm in violent weather, because "it was founded upon a rock" (Matthew 7:25).

The message of this parable is that almost any foundation will do when the weather is good. But only a faith based on the solid Foundation known as Jesus Christ can withstand the gales and floods of life.

Several centuries before Jesus was born, the prophet Isaiah looked ahead to the coming of the Messiah and referred to Him as the Sure Foundation (Isaiah 28:16).

FOUNTAIN

> In that day there shall be a **fountain** opened to the house of David and to the inhabitants of Jerusalem for sin and for uncleanness [NIV: to cleanse them from sin and impurity].
> ZECHARIAH 13:1

This verse from the prophet Zechariah looks forward to the day when the nations of Israel and Judah would be restored to moral purity. They had rebelled against God and were worshipping false gods. The Lord would provide a fountain in which they could wash and be cleansed of their sin.

The word *fountain* in the Bible generally refers to a spring or some source of fresh water, such as a well or a free-flowing stream. This type of water was preferable to standing water that was stored in cisterns. The prophet Isaiah used this image of a fountain in referring to God (see *Fountain of Living Waters* in part 1, Names of God the Father).

This passage from Zechariah has been interpreted as a reference to Jesus Christ. He is the Fountain whose blood provides cleansing from sin. This Fountain is available to everyone—nobles ("the house of David") as well as commoners ("the inhabitants of Jerusalem").

As the Fountain of salvation, Jesus invites us to drink freely of the living water that He provides. "Whosoever drinketh of the water that I shall give him shall never thirst," He told the woman at the well. "The water that I shall give him shall be in him a well of water springing up into everlasting life" (John 4:14).

Jesus as the Fountain of Life is memorialized in the hymn "There Is a Fountain," written by William Cowper.

> There is a fountain filled with blood
> Drawn from Immanuel's veins;
> And sinners plunged beneath that flood
> Lose all their guilty stains.
> Lose all their guilty stains,
> Lose all their guilty stains;
> And sinners plunged beneath that flood
> Lose all their guilty stains.

FRIEND OF PUBLICANS AND SINNERS

With these words, Jesus condemned the Pharisees, who were criticizing Him for associating with people whom they considered the outcasts of society.

But Jesus took their criticism as a compliment. He had been sent into the world to become the Savior of sinners. On one occasion, He told the scribes and Pharisees, "They that are whole have no need of the physician, but they that are sick: I came not to call the righteous, but sinners to repentance" (Mark 2:17).

In addition to befriending all sinners, Jesus was also a special friend to His disciples—the twelve ordinary men whom He trained to carry on His work after He was gone. In His long farewell address to them in the Gospel of John, He tells them, "Henceforth I call you not servants. . .but I have called you friends; for all things that I have heard of my father I have made known unto you" (John 15:15).

Most of us get to know a lot of people during our lifetime—teachers, neighbors, fellow church members, work associates. But few of these become true friends. In this select group whom we consider friends, one stands out above all others—our Lord Jesus Christ. He is the Friend who made the ultimate sacrifice on our behalf. "Greater love hath no man than this," He declared, "that a man lay down his life for his friends" (John 15:13).

The Son of man came eating and drinking, and they say, Behold a man gluttonous, and a winebibber [NIV: Here is a glutton and a drunkard], a **friend of publicans and sinners**.
MATTHEW 11:19
[NASB, NIV, NRSV: **friend of tax collectors and sinners**]

"Jesus Is All the World to Me," a hymn by Will L. Thompson, focuses on the never-failing friendship of Jesus for all believers.

Jesus is all the world to me,
My life, my joy, my all;
He is my strength from day to day,
Without Him I would fall:
When I am sad, to Him I go,
No other one can cheer me so;
When I am sad
He makes me glad,
He's my friend.

FULLERS' SOAP

This verse from the next to last chapter in the Old Testament refers to the coming Messiah. The Jewish people expected Him to be a conquering hero. But the prophet Malachi declared that He would come in judgment against the sinful nation of Israel.

A fuller, or launderer, made his living by washing and dyeing clothes or cloth. Soap as we know it did not exist in Bible times, so the fuller used a strong alkaline substance to get clothes clean. It was made from a plant that was reduced to ashes to form potash or lye.

The name Fullers' Soap emphasizes the judgment side of Jesus' ministry. He will return to earth in judgment against those who refuse to accept Him as Lord and Savior (see 2 Corinthians 5:10).

GATE. See *Door.*

GIFT OF GOD

Jesus spoke these words to the woman at the well outside the village of Sychar (see John 4:5–26). In His long conversation with this sinful woman, Jesus made it clear that He was the Gift of God who had been sent into the world by God the Father as His agent of salvation.

Jesus answered and
said unto her, If thou
knewest the **gift of
God**, and who it
is that saith to thee,
Give me to drink; thou
wouldest have asked
of him, and he would
have given thee
living water.
JOHN 4:10

The dictionary defines a gift as "something voluntarily transferred by one person to another without compensation." This is a fancy way of saying that a gift is something a person gives without expecting anything in return. Speaking in spiritual terms, we might add the element of grace to this definition: God through His Son gave us a gift that we could never earn and certainly did not deserve.

Some earthly gifts are better than others. Most of us have received gifts that we couldn't use or that had to be returned to the store because they were the wrong size or the wrong color. But not so with God's gift of His Son. We needed this gift more than anything in the world; it was selected with great care; and it was given in love. This familiar verse from the Gospel of John says it all: "For God so loved the world, that he gave his only begotten Son, that whosoever believeth in him should not perish, but have everlasting life" (John 3:16).

Another name of God the Son that means essentially the

same thing as Gift of God is Unspeakable Gift (2 Corinthians 9:15).

God's Greatest Gift

- "For the wages of sin is death; but the gift of God is eternal life through Jesus Christ our Lord" (Romans 6:23).
- "For by grace are ye saved through faith; and that not of yourselves: it is the gift of God: not of works, lest any man should boast" (Ephesians 2:8–9).

GLORY OF ISRAEL

This verse is part of the prayer of Simeon in the temple when he recognized the infant Jesus as the Messiah whom God had sent into the world (see *Consolation of Israel* above). God revealed to Simeon that Jesus would grow up to become not only a light to the Gentiles but the Glory of Israel as well.

As God's chosen people, the nation of Israel was charged with the responsibility of leading other nations to come to know and worship the one true God. Jesus was born into the world as a Jew and a native of Israel. In this sense, He was the Glory of Israel, showing that God had not given up on His promise to bless the entire world through Abraham and his descendants (see Genesis 12:1–3).

> For my eyes have seen thy salvation. . . a light to lighten the Gentiles [NIV: a light for revelation to the Gentiles], and the **glory of thy people Israel**.
> LUKE 2:30, 32

The tragedy is that Jesus was rejected by His own people. They were tripped up by their expectations of a Messiah who would restore Israel to its golden days as a political power. But God's purpose was not turned aside by their refusal to ac-

The impressive and brilliant flame of a rocket launch is nothing compared to the "glory of Israel," the spiritual light that Jesus brings!

cept Him and His spiritual mission. The glory of one nation, Israel, went on to become a light to the Gentiles, as Simeon predicted. At His return He will become the Glorified One among all the peoples of the world (see Philippians 2:11).

Then saith he to
Thomas, Reach hither
thy finger [NIV: Put
your finger here], and
behold [NIV: see] my
hands, and reach
hither thy hand [NIV:
reach out your hand],
and thrust it into my
side: and be not
faithless, but believing
[NIV: stop doubting
and believe]. And
Thomas answered
and said unto him, my
Lord and my **God**.
JOHN 20:27–28

GOD

These verses from the Gospel of John describe an appearance of Jesus to His disciples after His resurrection. He had revealed Himself to them before at a time when Thomas the disciple was not present. Thomas had declared that he would not believe that Jesus was alive unless he could see Him with his own eyes.

When Thomas finally saw the resurrected Lord, he not only believed, but he also acknowledged Jesus as God in the flesh. This is one of the clearest statements in all the New Testament of the divinity of Jesus and His oneness with the Father.

Thomas, like all the other disciples of Jesus, had lived and worked with Him for about three years. They had walked with Him among the people, observing His miracles and listening to His teachings on the kingdom of God. But they were slow to understand that Jesus was actually God come to earth in human form. Theologians call this the doctrine of incarnation, a word that derives from a Latin term, *in carne*, meaning "in flesh."

As the God-man, Jesus is both the all-powerful Father, for whom nothing is impossible, and the man of sorrows, who can sympathize with us in our human weakness. He is the all-sufficient Savior.

Other names of God the Son that express His divinity and oneness with the Father are God Blessed For Ever (Romans 9:5), God Manifest in the Flesh (1 Timothy 3:16), God Our Saviour (1 Timothy 2:3), and True God (1 John 5:20).

Jesus' Oneness with God in John's Gospel

- "In the beginning was the Word, and the Word was with God, and the Word was God" (John 1:1).
- "I and my Father are one" (John 10:30).
- "He that hath seen me hath seen the Father" (John 14:9).

GOD BLESSED FOREVER. See *God*.

GOD MANIFEST IN THE FLESH.
See *Flesh*; *God*.

GOD OUR SAVIOUR. See *God*.

GOD WITH US. See *Immanuel/Emmanuel.*

GOOD MASTER

This account of Jesus' encounter with a man seeking eternal life appears in all three Synoptic Gospels—Matthew, Mark, and Luke. Matthew tells us that the man was young (see Matthew 19:22); Mark reveals that he was rich (see Mark 10:22); and Luke informs us that he was a ruler (see Luke 18:18). Thus, the man is known as the rich young ruler.

This young man called Jesus "Good Master" and bowed before Him. This shows that he was respectful toward Jesus and recognized Him as a teacher of some authority. But Jesus gently corrected him for calling Him "good." "There is none good but one," He replied, "that is, God" (Mark 10:18).

Why did Jesus resist this name? Perhaps He saw it as meaningless flattery. Or, it may have been His way of testing the young ruler's commitment to God the Father, who held the keys to eternal life—the very thing the man was seeking. He wanted to know what he could *do* to have eternal life. Jesus made it clear that it is a gift that God bestows on those who follow His commands.

The message of this account is that flattery gets us nowhere with God. He grants His grace to those who commit to follow Him in absolute obedience. The rich young ruler was more committed to his riches than he was to following the Lord. This kept him from finding the eternal life that he sought.

> And when he was gone forth into the way, there came one [NIV: a man] running, and kneeled to him, and asked him, **Good Master**, what shall I do that I may inherit eternal life?
> MARK 10:17
> [NASB, NIV, NRSV: **Good Teacher**]

GOOD SHEPHERD

This verse is part of a long monologue by Jesus, in which He compares His followers to sheep and identifies Himself as the Shepherd who leads His flock (see John 10:1–16).

In the Old Testament, God is also known by this name (see *Shepherd* in part 1, Names of God the Father). Sheep are helpless animals that have no natural defenses against predators such as wolves and lions. They wander away from the flock and find themselves in danger unless they are watched constantly. They have to be led from one grassy area to another to find new sources of food and water. Sheep need a vigilant leader—a shepherd—to provide all these resources.

But Jesus is more than just another shepherd. He is the *Good* Shepherd. The "good" in this name shows that Jesus

> I am the **good shepherd**: the **good shepherd** giveth his life for the sheep.
> JOHN 10:11

was deliberately contrasting Himself with the religious leaders of Israel—the scribes and Pharisees—who were leading the people astray. They were like "hirelings" (John 10:12), or hired hands who were paid to do a job but had no personal interest in the sheep they were leading. But Jesus is different.

- He knows His sheep personally and calls them by name (John 10:3).
- He doesn't drive His sheep; He guides them by showing the way (John 10:4).
- He is the door of the sheepfold that offers shelter and safety for His sheep (John 10:9).
- Unlike hired shepherds, He is willing to put His own life on the line for His sheep (John 10:11–12).
- He loves His sheep (John 10:13–15).

Some people might consider it an insult if we referred to them as sheep. But Christians don't mind, because we, as God's sheep, are in the care of the Good Shepherd.

Other names of God the Son that use the imagery of a shepherd are Chief Shepherd (1 Peter 5:4), Door of the Sheep (John 10:7), Great Shepherd of the Sheep (Hebrews 13:20), and Shepherd of Your Souls (1 Peter 2:25).

The image of Christ as the "Good Shepherd" was captured in art by the early Christian church as represented in statuettes like this one from the 4th century.

Led by the Good Shepherd

In her hymn "Saviour, Like a Shepherd Lead Us," Dorothy A. Thrupp prays for the tender leadership of the Good Shepherd.

Saviour, like a shepherd lead us,
Much we need thy tender care;
In thy pleasant pastures feed us,
For our use thy folds prepare.
Blessed Jesus, blessed Jesus,
Thou hast bought us, Thine we are.
Blessed Jesus, blessed Jesus,
Thou hast bought us, Thine we are.

GOOD TEACHER. *See Good Master.*

GOVERNOR

When Jesus was born in Bethlehem, wise men came from a far country to find Him after a strange star appeared in the eastern sky. They stopped in Jerusalem to find out where this new ruler had been born. The Jewish scholars of Jerusalem quoted this verse from the prophet Micah to tell these wise men that this ruler was supposed to be born in Bethlehem (see Micah 5:2). The name that they used for Jesus was Governor, a generic term for a ruler, administrator, leader, or civil official.

The world into which Jesus was born knew all about governors. These officials were sent by Rome to rule over the provinces—territories similar to states—into which the Roman government had divided its empire. A provincial governor was responsible for collecting taxes for the Roman treasury, keeping the peace, and administering the rule of Rome in the territory to which he was assigned. Three Roman governors are mentioned in the New Testament: Cyrenius (Luke 2:2), Pontius Pilate (Matthew 27:2), and Felix (Acts 23:24).

But Jesus is a Governor of a different type. He was sent as a spiritual ruler to guide and direct His people in the ways of the Lord. He rules by love and not by force. As Christians, our lives should reflect more of His rule every day as we grow in our commitment to Him and His teachings.

Governors of states and nations come and go, but Jesus' rule over His followers is eternal. As the prophet Isaiah declares, "Of the increase of his government and peace there will be no end" (Isaiah 9:7 NIV).

In other passages about the Messiah's rulership, Jesus is called a Leader and Commander (Isaiah 55:4) and a Ruler in Israel (Micah 5:2).

GREATER THAN JONAS/GREATER THAN SOLOMON

In these verses, Jesus condemns the scribes and Pharisees for their unbelief. Although they had seen Him perform many miracles, they were biased against Him and His teachings. They kept asking Him to perform more spectacular signs. Jesus uses two case studies from the Old Testament to make a

> And thou Bethlehem, in the land of Juda, art not the least [NIV: are by no means least] among the princes [NIV: rulers] of Juda: for out of thee shall come a **Governor**, that shall rule my people Israel.
> MATTHEW 2:6

point about their hopeless skepticism.

First, Jesus asks them to think about the citizens of the pagan city of Nineveh, who had repented at the preaching of the reluctant prophet Jonah. These pagan Ninevites were a judgment against Jesus' generation. He was Greater Than Jonah would ever be, but still the scribes and Pharisees refused to accept Him or His message.

Then Jesus reminds them of the queen of Sheba and draws a contrast between her attitude and theirs. She had traveled many miles to learn from King Solomon (and did so gladly), but the Jewish religious leaders were unwilling to listen to Jesus, who stood among them as a ready and accessible teacher. The queen of Sheba was eager to learn from Solomon, but the scribes and Pharisees were hardened in their attitude toward Jesus. The queen also stood in judgment against Jesus' generation because they had rejected the teachings of the One who was Greater Than Solomon.

The problem with the scribes and Pharisees was that their minds were like concrete—permanently set. For generations, they had been expecting God to send the Messiah into the world; yet, when He stood among them, they didn't recognize Him. They were trapped by their expectations of what the Messiah would be like.

Jesus always has been and always will be a "greater than" personality. His grace exceeds our understanding. He always has more truth to teach us than we are willing to accept. He has prepared a place for us in heaven that is more glorious than we can imagine. This means that we as Christians need open and teachable minds. Hold on for the ride; God is not finished with us yet.

GREAT HIGH PRIEST

The worship rituals of Old Testament times were presided over by the priesthood. Priests offered various types of sacrifices on behalf of the people to atone for their sins. This name of Jesus from the book of Hebrews picks up on this priestly imagery.

At the top of the priestly hierarchy stood the high priest. His responsibility as supreme priest was to see that all the functions of the priesthood were carried out appropriately (see 2 Chronicles 19:11). Below him were the priests, who performed sacrificial rituals at the altar. On the lower end of

Seeing then that we have a **great high priest**, that is passed into the heavens, Jesus the Son of God, let us hold fast our profession [NIV: hold firmly to the faith we profess].
HEBREWS 4:14

the priesthood were the Levites, who performed menial jobs as assistants to the priests, doing such chores as preparing animals for sacrifice, cleaning sacrificial vessels, and taking care of the tabernacle and the temple.

In this verse from Hebrews, the writer adds another level to this priesthood hierarchy by referring to Jesus as the Great High Priest. He stands above even the high priest of Israel, because He laid down His own life as the perfect sacrifice for sin.

The book of Hebrews might be called the priestly book of the New Testament. It is filled with references to Jesus as our Priest or our High Priest (see sidebar). In modern terms, a priest is usually understood as a religious leader who intercedes between God and man on behalf of sinful people. As Christians, we need no human intermediary to represent us before God. We can come directly into His presence through "one mediator between God and men, the man Christ Jesus" (1 Timothy 2:5).

Other priestly names of God the Son that express basically the same idea as Great High Priest are High Priest For Ever (Hebrews 6:20), High Priest of Our Profession (Hebrews 3:1), Merciful and Faithful High Priest (Hebrews 2:17), and Priest For Ever (Hebrews 7:17).

> The High Priest in Bibles times was overseer of all the priestly functions, including the sacrifices. Jesus stands above all other priests as the True High Priest who also came to lay down his life as the one true sacrifice for sin.

EARTHLY PRIESTS COMPARED TO JESUS' PRIESTHOOD

Human Priests	Jesus Our Priest
Became priests through human succession (Hebrews 5:1)	Appointed a priest by God (Hebrews 5:5, 10)
Required to offer sacrifice for their own sin (Hebrews 7:27–28)	Had no sin (Hebrews 4:15)
Animal blood could not take away sin (Hebrews 10:1–4)	Offered His own blood as atonement for human sin (Hebrews 9:12)
Subject to death (Hebrews 7:23)	Has an eternal priesthood; lives forever (Hebrews 7:24–25)

GREAT PROPHET

This verse describes the reaction of the people of Nain when Jesus brought back to life the son of a widow of that town. Perhaps they were comparing Jesus to Elijah, the famous prophet of Old Testament times, who also brought back from the dead the son of a poor widow (see 1 Kings 17:17–24).

Their reaction was similar to that of those whom Jesus fed when He multiplied five loaves and two fish to feed more than five thousand people. They declared, "This is of a truth that prophet that should come into the world" (John 6:14). They were referring to a promise God had made to Moses many centuries before that a prophet similar to Moses would one day appear among His people (see Deuteronomy 18:18). Jesus was the promised Prophet.

Jesus was the ultimate Prophet in a long line of prophets whom God had sent to His people, the Israelites, across many centuries. The classic definition of a prophet in the Jewish tradition is that he should declare God's message to His people and he should foretell the future. Jesus fit this definition perfectly.

As the Master Teacher, He expounded God's timeless truth to people as they had never been taught before. He taught about the kingdom of God and how people could become citizens of this heavenly realm. He also drew back the curtain to reveal the end time, encouraging people to get ready for the time when God would bring the world to its appointed conclusion.

A true prophet must be committed to declaring God's truth, no matter how his message is received. He accepts the fact that he will never be the most popular person in town. It was no different with Jesus. Some of the saddest words He ever uttered were spoken after He was rejected by the people of His own hometown: "Only in his hometown and in his own house is a prophet without honor" (Matthew 13:57 NIV).

Other names of God the Son that emphasize his role as Prophet are Prophet Mighty in Deed and Word (Luke 24:19) and Prophet of Nazareth of Galilee (Matthew 21:11).

GREAT SHEPHERD OF THE SHEEP.

See *Good Shepherd*.

GUARDIAN OF YOUR SOULS. See *Bishop of Your Souls.*

HEAD OF ALL PRINCIPALITY AND POWER

In this verse, the apostle Paul deals with a false teaching in the church at Colossae. Some were claiming that Jesus was a member of an order of angels, thus a created being like all other things created by God. Paul declared that Jesus was actually the Head of All Principality and Power—a non-created being who was above all heavenly beings, with the exception of God Himself. And even in His relationship to God, Jesus reflected "all the fulness of the Godhead."

Just as Jesus is supreme in the heavens, He also exercises dominion over all the earth. This truth should drive us to our knees in worship and praise. In her hymn "Praise Him! Praise Him!" this is how Fanny J. Crosby expresses it:

Praise Him! Praise Him! Jesus our blessed Redeemer!
Sing, O Earth, His wonderful love proclaim!
Hail Him! Hail Him! highest archangels in glory;
Strength and honor give to His holy name!

Other names of God the Son that express His supreme headship are Head of Every Man (1 Corinthians 11:3) and Head Over All Things (Ephesians 1:22).

HEAD OF EVERY MAN. See *Head of All Principality and Power.*

HEAD OF EVERY RULER AND AUTHORITY. See *Head of All Principality and Power.*

HEAD OF THE CHURCH

Only here and in one other place in the New Testament (see Colossians 1:18) is Jesus called the Head of the Church. This is not surprising, because very little is said about the church in any of the New Testament writings. But there is little doubt that Jesus had the church in mind from the very beginning of His ministry.

The first evidence of His commitment to the church was His selection of twelve disciples to join Him in ministry. The word *disciple* means "learner"—and that's exactly what they

> For in him dwelleth all the fulness of the Godhead bodily [NIV: in Christ all the fullness of the Deity lives in bodily form]. And ye are complete in him, which is the **head of all principality and power**.
> COLOSSIANS 2:9–10
> [NASB: **head over all rule and authority**; NIV: **head over every power and authority**; NRSV: **head of every ruler and authority**]

> For the husband is the head of the wife, even as Christ is the **head of the church**: and he is the saviour of the body.
> EPHESIANS 5:23

were. They learned from Jesus—who He was, the mission on which He had been sent, the characteristics of citizens of the kingdom of God, and God's love for all people, Gentiles included. Jesus trained these common, ordinary men to carry on His work after He was gone.

Jesus also spoke openly several times about the church. On one occasion, he told Peter, "Upon this rock I will build my church" (Matthew 16:18). Peter had just declared his belief that Jesus was the long-awaited Messiah and "the Son of the living God" (Matthew 16:16). Jesus was saying that His church would be built on confessions of faith just like the one Peter had made. The church would consist of people who accepted Jesus as Savior and Lord and committed themselves to His work of redemption in the world.

Church buildings come in every color, shape, and size. But if they truly worship Jesus, they all have the same "head."

Other clues about Jesus' commitment to the church appear in the Gospel of John. He promised His disciples that He would send the Holy Spirit to comfort and guide them after He returned to God the Father (see John 14:16–18). He sealed this promise some time later with a fervent prayer on their behalf. He asked God to protect His disciples and keep them committed to the mission for which He had trained them. "As you sent me into the world," He prayed, "I have sent them into the world" (John 17:18 NIV).

The church is still the key element in Jesus' strategy to bring the world into the kingdom of God. He is the Head of the Church, and we as believers make up the body. A body without a head is useless, but a body joined to a head becomes a living, breathing, working organism. There's no limit to what it can accomplish for the cause of Christ our Head.

Love for the Church

If Jesus loved the church enough to die for it, Christians should love it, too. This is the message of "I Love Thy Kingdom, Lord," a hymn by Timothy Dwight.

I love Thy kingdom, Lord,
The house of Thine abode,
The church our blessed Redeemer saved
With His own precious blood.
For her my tears shall fall;
For her my prayers ascend;
To her my cares and toils be given
Till toils and cares shall end.

HEAD OF THE CORNER

Jesus directed these words to the religious leaders of His day who were questioning His authority. He quoted Psalm 118:22–23, an Old Testament passage that they probably knew well. His point was that He was destined to be rejected by them as the Messiah.

But He, the rejected Stone, would become the center-piece of a new building that would include all people who accepted Him as Savior and Lord. This building would be the church, a fresh, new organism that would be born out of the ashes of the old religious order based on the Jewish law.

The apostle Peter also quoted this same verse from the Psalms (see 1 Peter 2:7). Peter went on to say that Jesus, the rejected Stone, was also a Stone of Stumbling and a Rock of Offence (see 1 Peter 2:8) to those people who thought the Messiah would be a powerful political and military leader. It was unthinkable to them that He would come as a spiritual deliverer who would suffer and die on a cross.

Jesus as the Head of the Corner expresses the same idea as His name, Cornerstone (see *Chief Cornerstone* above).

HEAD OVER ALL RULE AND AUTHORITY. See *Head of All Principality and Power.*

HEAD OVER ALL THINGS. See *Head of All Principality and Power.*

Jesus saith unto them, Did ye never read in the scriptures, The stone which the builders rejected, the same is become the **head of the corner**: this is the Lord's doing, and it is marvellous in our eyes?
MATTHEW 21:42
[NASB: **CHIEF CORNER STONE**; NIV: **capstone**; NRSV: **cornerstone**]

HEAD OVER EVERY POWER AND AUTHORITY. See *Head of All Principality and Power.*

HEIR OF ALL THINGS

The dictionary defines an heir as "one who receives or is entitled to receive some endowment or quality from a parent or predecessor." Most heirs receive only a small amount of property or cash that their parents have managed to accumulate during a lifetime of working and saving. But the writer of Hebrews declares that Jesus is the Heir of All Things, and this endowment was granted to Him by none other than God the Father.

The heirship of Jesus is both material and spiritual. He participated with God in the creation of the world (see John 1:3), so God has granted Him ownership and dominion over the universe. In the spiritual sense, He sets the terms by which all people will be judged for their sins. Then He Himself became the means by which people could be made righteous in God's sight. This was accomplished through His death on the cross.

The great thing about Jesus' spiritual heirship is that He shares His inheritance with us. As the apostle Paul expresses it, we are "joint-heirs with Christ" (Romans 8:17) because He lives eternally with the Father and He has made it possible for us to enjoy eternal life with Him.

God, who. . .spake in time past unto the fathers by the prophets, hath in these last days spoken unto us by his Son, whom he hath appointed **heir of all things**, by whom also he made the worlds.
HEBREWS 1:1–2

La lecture du Testament

Heirs nervously hear "The Reading of the Will," the name of this nineteenth-century illustration by Boilly. While human beings often fight over wills, Jesus gladly shares His heavenly inheritance with all who believe in Him.

HIGH PRIEST. See *Great High Priest.*

HIGH PRIEST ACCORDING TO THE ORDER OF MELCHIZEDEK. See *High Priest after the Order of Melchisedec.*

HIGH PRIEST AFTER THE ORDER OF MELCHISEDEC

This name of Jesus refers to one of the most mysterious personalities of the Bible. Melchisedec was the king of Salem—

an ancient name for Jerusalem—and a priest of the Most High God. He appeared to Abraham and his servants after they defeated several kings who had carried Abraham's nephew, Lot, away as a captive.

When Abraham returned from battle with the spoils of war he had taken from these kings, Melchisedec met him, blessed him, and gave him and his hungry men bread and wine to eat. In return, Abraham presented Melchisedec with a tithe—one-tenth of the spoils of war he had taken from the conquered kings (see Genesis 14:12–20).

The author of Hebrews calls Jesus a High Priest after the Order of Melchisedec because Melchisedec did not become a priest by virtue of his birth. He was not a descendant of Aaron, the first high priest of Israel through whose family line all succeeding priests of Israel emerged.

Like Melchisedec, Jesus did not inherit His priestly responsibilities. He was appointed to this role by God the Father. His priesthood is eternal, without beginning or end, and thus superior to the priests and the sacrificial system of the Old Testament (see Hebrews 7:16, 24).

> And being made perfect, he became the author of eternal salvation unto all them that obey him; called of God an **high priest after the order of Melchisedec**. HEBREWS 5:9–10 [NASB, NRSV: **high priest according to the order of Melchizedek**; NIV: **high priest in the order of Melchizedek**]

HIGH PRIEST FOR EVER. See *Great High Priest*.

HIGH PRIEST IN THE ORDER OF MELCHIZEDEK. See *High Priest after the Order of Melchisedec*.

HIGH PRIEST OF OUR PROFESSION. See *Great High Priest*.

HOLY CHILD JESUS. See *Child Jesus*.

HOLY AND RIGHTEOUS ONE. See *Holy One/Holy One of God*.

HOLY ONE/HOLY ONE OF GOD

This name of Jesus is also applied to God and the Holy Spirit (see *Holy One* in part 1, Names of God the Father, and part 3, Names of God the Holy Spirit). In Paul's sermon in the book of Acts, he calls Jesus by this name to contrast the righteousness of Jesus with the unrighteousness of Barabbas, a

But ye denied the **Holy One** and the Just, and desired a murderer to be granted unto you.
ACTS 3:14
[NASB, NIV, NRSV: **Holy and Righteous One**]

Saying, Let us alone; what have we to do with thee, thou Jesus of Nazareth? art thou come to destroy us? I know thee who thou art, the **Holy One of God**.
MARK 1:24

Actor Max von Sydow performs an exorcism in the 1973 film *The Exorcist*. It was a demon-possessed man who identified Jesus as "the Holy One of God."

To whom God would make known what is the riches of the glory of this mystery among the Gentiles; which is Christ in you, the **hope of glory**.
COLOSSIANS 1:27

criminal whom the crowd released instead of Jesus on the day of Christ's crucifixion (see Matthew 27:15–26). In the verse from Mark's Gospel, even the evil spirit that Jesus casts out of a demented man recognizes Jesus as the Holy One of God.

Jesus can be called the Holy One because He is the only sinless person who ever lived. Perfect in holiness before He was born, He managed to resist sin throughout His entire life because of His close relationship with God the Father.

We as Christians will never achieve complete holiness in this life. We will always struggle with temptation and our sinful human nature. But we ought to be growing more and more like Jesus in this important dimension of the Christian life. The apostle Peter admonishes us, "Just as he who called you is holy, so be holy in all you do" (1 Peter 1:15 NIV).

In a messianic passage in the book of Daniel, Jesus is also called the Most Holy (Daniel 9:24).

HOPE OF GLORY

The apostle Paul is known as the apostle to the Gentiles, but he could also be called the apostle of hope. His writings abound with the theme of the hope that believers have in the promises of Jesus Christ (see sidebar).

In this verse from his letter to the Colossian church, he called Jesus the Hope of Glory. If we know Christ as our Savior and Lord, we are assured that we will live with Him in His full glory when we reach our heavenly home.

To hope in something is to look forward to its fulfillment with confident expectation. Notice that Paul says in this verse that "Christ in you" is your Hope of Glory. With Jesus as a constant presence in your life, you can be as certain of heaven as if you were already there.

Jesus as Our Hope in Paul's Writings
- "Now the God of hope fill you with all joy and peace in believing, that ye may abound in hope" (Romans 15:13).
- "Be not moved away from the hope of the gospel, which ye have heard" (Colossians 1:23).
- "Being justified by his grace, we should be made heirs according to the hope of eternal life" (Titus 3:7).

HORN OF SALVATION

These verses are part of the song of praise, known as the "Bene-dictus," that Zacharias sang at the birth of his son John, the forerunner of Jesus (see Luke 1:67–79). This name was also applied to God by the psalmist David in Psalm 18 (see *Horn of My Salvation* in part 1, Names of God the Father).

An animal horn was used as a container for the oil that was poured on the head of a king in an anointing ceremony (see 1 Samuel 16:13). Thus, Zacharias implied that Jesus was the King of salvation from the kingly line of David. A horn was also considered a symbol of strength (see Psalm 112:9). This imagery, as applied to Jesus, declares that He would be a powerful Savior.

As the Horn of Salvation, Jesus is the all-sufficient Savior, who sprang from the line of David. In Bible times, a trumpet (*shofar*, or ram's horn) was made from an animal horn, so

> Blessed be the Lord God of Israel: for he hath visited and redeemed his people, and hath raised up an **horn of salvation** for us in the house of his servant David.
> LUKE 1:68–69
> [NRSV: **mighty savior**]

Since early Bible times the "shofar" has been used on many Jewish holidays to remind the hearers that God is King and Rescuer.

we can carry this horn analogy one step further: Our role as Christians is to "sound the trumpet" about God's love and grace to an unbelieving world.

Another name of Jesus on the theme of salvation is Salvation of God (Luke 3:6).

I AM

This name that Jesus called Himself is the equivalent of the name with which God identified Himself to Moses at the burning bush (see *I Am That I Am* in part 1, Names of God the Father).

Just like the great I Am of the Old Testament, Jesus was claiming to be eternal, timeless, and unchanging. He had always been and He would always be. In other words, He was of the same divine essence as God the Father.

This claim of divinity was seen as blasphemy by the Jewish religious leaders, so they picked up stones to execute Jesus—the penalty for such a crime as spelled out in the Old Testament law (see Leviticus 24:16). But Jesus' escape proved the claim He was making. He easily avoided their death threat as He slipped miraculously "through the midst of them." Only when the time was right, in accordance with God's plan, would He allow Himself to be captured and crucified.

IMAGE OF GOD. See *Express Image of God.*

IMAGE OF THE INVISIBLE GOD.

See *Express Image of God.*

IMMANUEL/EMMANUEL

This prophecy from the prophet Isaiah was gloriously fulfilled with the birth of Jesus, as described in these two verses from Matthew's Gospel. Matthew adds the phrase that gives the meaning of the name Immanuel: "God with us."

Even before Jesus was born, this name was given to Him by an angel who appeared to Joseph. Joseph needed divine assurance that Mary's pregnancy was an act of the Holy Spirit, and that he should proceed to take her as his wife.

The promise of God's presence among His people goes back to Old Testament times. For example, when God called Moses to return to Egypt to free His people from slavery, He told him, "I will be with you" (Exodus 3:12 NIV). Likewise, when God called the prophet Jeremiah to the difficult task of delivering a message of judgment to His wayward people, He promised the prophet, "I am with you and will rescue you" (Jeremiah 1:8 NIV).

King David declared that God's presence would follow him wherever he went: "If I take the wings of the morning, and dwell in the uttermost parts of the sea; even there shall thy hand lead me, and thy right hand shall hold me" (Psalm 139:9–10).

These promises of God's presence with His people reached their peak in His Son, Jesus Christ, who came to earth in the form of a man to show mankind that God is for us in our weak, sinful, and helpless condition. As a man, Jesus understands our temptations and shortcomings. As God, He can meet all these needs through His love and grace.

Just as Matthew's Gospel begins with the affirmation that God is with us, so it ends with Jesus' promise of His abiding presence: "Lo, I am with you always, even unto the end of the world" (Matthew 28:20).

> Therefore the Lord himself shall give you a sign; Behold, a virgin shall conceive, and bear a son, and shall call his name **Immanuel**.
> ISAIAH 7:14
>
> Now all this was done, that it might be fulfilled which was spoken of the Lord by the prophet. . . . And they shall call his name **Emmanuel**, which being interpreted is, God with us.
> MATTHEW 1:22–23
> [NASB, NIV: **Immanuel**]

Saint Patrick, a missionary to Ireland in the fourth century, expressed the reality of Jesus as God with Us in this beautiful prayer:
Christ be beside me, Christ be before me,
Christ be behind me, King of my heart;
Christ be within me, Christ be below me,
Christ be above me, never to part.
Christ on my right hand, Christ on my left hand,
Christ all around me, shield in the strife;
Christ in my sleeping, Christ in my sitting,
Christ in my rising, light of my life.

INNOCENT MAN. See *Just Man*.

INSTRUCTOR. See *Master*.

JESUS

Jewish custom dictated that a male child be circumcised and named on the eighth day after he was born. Mary and Joseph followed this custom with Jesus. They had been told by an angel, even before Jesus was born, that His name would be Jesus (Matthew 1:21; Luke 1:31). They followed the angel's instruction by giving Him this name.

The name *Jesus* is the equivalent of the Old Testament name rendered variously as Jehoshua (Numbers 13:16), Jeshua (Ezra 2:2), and Joshua (Exodus 17:9). It means "Jehovah (or Yahweh) Is Salvation." Thus, Jesus' personal name indicated from the very beginning that He was to be God's agent of salvation in a dark and sinful world.

Jesus was actually a common name among the Jewish people when He was born, similar to the popularity of John or Robert in our society. For example, a believer named Jesus Justus was mentioned by the apostle Paul in his letter to the Christians at Colossae (see Colossians 4:11). But the name has become so closely associated with Jesus of Nazareth, the Son of God, that few people are given this name in our time. In the words of Paul, it is the "name. . .above every name" (Philippians 2:9).

The name Jesus appears often by itself in the Gospels (see Matthew 17:18; Mark 14:62; Luke 10:37; John 20:14). But outside the Gospels, it often appears in combination with other names such as Jesus Christ (Acts 8:37), Jesus Christ Our Lord (Romans 6:11), Lord Jesus (Colossians 3:17), and Lord Jesus Christ (James 2:1).

His Wonderful Name

Christians never seem to tire of hearing the name of Jesus, according to the hymn "There Is a Name I Love to Hear," written by Frederick Whitfield.

There is a Name I love to hear,
I love to sing its worth;
It sounds like music in mine ear,
The sweetest Name on earth.
Oh, how I love Jesus,
Oh, how I love Jesus,
Oh, how I love Jesus,
Because He first loved me.

JESUS CHRIST. See *Christ*; *Jesus*.

JESUS CHRIST OUR LORD. See *Christ*; *Jesus*.

JESUS OF GALILEE/JESUS OF NAZARETH

Galilee was one of three provinces, or regions, into which Palestine was divided during New Testament times. Nazareth, the hometown of Jesus (see Luke 2:51), was a small, insignificant village in the province of Galilee.

The verse from Matthew in which Jesus was called Jesus of Galilee, describes the final days of His ministry in Jerusalem. This city was located in the southernmost province of Judea, about ninety miles from the province of Galilee. This young

> Now Peter sat without in the palace [NIV: out in the courtyard]: and a damsel [NIV: servant girl] came unto him, saying, Thou also wast with **Jesus of Galilee**.
> MATTHEW 26:69
> [NASB, NRSV: **Jesus the Galilean**]

People at the time of Christ would not recognize Nazareth today. It has changed from a small village not much larger than a football field to one of Israel's larger cities.

woman questioned Peter about his association with Jesus because Galilee to the north was Jesus' home province and the place where He had spent most of His time of ministry.

In the verse from John's Gospel, Phillip's reference to Jesus as a person from Nazareth shows his prejudice against this tiny village. He was convinced that no one of any importance could come from this little "hick town."

But Nathanael changed his mind when he met Jesus in person. When Jesus told him that He knew all about him, Nathanael acknowledged Him as "the Son of God" and "the King

> Philip findeth Nathanael, and saith unto him, We have found him, of whom Moses in the law, and the prophets, did write, **Jesus of Nazareth**, the son of Joseph.
> JOHN 1:45

of Israel" (John 1:49). Nathanael eventually became one of Jesus' disciples—the one referred to as Bartholomew (see Mark 3:18).

The significance of these names—Jesus of Galilee and Jesus of Nazareth—is that they attest to the historicity of Jesus Christ. He was not a make-believe figure who emerged from a fiction writer's imagination. He was a real person, who grew up in humble circumstances and spent most of His ministry among the common people. Some skeptics may say otherwise, but Christians declare that the Gospels are eyewitness accounts of the life of a miracle-working Savior, who hailed from a little village in a backwater province.

If Jesus had been created by a fiction writer, He probably would have been born into society's upper class in the influential city of Jerusalem. He certainly would not have been executed on a Roman cross like a common criminal.

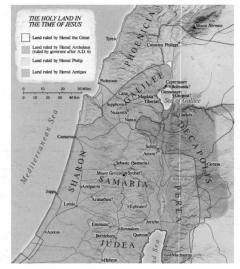

JESUS THE GALILEAN. See *Jesus of Galilee/Jesus of Nazareth.*

JUDGE OF QUICK AND DEAD

This name of Jesus appears in the sermon that the apostle Peter preached to the Roman centurion Cornelius, a Gentile (see Acts 10:25–43). Peter made it clear to Cornelius that Jesus had been appointed by God the Father as the supreme Judge of all things—the living and the dead.

God's activity as Judge is one of the key themes of the Old Testament (see *Judge* and *Judge of All the Earth* in part 1, Names of God the Father). But after God sent His Son, Jesus, into the world, He established a new way of rendering His judgment. According to the Gospel of John, with the coming of Jesus, God the Father "committed all judgment unto the Son" (John 5:22). Jesus is now the agent through whom divine judgment is handed down.

As the Judge of Quick and Dead, Jesus is the great dividing line in history. At the great white throne judgment in the end time, He will send into eternal punishment those who have refused to accept Him as Savior and Lord (see Revelation 20:11–15). Christians will not be involved in this judgment, because they have accepted by faith the sacrifice that Jesus has made on their behalf.

But Christians will not totally escape divine judgment; they will be subjected to an evaluation known as the judgment seat of Christ. At this judgment, the service they have rendered for Jesus Christ will be judged and rewarded accordingly (see sidebar). The exact nature of this judgment and the rewards are unclear. But the fact that we will face this time of accountability before the Lord should motive us to loyal service in the cause of God's kingdom.

Another name of Jesus that emphasizes His role as Judge is Righteous Judge (2 Timothy 4:8).

And he commanded us to preach unto the people, and to testify that it is he which was ordained of God to be the **Judge of quick and dead**. Acts 10:42 [NASB, NIV, NRSV: **Judge of the living and the dead**]

Paul's Teachings on Christians Facing the Judgment Seat of Christ

- "For we must all appear before the judgment seat of Christ, that each one may receive what is due him for the things done while in the body, whether good or bad" (2 Corinthians 5:10 NIV).
- "So then, each of us will give an account of himself to God" (Romans 14:12 NIV).
- "His work will be shown for what it is, because the Day will bring it to light. . . . If what he has built survives, he will receive his reward. If it is burned up, he will suffer loss; he himself will be saved, but only as one escaping through the flames" (1 Corinthians 3:13–15 NIV).

JUDGE OF THE LIVING AND THE DEAD. See *Judge of Quick and Dead*.

JUST MAN

When he [Pilate] was set down on the judgment seat, his wife sent unto him, saying [NIV: sent him this message], Have thou nothing to do with that **just man**: for I have suffered many things this day in a dream because of him. MATTHEW 27:19 [NASB: **righteous Man**; NIV, NRSV: **innocent man**]

Pontius Pilate, the Roman governor who condemned Jesus to death, received this message from his wife while Jesus was on trial. She tried to get Pilate to release Jesus, because it had been revealed to her in a dream that He was innocent of the charges against Him.

Pilate also knew that Jesus was not guilty, but he caved in to political pressure from the Jewish religious leaders and pronounced the death penalty against Jesus. Pilate washed his hands before the crowd and declared, "I am innocent of the blood of this just person" (Matthew 27:24).

The word *just*, as applied to Jesus by Pilate and his wife, means "innocent." But in other contexts in the New Testament, the names Just (Acts 3:14) Just One (Acts 7:52; 22:14), and Righteous Man (Luke 23:47) refer to Jesus' righteousness and holiness.

Jesus, the Sinless and Righteous One, was not guilty of any crime or wrongdoing. This makes His death on our behalf all the more meaningful. He willingly laid down His life on the cross as the sacrifice for our sin.

KING

The whole multitude [NIV: crowd] of the disciples began to rejoice and praise God with a loud voice for all the mighty works that they had seen; saying, Blessed be the **King** that cometh in the name of the Lord: peace in heaven, and glory in the highest. LUKE 19:37–38

When Jesus made His triumphal entry into Jerusalem, He was hailed as King by the crowds that had seen His miracles during His public ministry. They acknowledged Him as the wonder-working Messiah, whom God had been promising to send to His people for many centuries.

In the Old Testament, God the Father is also referred to by this name (see *King* in part 1, Names of God the Father). But the Jewish people rejected God's kingship in favor of rule by an earthly king in the time of the prophet Samuel (see 1 Samuel 8:4–9).

Saul, Israel's first king, was followed by many other kings throughout history. But by Jesus' time, no king had ruled over the Jews for a period of about five hundred years. They thought their long-promised Messiah would be a powerful king who would restore their nation to its glory days as a political power. When the crowds greeted Jesus as King when

He entered Jerusalem, they were thinking of Him in these terms.

Jesus faced this problem throughout His ministry. After the miracle of the feeding of the five thousand, He realized that the crowds "would come and take him by force, to make him a king" (John 6:15). He avoided them by slipping away to a secluded spot on a nearby mountain.

There was nothing Jesus could do to avoid the crowds on the day when He entered Jerusalem. But He rode a donkey, a symbol of humility and peace, rather than a prancing white horse, the steed of choice for military heroes of the day (see Matthew 21:1–5). This showed that He was not a political king but a spiritual King—one who had come into the world to conquer sin and death.

This artwork is from the Church of Bethpage, located on the Mount of Olives, and represents how the people saw Jesus as King on His triumphal entry into Jerusalem.

KING OF ISRAEL. See *King of the Jews.*

KING OF KINGS

The nineteenth chapter of Revelation describes the return of Jesus Christ to earth in the end time, when He will triumph

And he hath on his vesture [NIV: robe] and on his thigh a name written, **KING OF KINGS**, AND LORD OF LORDS.
REVELATION 19:16

over all His enemies. According to verse 16, He will wear a banner across His royal robe. It will be emblazoned with the phrase "King of Kings." This name, emphasizing His supreme rule over all the earth, will be prominently displayed for everyone to see.

In Old Testament times, the title "king of kings" was assigned to a ruler with an empire that covered a wide territory. Often, a king of an empire would allow the rulers of conquered nations or tribes to keep their royal titles for political and economic reasons. But it was clear that the "king of kings" was the undisputed ruler of his vast domain. Thus, the Persian ruler Artaxerxes referred to himself as "king of kings" in a letter that he sent to Jerusalem with Ezra the priest (Ezra 7:12).

When Jesus returns in glory, He will be the sole ruler of the universe. Meanwhile, He rules over His kingdom, known as the church. If we belong to Him, we are subjects of His kingdom. He should already be King of Kings in our lives.

In a passage that looked forward to the birth of the Messiah, the prophet Zechariah called Jesus the King over All the Earth (Zechariah 14:9).

Our Matchless King

The hymn "Crown Him with Many Crowns," by Matthew Bridges and Godfrey Thring, praises the Lord Jesus for His role as King of Kings in the lives of Christians.

Crown Him with many crowns,
The Lamb upon His throne;
Hark! How the heavenly anthem drowns
All music but its own:
Awake, my soul, and sing
Of Him who died for thee,
And hail Him as thy matchless King
Through all eternity.

KING OF SAINTS

Most people think of saints as people who have been beatified and honored by a church body because of their dedicated service to God. But *saints* when it appears in the New Testament is a term for Christians. Any person who has accepted Jesus as Savior and who follows Him as Lord of his life is a saint. Christians as saints make up the church, the body of Christ.

Thus, Jesus' name as King of Saints is similar to his title as Head of the Church. He watches over His saints and energizes them through His Holy Spirit for the task of carrying out His work in the world.

In this verse from Revelation, the saints of God sing two songs—the song of Moses and the song of the Lamb. These songs celebrate redemption and deliverance. Just as Moses' song celebrates Israel's deliverance from Egyptian slavery (see Exodus 15:1–19), so the song of the Lamb rejoices in our deliverance from Satan and the bondage of sin and death.

> And they sing the song of Moses the servant of God, and the song of the Lamb, saying, Great and marvellous are thy works, Lord God Almighty; just and true are thy ways, thou **King of saints**.
> REVELATION 15:3
> [NASB, NRSV: **King of the nations**; NIV: **King of the ages**]

KING OF THE JEWS

This question asked by Pontius Pilate, the Roman official who condemned Jesus to death, appears in all four Gospels (see Mark 15:2; Luke 23:3; John 18:33). The Gospel writers considered this name important, because it was the basis of the charge that led to Jesus' execution.

> And Jesus stood before the governor: and the governor asked him, saying, Art thou the **King of the Jews**? And Jesus said unto him, Thou sayest [NIV: Yes, it is as you say].
> MATTHEW 27:11

The Jewish religious leaders who turned Jesus over to Pilate were enraged by what they considered His blasphemy, or His claim to be the divine Son of God (see Matthew 26:63–66). But they knew that the Romans would never condemn Jesus to death on the basis of their religious laws alone (see John 18:29–32). So they claimed that Jesus was guilty of sedition against the Roman government by claiming to be a king (see Luke 23:2). The implication of this charge is that Jesus was plotting to overthrow Roman rule.

This charge against Jesus was guaranteed to get action from Pilate. One thing his superiors in Rome would not tolerate was unrest or rebellion in the territory over which he ruled.

Jesus never claimed to be a political king (see *King* above). So why didn't He deny that He was the King of the Jews when Pilate asked Him if the charge against Him was true? He refused to answer this question to Pilate's satisfaction because He knew the time for His sacrificial death had

This mosaic from the French Basilica of Our Lady of the Rosary shows Pontius Pilate holding a sign that translates as "Jesus of Nazareth, King of the Jews."

arrived. He would allow events to run their course without any intervention on His part, because it was His destiny to die on the cross. He would be sacrificed willingly as the King of the Jews in order to provide salvation for the entire world.

Another name of Jesus that is similar to King of the Jews is King of Israel (John 1:49; 12:13).

The Right Time for Redemption

During His earthly ministry, Jesus was aware that the timing of His death would be in accordance with God's plan. For example, He told His skeptical brothers, who wanted Him to declare His purpose openly to others: "The right time for me has not yet come" (John 7:6 NIV). But just a few days before His crucifixion, He told His disciples, "My appointed time is near" (Matthew 26:18 NIV).

Looking back on the cross and Jesus' sacrificial death, the apostle Paul declares, "When the fulness of time was come, God sent forth his Son, made of a woman, made under the law, to redeem them that were under the law, that we might receive the adoption of sons" (Galatians 4:4–5).

KING OF THE AGES. See *King of Saints.*

KING OF THE NATIONS. See *King of Saints.*

KING OVER ALL THE EARTH. See *King of Kings.*

LAMB

In this verse from the book of Revelation, the apostle John describes Jesus as the sacrificial Lamb who laid down His life as redemption for the sins of the world. Notice the things that John declares Jesus the Lamb is worthy to receive.

- Power. The Lamb exercises ultimate power over the universe as well as the lives of Christians.
- Riches. All the material possessions we have accumulated belong to Him.
- Wisdom. Jesus is the all-wise One who grants wisdom to those who follow Him.
- Strength. Our physical powers should be dedicated to the service of the Lamb.

And I beheld, and I heard the voice of many angels round about the throne and the beasts and the elders. . .saying with a loud voice, Worthy is the **Lamb** that was slain to receive power, and riches, and wisdom, and strength, and honour, and glory, and blessing.
REVELATION 5:11–12

- Honor. Our behavior as Christians should bring honor to the One whom we profess to follow.
- Glory. Jesus' glory, His excellence and moral superiority, is magnified when Christians are fully devoted to Him and His cause.
- Blessing. In this context, *blessing* means "praise." We should praise the Lamb with our lives as well as our words.

Jesus as the Lamb is one of the major themes of the book of Revelation. As the Lamb, He is worthy to open the scroll that describes God's judgment against the world (see Revelation 5:4; 6:1). The Lamb provides the light for the heavenly city, or New Jerusalem (see Revelation 21:22–23). Those who belong to Jesus have their names written in the Lamb's book of life (see Revelation 21:27).

LAMB OF GOD

On two successive days John the Baptist, forerunner of Jesus, referred to Jesus by this name (see John 1:35–36). Of all the names John could have used—King, Messiah, Prophet—he chose to identify Jesus as the Lamb of God. Lambs were choice young sheep that were used as sacrificial animals in Jewish worship rituals (see Leviticus 14:11–13; 1 Samuel 7:9). Thus, at the very beginning of Jesus' ministry, John

The next day John seeth Jesus coming unto him, and saith, Behold the **Lamb of God**, which taketh away the sin of the world.
JOHN 1:29

The image of Jesus as the Lamb of God carried more meaning at the time of Christ as lambs like this were part of the Jewish religious life, central to the Temple sacrifices.

realized the sacrificial role that Jesus was destined to fill.

The prominence of lambs in the Jewish sacrificial system began with the deliverance of the Israelites from Egyptian slavery, many centuries before Jesus' time. The Lord commanded the people to smear the blood of lambs on the doorposts of their houses. This indicated that they would be passed over when God struck the land with the death of the firstborn (see Exodus 12:21–23). The Jewish festival known as Passover was commemorated from that day on with the eating of unleavened bread and the sacrifice of lambs.

One of the great messianic passages of the Old Testament predicted that Jesus would die like a sacrificial lamb. About seven hundred years before Jesus was born, the prophet Isaiah declared of Him, "He was oppressed, and he was afflicted, yet he opened not his mouth: he is brought as a lamb to the slaughter, and as a sheep before her shearers is dumb, so he opened not his mouth" (Isaiah 53:7).

On the night before His crucifixion, Jesus picked up on the sacrificial lamb imagery that John the Baptist had used of Him when He began His public ministry. He gathered with His disciples to eat a meal that was part of the observance of the Jewish Passover. But He turned it into a meal that we know as the Memorial Supper or the Lord's Supper.

Just as the blood of the first Passover lamb had been an agent of deliverance for the Israelites in Egypt, so the shed blood of Jesus would provide divine redemption for the entire world. As Jesus passed the cup among His disciples, He told them, "This is my blood of the new testament, which is shed for many for the remission of sins" (Matthew 26:28).

Saved by the Blood of the Lamb of God

- "In Christ Jesus ye who sometimes were far off are made nigh by the blood of Christ" (Ephesians 2:13).
- "Neither by the blood of goats and calves, but by his own blood he entered in once into the holy place, having obtained eternal redemption for us" (Hebrews 9:12).
- "Ye were not redeemed with corruptible things. . .but with the precious blood of Christ, as of a lamb without blemish and without spot" (1 Peter 1:18–19).
- "The blood of Jesus Christ. . .cleanseth us from all sin" (1 John 1:7).

LAMB SLAIN FROM THE FOUNDATION OF THE WORLD

The affirmation of this verse is that Jesus was not only the Lamb who was sacrificed for our sins, but He also was selected for this task before the world was created (see *Foreordained before the Foundation of the World* above).

God the Father looked down through the centuries and determined that His Son, Jesus, would die at some time in the future as an atonement for sin. Jesus' death was no accident of history, and no afterthought in the mind of God. It was the fulfillment of God's eternal plan.

How long did it take for this plan to work itself out? As long as it took. This answer may seem nonsensical and ridiculous, but it's as close as we can get to understanding God and His mysterious ways. The apostle Peter expresses it like this: "One day is with the Lord as a thousand years, and a thousand years as one day" (2 Peter 3:8).

> And all that dwell upon the earth shall worship him, whose names are not written in the book of life of the **Lamb slain from the foundation of the world**.
> REVELATION 13:8
> [NIV: **Lamb. . .Slain from the creation of the world**]

LAST. See *Alpha and Omega.*

LAST ADAM

This is the only place in the Bible where Jesus is called by this name. The apostle Paul in this verse draws a contrast between Jesus as the Last Adam and the Adam of the book of Genesis, who was the first man created. This contrast appears at several points throughout the fifteenth chapter of 1 Corinthians.

After God created Adam and placed him in the Garden of Eden, He told him he could eat the fruit from every tree in the garden except one—"the tree of the knowledge of good and evil" (Genesis 2:17). But Adam deliberately disobeyed God and ate the forbidden fruit (see Genesis 3:6). This act of rebellion placed Adam and all his descendants—including everyone born since Adam's time—under the curse of sin and death.

But according to Paul, God had good news for those who were tainted by Adam's sin. He sent another Adam—the Last Adam, Jesus Christ—to undo what the first Adam had caused. Paul expresses it like this: "As in Adam all die, even so in Christ shall all be made alive" (1 Corinthians 15:22). The first Adam's legacy of death has been nullified by the Last Adam's perfect obedience to God the Father, and His sacrificial death on our behalf.

> And so it is written, The first man Adam was made a living soul; the **last Adam** was made a quickening spirit.
> 1 CORINTHIANS 15:45

As Paul continues in this passage from 1 Corinthians, he refers to Jesus as the Second Man. Adam (the first man) was a created being, formed from the dust of the earth (see Genesis 2:7), and thus, "of the earth, earthy" (1 Corinthians 15:47); but Jesus, as the Second Man, came from heaven.

LAUNDERER'S SOAP. See *Fullers' Soap.*

LEADER. See *Master; Prince.*

LEADER AND COMMANDER TO THE PEOPLE

Behold, I have given him for [NIV: made him] a witness to the people, a **leader and commander to the people**.
ISAIAH 55:4

The fifty-fifth chapter of Isaiah is one of many messianic passages in his book. In this verse, the coming Messiah is portrayed as One who will serve as a Leader and Commander for the people to whom He is sent by the Lord.

A leader is a person who guides others in the pursuit of a goal. He enlists others to work toward the goal, motivates and inspires them, encourages them through personal example, and keeps them focused on their objective. The name *commander* conjures up a military image. He is more directive in his approach to leadership. He knows what has to be done to win a battle, and he marshals his troops to engage the enemy in such a way that victory is assured.

As Christians, we have both a Leader and a Commander in Jesus Christ. His objective is to bring others into His kingdom. Our task is to follow His leadership as we bear witness for Him in the world. As our Commander, He has the right to demand our unquestioning obedience.

LIFE

When Christ, who is our **life**, shall appear, then shall ye also appear with him in glory.
COLOSSIANS 3:4

We are accustomed to thinking of Jesus in terms of the eternal life that He promises to believers. But in this verse from the apostle Paul's letter to the Colossians, he describes Jesus as the Life of believers in the here-and-now. We don't have to wait until we die to enjoy life with Jesus. He is our Life today—in this present world.

With Jesus as our Life, we can live each day with joy, in spite of the problems and frustrations that come our way. He is the very essence of the truly good life, and He promises the same to those who follow Him: "I am come that they might have life, and that they might have it more abundantly" (John 10:10).

Other names of God the Son that emphasize the meaningful life He offers Christians are Prince of Life (Acts 3:15) and Word of Life (1 John 1:1).

Walking with Jesus Every Day

The old gospel hymn "Ev'ry Day with Jesus," by Robert C. Loveless, expresses the joy of life with Jesus, our Life, during every day of our earthly journey.

> Ev'ry day with Jesus
> Is sweeter than the day before,
> Ev'ry day with Jesus
> I love Him more and more;
> Jesus saves and keeps me,
> And He's the One I'm waiting for;
> Ev'ry day with Jesus
> Is sweeter than the day before.

LIFE-GIVING SPIRIT. See *Quickening Spirit.*

LIGHT

These verses from the prologue of John's Gospel contain one of the more meaningful names of God the Son in the entire New Testament. Jesus was the Light whom God sent into a world that was stumbling around in the darkness of sin.

This name of Jesus is also used for God the Father (see *Light* in part 1, Names of God the Father) because God is the Creator of light. The earth was shrouded in darkness until He declared, "Let there be light" (Genesis 1:3), and light appeared to illuminate the earth.

Light is something we take for granted until it disappears. Most of us know what it's like to grope around in a dark house after the electricity goes out unexpectedly. We are virtually helpless until we locate that flashlight we had placed in a closet for just such an emergency.

As the Light, Jesus pushes back the darkness and helps us find our way in a chaotic world. He reveals God in all His righteousness, and He bridges the gap that separates sinful humankind from a holy God. He gives us insights from God's written Word, the Bible, that enable us to make wise

There was a man sent from God, whose name was John. The same came for a witness, to bear witness of the **Light**, that all men through him might believe.
JOHN 1:6–7

decisions and live in accordance with His will.

Just as Jesus is the Light of our lives, He expects us as Christians to reflect His light to others. In His Sermon on the Mount, He called us "the light of the world" (Matthew 5:14). Then He challenged us to "let your light so shine before men, that they may see your good works, and glorify your Father which is in heaven" (Matthew 5:16).

The apostle John also refers to Jesus as the True Light (John 1:9).

LIGHT OF THE GENTILES. See *Light of the World.*

LIGHT OF THE WORLD

Jesus referred to Himself by this name in a conversation with the Pharisees, His constant critics. They thought He was nothing but a religious quack and a troublemaker. But Jesus claimed to be the Son of God, who had been sent on a redemptive mission as the Light of the World. He also used this name for Himself after restoring the sight of a blind man (see John 9:5).

The Jewish people of Jesus' time—especially religious leaders such as the Pharisees—were filled with religious and national pride. They realized that God had blessed them as His special people. They thought of His favor as something they deserved because of their moral superiority to the people of other nations. But they forgot that God had blessed them because He wanted them to serve as His witnesses to the rest of the world. Centuries before, God had told their ancestor Abraham, "I will make of thee a great nation. . .in thee shall all families of the earth be blessed" (Genesis 12:2–3).

Jesus was born into the world as a Jew, but His commitment as Savior was to the entire world. This is one reason why He was rejected by the Jewish religious leaders of His time. How could God the Father possibly love the pagan peoples of the world as much as He loved them? They wanted to put limits on God's love and concern.

This problem is still with us today. Some people want to make Jesus into the Light of the middle class, or the Light of Western society, or the Light of the beautiful. But He refuses to be bound by such restrictions. He is also the Light of the poor, the Light of the Third World, and the Light of the

Then spake Jesus again unto them, saying, I am the **light of the world**: he that followeth me shall not walk in darkness, but shall have the light of life.
JOHN 8:12

homely. No matter what your earthly circumstances, Jesus is *your* Light.

Another name of Jesus that expresses the same truth as Light of the World is Light of the Gentiles. To the Jews, "Gentiles" was a catch-all term for all non-Jewish peoples. In a famous messianic passage, the prophet Isaiah declared that Jesus would come into the world as a Light of the Gentiles (see Isaiah 42:6).

Light for a Dark World

Jesus is the Light for a dark world, according to the hymn "The Light of the World Is Jesus" by Philip P. Bliss.

The whole world was lost in the darkness of sin,
The Light of the world is Jesus;
Like sunshine at noonday His glory shone in,
The Light of the world is Jesus.
Come to the Light, 'tis shining for thee;
Sweetly the Light has dawned upon me,
Once I was blind, but now I can see:
The Light of the world is Jesus.

LION OF THE TRIBE OF JUDAH

This name of Jesus appears in one of the visions of the apostle John in the book of Revelation. Only Jesus as the Lion of the Tribe of Judah is worthy to open the scroll that contains God's judgment against the world in the end time. God the Father has delegated to His Son the authority and power to serve as supreme Judge over all things.

The lion, known as the "king of beasts," is legendary for its strength and ferocious nature. Lions do not roam the land of Israel today, but they were common in Bible times. For example, David killed a lion that was threatening his father's sheep (see 1 Samuel 17:37). The judge Samson, one of the superheroes of the Bible, killed a young lion with his bare hands (see Judges 14:5–6). God the Father also compared His forthcoming judgment against His rebellious people—the nation of Israel (spoken of symbolically as Ephraim) and the nation of Judah—to the fierceness of a lion (see Hosea 5:14).

Jesus as the Lion of the Tribe of Judah probably has its origin in the prophecy of Jacob in the book of Genesis. He declared that his son Judah was destined to become the

> And one of the elders saith unto me, Weep not: behold, the **Lion of the tribe of Judah**, the Root of David, hath prevailed [NIV: triumphed] to open the book, and to loose the seven seals thereof.
> REVELATION 5:5

This statue of the "Lion of Judah" stands in the Ethiopian capital of Addis Ababa.

greatest among all his twelve sons, whose descendants would become the Israelites, God's chosen people. Jacob described Judah, symbolically, as a lion, or a fearless ruler, who would lead God's people (see Genesis 49:8–12).

This prophecy was fulfilled dramatically throughout the Bible. The tribe of Judah, composed of Judah's descendants, took the lead on the Israelites' trek through the wilderness after they left Egypt (see Numbers 10:14). Moses' census of the people in the wilderness revealed that the tribe of Judah was the largest of the twelve tribes (see Numbers 1:27; 26:22). King David, the popular ruler of Israel, against whom all future kings were measured, was a Judahite, a native of Bethlehem in the territory of Judah (see 1 Samuel 16:1).

Most significantly of all, Jesus the Messiah sprang from the line of Judah. The genealogy of Jesus in the Gospel of Matthew traces His lineage back to Judah (spelled "Judas" in the KJV; see Matthew 1:2–3). Thus, Jesus is the Lion of the Tribe of Judah, who rules among His people as supreme Savior and Lord.

LIVING BREAD. See *Bread*.

LIVING STONE

To whom coming, as unto a **living stone**, disallowed [NIV: rejected] indeed of men, but chosen of God, and precious [NIV: precious to him].
1 PETER 2:4

In this verse, the apostle Peter compares Jesus to a stone used in the construction of a building. The imagery of a stone is also applied to Jesus in other New Testament passages (see *Chief Cornerstone* and *Head of the Corner* above). But Peter refers to Jesus here as a Living Stone, emphasizing His resurrection from the dead and His close relationship with believers as the living Christ.

In the next verse, Peter describes Christians as "lively stones" (1 Peter 2:5). Just as Jesus is the living and breathing Head of the Church, so believers make up the body of the church. Thus, the church is a living organism devoted to the service of Jesus and His kingdom in the time between His ascension to God the Father and His second coming.

Peter summarizes the mission of the church by stating

that Christians are "a chosen generation, a royal priesthood, an holy nation, a peculiar people; that ye should shew forth the praises of him who hath called you out of darkness into his marvellous light" (1 Peter 2:9).

Maybe you never thought about it before, but if you belong to Jesus, you have the spirit of the Living Stone in your life. We bring honor to Him when we serve as "lively stones" in the world.

A large crowd of Christians "shew forth the praises" of their Living Stone, Jesus.

LORD

Lord is one of the most popular names of God the Son in the New Testament, appearing hundreds of times. These two verses show that this name, from the Greek word *kurios*, is used in two distinct ways in the New Testament.

In the first verse, from Luke's Gospel, the "Lord" used of Jesus is a term of respect, similar to our use of *mister* or *sir* in modern society. This "certain man" respected Jesus, but he apparently had no intention of committing his life to Him as his spiritual Lord and Master. He did not reply when Jesus told him about the sacrifice He required of His followers (see Luke 9:58).

Even Jesus' disciples sometimes called Him Lord in this polite, respectful sense. For example, Jesus once told a parable about the need for people to wait and watch expectantly for

And it came to pass, that, as they went in the way, a certain man said unto him, **Lord**, I will follow thee whithersoever thou goest [NIV: wherever you go].
LUKE 9:57

His return. Peter approached Him and asked, "Lord, speakest thou this parable unto us, or even to all?" (Luke 12:41).

As Jesus' earthly ministry unfolded, the polite title of Lord that people used of Him was transformed into a declaration of faith in Him as the divine Son of God the Father. This is the sense in which the apostle Paul calls Jesus "Lord" in 1 Corinthians 15:58.

After His resurrection and ascension, Jesus became the Lord of history, the Lord of the church, and the Lord of individual Christians. When we declare that "Jesus is Lord," we submit to His lordship and crown Him as the supreme ruler over our lives.

> Therefore, my beloved brethren, be ye stedfast, unmoveable, always abounding in the work of the **Lord**, forasmuch as ye know that your labour is not in vain in the **Lord**.
> 1 CORINTHIANS 15:58

LORD AND SAVIOUR JESUS CHRIST.
See *Christ Jesus Our Lord.*

LORD CHRIST. See *Christ Jesus Our Lord.*

LORD FROM HEAVEN

This verse appears in the apostle Paul's famous passage about Jesus' sinlessness in contrast to Adam's sin as the first man (see *Last Adam* above). Here, Adam's origin as a being created from the dust of the earth (see Genesis 3:19) is contrasted with Jesus' divine origin as the Lord from heaven.

When Jesus completed His mission on earth as our Redeemer, He returned to His Father in heaven (see Acts 1:9–11). He is now seated in heaven at God's right hand (see Colossians 3:1), where He intercedes on our behalf with God the Father (see Romans 8:34).

> The first man is of the earth, earthy: the second man is the **Lord from heaven**.
> 1 CORINTHIANS 15:47

The One from Heaven

Jesus' coming to earth from heaven the first time, as well as His future return, is celebrated in the hymn "One Day," by J. Wilbur Chapman.

One day when heaven was filled with His praises,
One day when sin was as black as could be,
Jesus came forth to be born of a virgin,
Dwelt among men, my example is He!
Living, He loved me; dying, He saved me;
Buried, He carried my sins far away;
Rising, He justified freely forever:
One day He's coming—O glorious day!

Just as Jesus came into the world from heaven when the time was right (see Galatians 4:4), so, too, will He return one day to bring the earth as we know it to its conclusion, in accordance with God's plan. As Christians, we should be looking forward with watchful readiness to that glorious day (see Matthew 25:13).

LORD JESUS. See *Jesus*.

LORD JESUS CHRIST. See *Jesus*.

LORD JESUS CHRIST OUR SAVIOUR.
See *Christ Jesus Our Lord*.

LORD OF GLORY. See *Brightness of God's Glory*.

LORD OF LORDS
This name emphasizes Jesus' supreme authority in the end time, when He returns to earth in victory over all His enemies. He is also called Lord of Lords in two other places in the New Testament (see 1 Timothy 6:15; Revelation 17:14; see also *King of Kings* above).

> And he hath on his vesture [NIV: robe] and on his thigh a name written, **KING OF KINGS, AND LORD OF LORDS.**
> Revelation 19:16

As Lord of Lords, Jesus is superior in power and authority to all the rulers of the earth. Some monarchs of the ancient world were worshipped as divine by their subjects. But only Jesus, as Lord of Lords, is worthy of our worship and total commitment.

Here is how the apostle Paul expresses the meaning of this name in his letter to the believers at Philippi: "God also hath highly exalted him, and given him a name which is above every name: that at the name of Jesus every knee should bow, of things in heaven, and things in earth, and things under the earth; and that every tongue should confess that Jesus Christ is Lord, to the glory of God the Father" (Philippians 2:9–11).

LORD OF PEACE
As the apostle Paul brought to a close his second letter to the Thessalonian Christians, he blessed them with this beautiful benediction. He wanted these Christians, who were going through disagreement and turmoil, to experience the peace that Jesus promises to those who abide in Him.

Now the **Lord of peace** himself give you peace always by all means [NIV: at all times and in every way]. The Lord be with you all.
2 THESSALONIANS 3:16

The dictionary defines peace as "freedom from disquieting or oppressive thoughts or emotions." This definition assumes that peace is the *absence* of elements such as conflict or negative feelings. But we as Christians know that peace is actually the *presence* of something. This presence is Jesus Christ, who brings peace and inner tranquillity to those who have placed their trust in Him. With Jesus as the Lord of Peace in our lives, we can have peace even in the midst of troubling circumstances.

When Jesus was born in Bethlehem, the angels celebrated His arrival by declaring "peace, good will toward men" (Luke 2:14). Jesus also told His disciples on one occasion, "Let not your heart be troubled: ye believe in God, believe also in me" (John 14:1). We don't have to go around with troubled looks on our faces if the Lord of Peace reigns in our hearts.

The apostle Paul referred to Jesus as Our Peace (Ephesians 2:14). The prophet Isaiah called the coming Messiah the Prince of Peace (Isaiah 9:6).

Promises from the Lord of Peace

- "Peace I leave with you, my peace I give unto you" (John 14:27).
- "Being justified by faith, we have peace with God through our Lord Jesus Christ" (Romans 5:1).
- "He is our peace, who hath. . .broken down the middle wall of partition between us" (Ephesians 2:14).
- "The peace of God, which passeth all understanding, shall keep your hearts and minds through Christ Jesus" (Philippians 4:7).

LORD OF THE DEAD AND LIVING

Whether we live therefore, or die, we are the Lord's. For to this end [NIV: For this very reason] Christ both died, and rose, and revived [NIV: returned to life], that he might be **Lord** both **of the dead and living**.
ROMANS 14:8–9

In this verse from Paul's letter to the believers at Rome, he refers to those who know, and have known, Christ as Lord and Savior. Jesus is the Lord of the millions of Christians who have lived in the past and who have now passed on to their reward. He is also the Lord of all believers still living who look forward to eternal life with Him in heaven after their days on earth are over.

Whether we are alive or dead, there is no better place to be than in the hands of our loving Lord.

LORD OF THE HARVEST

These verses describe the reaction of Jesus to the crowds in the region of Galilee who came to Him for help. His reputation as a healer and teacher had spread throughout the area. He was moved with compassion when He saw their needs. He longed for more workers to help Him as the Lord of the Harvest with the spiritual harvest that pressed in from every side.

> Pray ye therefore the **Lord of the harvest**, that he will send forth labourers into his harvest.
> MATTHEW 9:38

Jesus had unlimited power, so why didn't He just take care of all these needs Himself, rather than ask His disciples to pray for more workers? Perhaps it was because He knew His time on earth was limited. Even if He healed all the sick and taught all those who flocked after Him, others in the same condition would take their place after He was gone. He needed other committed workers, such as His disciples, who would carry on His work after His death, resurrection, and ascension.

Jesus is still in the harvesting business. His work on earth continues through His church, under the power of the Holy Spirit. He still needs workers to gather the harvest. When we get so concerned about the spiritual needs of others that we begin to pray to the Lord of the Harvest for more workers, we might just become the answer to our own prayers.

Agriculture was a way of life in Bible times. The image of laborers harvesting in the ripened fields was an easy metaphor for those who heard Christ speak about a spiritual harvest. Scenes like this can still be seen in modern day Israel.

LORD OF THE SABBATH

This verse from Mark's Gospel describes Jesus' response to the Pharisees when they criticized Him for picking grain on the Sabbath to feed Himself and His hungry disciples. He

> And he said unto them, The sabbath was made for man, and not man for the sabbath: Therefore the Son of man is **Lord** also **of the sabbath**.
> MARK 2:27–28

also claimed to be the Lord of the Sabbath when He was criticized for healing people on this sacred day (see Matthew 12:8–14; Luke 6:5–11).

The original law about Sabbath observance stated simply, "Remember the sabbath day, to keep it holy" (Exodus 20:8). The law went on to restrict people from working on this day—Saturday, the seventh day of the week—in the Jewish religious system.

Over the years, the Pharisees had added all sorts of rules or traditions to this simple law about honoring the Sabbath. For example, one restriction forbade people from traveling more than about one-half mile—or a "Sabbath's day journey" (Acts 1:12)—from their homes on this day. These silly rules had reduced the Sabbath from a spiritual principle to little more than an external observance.

When Jesus claimed to be the Lord of the Sabbath, He declared that He would not be bound by the human rules about Sabbath observance that the Pharisees had established. To Jesus, doing good on the Sabbath by healing people was more important than obeying ritualistic rules (see Matthew 12:12).

Jesus' claim to be the Lord of the Sabbath also placed Him on the same level as God the Father. It was God who had established the Sabbath (see Genesis 2:2–3). Jesus as the agent of Creation (John 1:1–3) was the authority over the Sabbath. The Creator is always greater than anything He has created.

LORD OVER ALL

> For there is no difference between the Jew and the Greek: for the same **Lord over all** is rich unto all [NIV: richly blesses all] that call upon him.
> ROMANS 10:12

The name of Jesus in this verse—Lord over All—may seem to express the same idea as Lord of Lords (see above). But there is an important distinction between these two names.

Lord of Lords refers to Jesus' supreme rule throughout the earth at His second coming. Lord over All declares that every person, whether Jew or Gentile, is on the same level in relationship to Jesus Christ. The apostle Paul declares in this verse that Jesus does not have one plan of salvation for the Jewish people and another for Greeks or non-Jews. Every person comes to salvation by accepting by faith the price Jesus paid on the cross to redeem us from our sin.

In New Testament times, the Jews looked upon Greeks, or Gentiles, as pagans who were excluded from God's favor. The learned Greeks, in turn, thought of all people who were not Greek citizens as uncultured barbarians. But Paul declared that Jesus wiped out all such distinctions between people. The ground was level at the foot of the cross. Everyone stood before God as wayward sinners who had no hope except the forgiveness they could experience at the feet of the crucified Savior.

Paul also makes it clear in this verse that something is required of sinners who want the salvation that Jesus provides. They must "call upon" Jesus the Son. This involves repenting of their sins, confessing Him as Savior, and committing their lives to His lordship. This is the New Testament equivalent of "calling upon" God the Father, which runs like a refrain throughout the Old Testament (see Genesis 12:8; 1 Samuel 12:17; Psalm 4:3; Isaiah 55:6).

"Whosoever" Means Everyone

"Whosoever Will," a hymn written by Philip P. Bliss, declares that everyone is included in Jesus' summons to accept Him as Savior and Lord.

> "Whosoever heareth," shout, shout the sound!
> Spread the blessed tidings all the world around;
> Tell the joyful news wherever man is found,
> "Whosoever will may come."
> "Whosoever will, whosoever will!"
> Send the proclamation over vale and hill;
> 'Tis a loving Father calls the wanderer home:
> "Whosoever will may come."

LORD'S CHRIST

The "him" in this verse refers to Simeon, a man who came to the temple when the infant Jesus was dedicated to the Lord by Mary and Joseph (see *Consolation of Israel* above). Simeon recognized the young child as the Lord's Christ.

The word *Lord's* in this context refers to God the Father. *Christ* derives from a Greek word *christos*, meaning "anointed" (see *Christ* above). Thus, Simeon recognized Jesus as God's Anointed One, or the Messiah, whom the Jewish people had been expecting God the Father to send since Old Testament times.

Even though Jesus was just a little baby in His mother's arms, Simeon realized the moment he saw Him that He was the Messiah. This insight came from the Holy Spirit. So all

> And it was revealed unto him by the Holy Ghost, that he should not see death, before he had seen the **Lord's Christ**.
> LUKE 2:26

three persons of the Godhead—God the Father, God the Son, and God the Holy Spirit—were present at this event. This makes Jesus' dedication at the temple one of the more dramatic passages on the Trinity in the entire New Testament.

MAN APPROVED OF GOD. See *Flesh*.

MAN CHRIST JESUS. See *Flesh*.

MAN OF GOD'S RIGHT HAND

In this verse, the psalmist asks God the Father to strengthen the One whom He has selected for a special task. This Man of God's Right Hand refers to Jesus, the Messiah and the agent of God's redemption in the world.

A person who sat at the right side of a king in Bible times was the most important official in the royal court. He was often the second in command, who acted as the chief administrator of the king's affairs. Even today, a leader's most important and trusted aide is often referred to as his "right-hand man."

As the Man of God's Right Hand, Jesus came into the world as the dispenser of divine justice and forgiveness. God the Father delegated to Him the task of restoring sinful humankind to fellowship with Him through His death on the cross. When this task was accomplished, the Father summoned His Son back to heaven, where He is seated in the place of authority at His Father's right hand (see Ephesians 1:20).

You've probably heard the old saying, "Don't send a boy to do a man's job." Aren't you glad that Jesus was man enough and faithful enough and determined enough and prayerful enough to accomplish the task that His Father sent

> Let thy hand be upon the **man of thy right hand**, upon the son of man whom thou madest strong for thyself [NIV: you have raised up for yourself].
> PSALM 80:17

Jesus at His Father's Right Hand

- "It is Christ. . .who is even at the right hand of God, who also maketh intercession for us" (Romans 8:34).
- "Seek those things which are above, where Christ sitteth on the right hand of God" (Colossians 3:1).
- "This man, after he had offered sacrifice for sins for ever, sat down on the right hand of God" (Hebrews 10:12).
- "Who is. . .on the right hand of God; angels and authorities and powers being made subject to him" (1 Peter 3:22).

Him to do? No person has ever been sent on a more important mission, and He handled it perfectly as the Man of God's Right Hand.

MAN OF SORROWS

In our society, the words *sorrow* or *sorrows* suggest a state of deep remorse or regret over the loss of something or someone highly loved and esteemed. For example, we might say about a couple who have lost a child: "They are still in sorrow a year after the death."

If we apply this modern definition to this name of Jesus in Isaiah's prophecy—Man of Sorrows—we sense that an alternative translation of this name might be in order. Perhaps, as the NRSV suggests, Jesus was a Man of Suffering more than a Man of Sorrows.

Jesus was not a person who was immersed in a state of remorse or regret over a loss that He had experienced. He was an overcomer—a victorious person—in spite of the problems He faced during His earthly ministry. Even the suffering that led to His death on the cross was swallowed up in victory

> He is despised and rejected of men; a **man of sorrows**, and acquainted with grief: and we hid as it were our faces from him; he was despised, and we esteemed him not. Surely he hath borne our griefs, and carried our sorrows: yet we did esteem him [NIV: considered him] stricken, smitten of God, and afflicted.
> ISAIAH 53:3–4
> [NRSV: **man of suffering**]

An angel comforts Jesus as He prays the night before His crucifixion (Luke 22:43).

when He drew His last breath and declared, "It is finished" (John 19:30). He had accomplished the purpose for which He had been sent into the world.

There is no doubt that Jesus' suffering on the cross was real. So is the pain that we as Christians feel when we are ridiculed for our faith by an unbelieving world. But this should not drive us to sorrow or despair. The Man of Suffering has already "borne our griefs, and carried our sorrows" by dying on the cross in our place. He invites us to cast our cares upon Him during each day of our earthly journey.

Our inspiration for doing so is Jesus Himself, "who for the joy that was set before him endured the cross, despising the shame, and is set down at the right hand of the throne of God" (Hebrews 12:2).

MAN OF SUFFERING. See *Man of Sorrows*.

MAN WHOM GOD ORDAINED. See
Foreordained before the Foundation of the World.

MASTER

This name that Jesus used of Himself appears in the famous "woe" chapter of Matthew's Gospel, in which Jesus condemns the Pharisees. He was particularly critical of their hypocrisy and religious pride. They enjoyed being greeted in the streets with titles that recognized them for their learning and expertise in the Jewish law; but Jesus declared that He as God's Son was the only person who deserved the title of Master.

Master in this verse is a derivative of a Greek word that means "commander" or "ruler." Modern translations sometimes render this word as "teacher." But Jesus was claiming to be more than a teacher. He made it clear to His disciples and others who were listening that He had the right to serve as the supreme authority in their lives.

In New Testament times, slave owners were sometimes

> And call no man your father upon the earth: for one is your Father, which is in heaven. Neither be ye called masters: for one is your **Master**, even Christ.
> MATTHEW 23:9–10
> [NASB: **Leader**; NIV: **Teacher**; NRSV: **instructor**]

In the Master's Service

"O Master, Let Me Walk with Thee," Washington Gladden's famous hymn, expresses the believer's desire to serve others in the cause of Jesus Christ and His kingdom.

O Master, let me walk with thee
In lowly paths of service free;
Tell me Thy secret, help me bear
The strain of toil, the fret of care.
Help me the slow of heart to move
By some clear, winning word of love;
Teach me the wayward feet to stay,
And guide them in the homeward way.

called "masters" (see Colossians 4:1), implying their supreme control over every aspect of their slaves' lives. As Christians, we are also subject to the will of our Master, the Lord Jesus, who has redeemed us for His service.

MEDIATOR

A mediator is a person who serves as a middleman or go-between to bring two opposing parties together. For example, a mediator is often used in labor disputes. Both labor and management leaders agree to abide by the decision of an independent mediator. This avoids the expense and hassle of a lawsuit and often brings a quick resolution to the problem.

> For there is one God, and one **mediator** between God and men, the man Christ Jesus.
> 1 TIMOTHY 2:5

According to the apostle Paul, in this verse from his first letter to Timothy, Jesus also fills the role of spiritual Mediator in the world. He is the middleman, or go-between who reconciles God to mankind.

Man by nature is a sinner. In his sinful state, he is estranged from a holy God, who will not tolerate anything that is unholy or unclean. But Jesus eliminated this gap between God and man by sacrificing His life on the cross for our sins and purchasing our forgiveness. Cleansed of our sin through the blood of Jesus, we now have fellowship with God the Father. We have been reconciled to God through His Son's work as our Mediator.

Jesus is the perfect Mediator between God and man, because He had both divine and human attributes. As God, He understood what God the Father demanded of people in order to be acceptable in His sight. As a man, He realized the desperate situation of sinful human beings. He was the God-man who was able to bring these two opposites together in a way that brought glory to God and gave man access to God's blessings and His eternal presence.

U.S. President Jimmy Carter served as mediator, bringing Egyptian President Anwar Sadat and Israeli Prime Minister Menachem Begin together in a 1978 peace agreement.

Jesus our Mediator also expects His followers to serve as "middlemen" for others in a sinful world. Our job as Christians is to point others to Jesus Christ, who wants everyone to enjoy fellowship with God the Father. The

apostle Paul expresses it like this: "All things are of God, who hath reconciled us to himself by Jesus Christ, and hath given to us the ministry of reconciliation" (2 Corinthians 5:18).

MEDIATOR OF A BETTER COVENANT. See *Mediator of the New Testament.*

MEDIATOR OF A NEW COVENANT. See *Mediator of the New Testament.*

MEDIATOR OF THE NEW TESTAMENT

Testament is another word for covenant or agreement. Thus the "new testament" that the writer of Hebrews mentions here is the new covenant that God established with His people, based on the sacrificial death of Jesus Christ. Jesus is the Mediator of this new covenant.

The first covenant of God with His people was formalized in Old Testament times. God agreed to bless the Israelites and serve as their Guide and Protector if they would follow and worship Him. But the Jewish people broke this covenant time and time again as they fell into rebellion and idolatry.

Finally, God promised through the prophet Jeremiah that He would establish a new covenant with His people. This would be a spiritual covenant written on their hearts rather than a covenant of law (see Jeremiah 31:31–34). This covenant would accomplish for God's people what the old covenant had failed to do—bring them forgiveness and give them a new understanding of God the Father.

On the night before His crucifixion, Jesus declared that He was implementing this new covenant that had been promised by His Father. This covenant would be based on His blood, which would be shed to provide redemption and forgiveness of sin for God's people (see Matthew 26:28).

Unlike the old covenant, this new covenant has never been replaced. The Mediator of the New Covenant has promised that those who belong to Him will enjoy eternal life with Him in heaven. What could be better than that? We are willing to bet our lives that Jesus will deliver on His promise.

In Hebrews, Jesus is also called the Mediator of a Better Covenant (Hebrews 8:6) and the Surety of a Better Testament (Hebrews 7:22). These names express the same idea as Mediator of the New Testament.

And for this cause [NIV: for this reason] he is the **mediator of the new testament,** that by means of death, for the redemption of the transgressions that were under the first testament, they which are called might receive the promise of eternal inheritance.
HEBREWS 9:15
[NASB, NIV, NRSV: **mediator of a new covenant**]

MELCHISEDEK. See *High Priest after the Order of Melchisedec.*

MERCIFUL AND FAITHFUL HIGH PRIEST. See *Great High Priest.*

MESSENGER OF THE COVENANT

Jesus not only established the new covenant that God had promised for His people (see *Mediator of the New Testament* above). He was also the Messenger whom God sent to announce that this new covenant was now a reality. In this messianic passage, the prophet Malachi declares that Jesus the Messiah would come as the Messenger of the Covenant.

Throughout the history of Israel, God had sent many agents to deliver His message to His people. The greatest of His messengers were the prophets, who often delivered unpopular messages of divine judgment against the nation's sin and rebellion. But Jesus was the divine Messenger who stood out above all the others. He was the Messenger of the covenant of grace that God the Father had established with a sinful world.

About six hundred years before Jesus was born, the prophet Isaiah announced that God the Father would send His servant with a message of joy and comfort for all people. At the beginning of His public ministry, Jesus identified with this prophecy. He stood in the synagogue in his hometown of Nazareth and read these words from Isaiah: "The Spirit of the Lord is upon me, because he hath anointed me to preach the gospel to the poor; he hath sent me to heal the brokenhearted, to preach deliverance to the captives, and recovering of sight to the blind, to set at liberty them that are bruised, to preach the acceptable year of the Lord" (Luke 4:18–19). Then He declared, "This day is this scripture fulfilled in your ears" (Luke 4:21).

For more than three years, Jesus served as the faithful Messenger of God's new covenant of grace that He had been sent to establish. Then His earthly ministry ended with His death on the cross and His glorious resurrection. God's plan from the beginning was that His Messenger would eventually become the Message—the good news (gospel) about God's love for sinners.

> Behold, I will send my messenger, and he shall prepare the way before me: and the LORD, whom ye seek, shall suddenly come to his temple, even the **messenger of the covenant**, whom ye delight in: behold, he shall come, saith the LORD of hosts.
> MALACHI 3:1

MESSIAH

These two verses are part of the account in John's Gospel of Jesus' conversation with the Samaritan woman at the well. He admitted openly to her that He was the Messiah, the deliverer whom God had been promising to send to His people for hundreds of years.

The only other place in the New Testament where the word *Messiah* appears is also in John's Gospel. After meeting Jesus, Andrew told his brother, Simon Peter, "We have found the Messias" (John 1:41).

It's not surprising that *Messiah* appears rarely in the New Testament, because Jesus discouraged others from referring to Him by this title (see Matthew 16:20). The Jewish people expected their Messiah to be a political and military deliverer who would throw off the yoke of Rome and restore the fortunes of Israel. Jesus had come into the world as a spiritual Messiah, but He avoided this name because it would lead the people to expect Him to be something He was not.

Though the word *Messiah* is rare in the New Testament, the concept appears on almost every page. The Greek term *christos*, rendered as "Christ," means "anointed" or "anointed one"—a word referring to the Messiah or God's Chosen One (see *Chosen of God* and *Christ* above).

Even when the Messiah is mentioned in the Old Testament, the word itself is seldom used. Usually this leader who was to come is described as a Prince (Daniel 8:25), Ruler (Micah 5:2), or Servant (Isaiah 53:11). The rare exception is the book of Daniel, which contains a reference to Messiah the Prince (Daniel 9:25).

MESSIAH THE PRINCE. See *Messiah*.

MIGHTY GOD. See *Almighty*.

MIGHTY ONE OF ISRAEL. See *Almighty*.

MIGHTY ONE OF JACOB. See *Almighty*.

MIGHTY SAVIOUR. See *Horn of Salvation*; *Saviour*.

MINISTER OF THE TRUE TABERNACLE

One of the major themes of the book of Hebrews is the supremacy of Christ's priesthood over the Old Testament sacrificial system. In this verse, the writer of Hebrews claims that the priesthood established during Aaron's time (see Exodus 40:12–15) was only a shadow of the eternal priesthood provided for believers in heaven. Jesus is the priest of the heavenly sanctuary that God has established for His people; He is the Minister of the True Tabernacle.

The most sacred place in the Jewish religious system was the inner sanctuary of the tabernacle or temple, known as "the most holy" (NIV: Most Holy Place; NASB: holy of holies), which represented God's holy and awesome presence. Only the high priest could enter this section of the temple, and even he could do so only once a year, on the Day of Atonement. On this special occasion, he offered a sacrifice—first for his own sins and then for the sins of the people (see Leviticus 16:1–6).

When Jesus died on the cross, the heavy veil or curtain that sealed off this section of the temple was torn from top to bottom (see Matthew 27:50–51). This symbolized that all people now had access to God's presence and forgiveness through the sacrificial death of His Son, Jesus.

Jesus is now the perfect priest or Minister of the True Tabernacle in heaven. There, He conducts His ministry of intercession for all believers. "He is able to save completely those who come to God through him," the writer of Hebrews declares, "because he always lives to intercede for them" (Hebrews 7:25 NIV).

> We have such an high priest, who is set on the right hand of the throne of the Majesty in the heavens; a **minister** of the sanctuary, and **of the true tabernacle**, which the Lord pitched [NIV: set up], and not man.
> HEBREWS 8:1–2

This replica of the Tabernacle exemplifies how temporary the original one from Aaron's time was.

MORNING STAR. See *Bright and Morning Star.*

MOST HOLY. See *Holy One/Holy One of God.*

MY SON, THE BELOVED. See *Beloved Son.*

MY SON, WHOM I LOVE. See *Beloved Son.*

NAZARENE. See *Jesus of Galilee/Jesus of Nazareth.*

OFFSPRING OF DAVID. See *Root and Offspring of David.*

OFFSPRING OF THE WOMAN. See *Seed of the Woman.*

OMEGA. See *Alpha and Omega.*

ONE AND ONLY SON. See *Only Begotten Son.*

ONE CHOSEN OUT OF THE PEOPLE

Psalm 89 focuses on God's promise to King David that one of David's descendants would always occupy the throne of Israel (see 2 Samuel 7:8–17). Thus the "one chosen out of the people" in this verse refers to David, because he was chosen by the Lord from among the sons of Jesse to replace Saul as king (see 1 Samuel 16:10–13).

But this psalm also looks beyond David's time to its ultimate fulfillment in the Messiah, Jesus Christ. The angel Gabriel made this clear when he appeared to the virgin Mary to tell her that she would give birth to the Messiah, God's Chosen One. "He shall be great, and shall be called the Son of the Highest," Gabriel declared, "and the Lord God shall give unto him the throne of his father David" (Luke 1:32).

As the One Chosen out of the People, Jesus was not a king in the same sense as David. He did not seek political or military power. His kingship was spiritual in nature. He ushered in the kingdom of God, the dominion over which He reigns with all those who have accepted Him as Lord and Savior.

Then thou spakest in vision to thy holy one, and saidst, I have laid help [NIV: bestowed strength] upon one that is mighty; I have exalted **one chosen out of the people.**
PSALM 89:19 [NIV: **a young man from among the people**]

Sarcophagus frieze from the fourth century depicts the adoration of the shepherds over David's descendent—the infant Jesus—as the One Chosen Out of the People

ONE WHO SPEAKS TO THE FATHER IN OUR DEFENSE. See *Advocate*.

ONLY BEGOTTEN OF THE FATHER. See *Only Begotten Son*.

ONLY BEGOTTEN SON

Jesus used this name for Himself in His long discussion with Nicodemus about the meaning of the new birth (see John 3:1–21). This verse from that discussion is probably the best known passage in the entire Bible. Most Christians can quote it from memory. It has been called "the gospel in a nutshell" because its twenty-five words tell us so clearly and simply why Jesus came into the world.

The name Only Begotten Son describes Jesus' special relationship with the Father. He is unique—the one and only of His kind who has ever existed. The fact that He was God's one and only Son makes His role as our Savior all the more significant. God the Father sent the very best when He sent Jesus to die on the cross for our sins.

For God so loved the world, that he gave his **only begotten Son**, that whosoever believeth in him should not perish, but have everlasting life. JOHN 3:16 [NIV: **one and only Son**; NRSV: **only Son**]

This name of Jesus appears only in the writings of the apostle John (see John 1:18; 3:18; 1 John 4:9). John in his Gospel also referred to Jesus as the Only Begotten of the Father (John 1:14).

John 3:16: All the Greatest

An unknown author has explained in memorable terms why John 3:16 is a passage that appeals to all Christians.

God: The greatest lover.

So loved: The greatest degree.

The world: The greatest company.

That He gave: The greatest act.

His only begotten Son: The greatest gift.

That whosoever: The greatest opportunity.

Believeth: The greatest simplicity.

In him: The greatest attraction.

Should not perish: The greatest promise.

But: The greatest difference.

Have: The greatest certainty.

Everlasting life: The greatest possession.

ONLY POTENTATE. See *Blessed and Only Potentate.*

ONLY SON. See *Only Begotten Son.*

ONLY WISE GOD

These final two verses of the epistle of Jude form one of the most inspiring benedictions in the New Testament. Jude wanted his readers to experience the joy of their salvation and to continue to be faithful in their witness to their Only Wise God, whom he clearly identified as Jesus their Savior.

This is the only place in the Bible where Jesus is called by this name. The New King James Version translates this phrase as "God our Savior, who alone is wise." Only Jesus Christ has divine wisdom. Worldly wisdom is a poor substitute for the wisdom that God promises to those who follow Him as Savior and Lord.

Jesus the Son, and God the Father, impart wisdom to

Now unto him that is able to keep you from falling, and to present you faultless before the presence of his glory with exceeding joy, to the **only wise God** our Saviour, be glory and majesty, dominion and power, both now and for ever. Amen.
JUDE 1:24–25

believers by several methods—through the Holy Spirit, through the counsel of fellow Christians, and through the scriptures, the written Word of God. We will never be as wise as God, who is the fount of all wisdom. But we should be growing in this gift of grace as we walk with Him during our earthly journey. James advised the readers of his epistle: "If any of you lacks wisdom, he should ask God, who gives generously to all without finding fault, and it will be given to him" (James 1:5 NIV).

Another name of Jesus similar in meaning to Only Wise God is Wisdom of God (1 Corinthians 1:24).

Seeking Godly Wisdom

- "The wisdom of this world is foolishness with God. For it is written, He taketh the wise in their own craftiness" (1 Corinthians 3:19).
- "Be very careful, then, how you live—not as unwise but as wise, making the most of every opportunity, because the days are evil" (Ephesians 5:15–16 NIV).
- "Let the word of Christ dwell in you richly in all wisdom; teaching and admonishing one another in psalms and hymns and spiritual songs" (Colossians 3:16).

ORIGIN OF GOD'S CREATION. See *Beginning of the Creation of God.*

OUR PASCHAL LAMB. See *Our Passover.*

OUR PASSOVER

In this verse from his first letter to the believers at Corinth, the apostle Paul refers to the Jewish festival known as the Passover. This was the most important religious celebration among the Jews.

Passover commemorated the "passing over" of the houses of the Israelites when God destroyed all the firstborn of the land of Egypt. This occurred as God's final plague against Egypt to convince the pharaoh to release the nation of Israel from slavery. The Jews escaped God's judgment by following His command to mark their houses with the blood of sacrificial lambs (see *Lamb of God* above).

Jesus is Our Passover, Paul declares, because He shed His

Purge out therefore the old leaven, that ye may be a new lump, as ye are unleavened. For even Christ **our passover** is sacrificed for us.
1 CORINTHIANS 5:7 [NIV: **our Passover lamb**; NRSV: **our paschal lamb**]

blood to bring deliverance for God's people, just as the first sacrificial lambs inaugurated the first Passover. We remember His sacrifice with reverence every time we partake of Communion, the Lord's Supper.

The imagery of leaven in connection with Passover also appears in this verse. *Leaven* is another word for yeast, an ingredient used to cause bread to rise. But the Israelites left Egypt in such a hurry on the first Passover that they didn't have time to add leaven to their bread dough and wait for it to rise (see Exodus 12:34). Thus, whenever they observed this holiday from that day on, they were to eat unleavened bread. This part of Passover was known as the Feast of Unleavened Bread.

Paul refers to Christians in this verse as a "new lump," because they were "unleavened." Just as unleavened bread symbolizes the Israelites' freedom from Egyptian slavery, so Christians are unleavened, or separated from sin and death, by the perfect Passover Lamb, Jesus Christ.

Jesus celebrated the Passover meal with his disciples while reclining at the table. For centuries, the symbolism of this meal has pointed to Jesus as "Our Passover."

OUR PASSOVER LAMB. See *Our Passover*.

OUR PEACE. See *Lord of Peace*.

OVERSEER OF YOUR SOULS. See *Bishop of Your Souls.*

PERFECTER OF OUR FAITH. See *Author and Finisher of Our Faith.*

PHYSICIAN

These verses are part of the account of Jesus' calling of the tax collector, Matthew (also known as Levi), as His disciple. To celebrate the occasion, Matthew invited his tax collector associates and other friends to a "great feast" (Luke 5:29) for Jesus and His disciples.

The scribes and Pharisees were horrified that Jesus and His disciples would associate with such sinful people. But Jesus made it clear that He had been sent to people such as these. They needed a Savior and Deliverer. He was the Physician who could heal them of their desperate sickness known as sin.

Jesus' role as Physician is one of the more prominent in the Gospels. Most of His miracles were performed for people who were suffering from various physical problems—blindness, deafness, leprosy, and possession by evil spirits. But in many of these miracles, He went beyond healing the body to healing the soul and the spirit through forgiveness of sin. For example, after healing a paralyzed man, He told him, "Be of good cheer; thy sins be forgiven thee" (Matthew 9:2).

Jesus the Physician is still in the healing business. He

> But their scribes and Pharisees murmured against his disciples, saying, Why do ye eat and drink with publicans [NIV: tax collectors] and sinners? And Jesus answering said unto them, They that are whole [NIV: healthy] need not a **physician**; but they that are sick.
> LUKE 5:30–31
> [NIV: **doctor**]

Jesus touches a blind man's eyes to restore his sight in this relief from the eighteenth century.

offers hope to the discouraged, His abiding presence to the lonely, comfort to the grieving, and peace to the conflicted. But most of all, He brings deliverance from the most serious problems of the human race—sin and death. The apostle Paul expresses it like this: "The wages of sin is death; but the gift of God is eternal life through Jesus Christ our Lord" (Romans 6:23).

No Appointment Necessary

We as Christians don't need an appointment to see Jesus. He is always near, according to an old hymn by William Hunter titled "The Great Physician."

The great Physician now is near,
The sympathizing Jesus;
He speaks the drooping heart to cheer,
Oh, hear the voice of Jesus.
Sweetest note in seraph song,
Sweetest name on mortal tongue;
Sweetest carol ever sung,
Jesus, blessed Jesus.

PIONEER AND PERFECTER OF OUR FAITH. See *Author and Finisher of Our Faith.*

PIONEER OF SALVATION. See *Captain of Salvation.*

PLANT OF RENOWN

Is this verse from the prophet Ezekiel a description of the coming Messiah or a reference to the fertility of the renewed land of Israel? The KJV and NRSV translations treat the verse messianically, while the NASB and NIV render it as a reference to Israel.

The context of this verse provides support for the messianic interpretation. The entire thirty-fourth chapter of Ezekiel describes how God the Father will send a shepherd, His servant David, to feed His flock (see Ezekiel 34:23). As the Plant of Renown, this servant from David's line will provide God's people with all the food they need so "they shall be no more consumed with hunger."

And I will raise up for them a **plant of renown**, and they shall be no more consumed with hunger in the land, neither bear the shame of the heathen [NIV: scorn of the nations] any more.
EZEKIEL 34:29
[NASB: **renowned planting place**; NIV: **land renowned for its crops**; NRSV: **splendid vegetation**]

This name of God the Son is similar in meaning to His description of Himself as *Bread* (see above). Jesus is the spiritual sustenance that Christians need to keep their faith healthy and in tune with His will for their lives.

POTENTATE. See *Blessed and Only Potentate*.

POWER OF GOD

In this verse, the apostle Paul admits that many people were skeptical of a crucified Savior. If Jesus was such a great person, they reasoned, why did He wind up being executed on a Roman cross like a common criminal? To them His crucifixion was a sign of weakness, not a demonstration of strength.

On the contrary, Paul points out, Christ showed great power in His crucifixion. He was the very Power of God whom the Father sent to atone for the sins of the world through His death. The death of One on behalf of the many showed the extent of this divine power.

Jesus' power was demonstrated many times during His earthly ministry. He stilled a storm and calmed the waters on the Sea of Galilee (see Mark 4:37–39). He cast demons out of a demented man (see Luke 4:31–35). He raised His friend Lazarus from the dead (see John 11:43–44). But He refused to come down from the cross and save Himself, although the crowd taunted Him to do so (see Matthew 27:39–43).

This is a good example of power under control. Jesus could have called legions of angels to come to His rescue (see Matthew 26:53). But this would have nullified the purpose for which God the Father had sent Him into the world. His divine power was never greater than when He refused to use it.

> We preach Christ crucified, unto the Jews a stumblingblock, and unto the Greeks foolishness; but unto them which are called, both Jews and Greeks, Christ the **power of God**, and the wisdom of God.
> 1 CORINTHIANS 1:23–24

Christ as the Power of God in Paul's Writings

- "Your faith should not stand in the wisdom of men, but in the power of God" (1 Corinthians 2:5).
- "Though he was crucified through weakness, yet he liveth by the power of God" (2 Corinthians 13:4).
- "Be strong in the Lord, and in the power of his might" (Ephesians 6:10).
- "Be thou partaker of the afflictions of the gospel according to the power of God" (2 Timothy 1:8).

PRECIOUS CORNER STONE. See *Chief Cornerstone.*

PRIEST FOREVER. See *Great High Priest.*

PRINCE

The apostle Peter used this title for Jesus in his sermon before the Jewish Sanhedrin. He and the other apostles had just been released miraculously from prison by an angel after they were arrested for preaching about Jesus. Peter declared in his sermon that the Jewish religious leaders were guilty of crucifying Jesus, the Prince whom God the Father had sent into the world.

Prince is a title with at least three different meanings in the Bible. Peter could have had any one or all of these in mind when he referred to Jesus as a Prince.

1. A prince was the son of a king. If a king had several sons, his oldest was generally the one who succeeded his father on the throne. Perhaps Peter had Jesus as God's Son in mind when he called him a Prince.

2. *Prince* is a generic term often used in the Bible for a leader or ruler. For example, when Moses tried to stop a fight between two Israelites, one of them asked him, "Who made thee a prince and a judge over us?" (Exodus 2:14). When Peter called Jesus a Prince, he may have been saying that Jesus had been exalted by God to serve as a ruler over His people.

3. Sometimes the word *prince* is used as a synonym for *king* (see 1 Kings 11:34). By saying that Jesus was a Prince, Peter could have implied that He was the one and only sovereign ruler over God's people.

What Peter said about Jesus as a Prince boils down to this: He is the one and only Son of God appointed by the Father to rule over His people like a good king, administering justice and righteousness in His name.

The God of our fathers raised up Jesus, whom ye slew [NIV: killed] and hanged on a tree. Him hath God exalted with his right hand to be a **Prince** and a Saviour, for to give [NIV: that he might give] repentance to Israel, and forgiveness of sins.
ACTS 5:30–31
[NRSV: **Leader**]

Another Prince

Jesus is the Prince over God's kingdom. But He recognized there is another prince—Satan—who tries to undermine His work. He referred to Satan several times as "the prince of this world" (see John 12:31; 14:30; 16:11). The apostle Paul called Satan "the prince of the power of the air" (Ephesians 2:2).

PRINCE OF LIFE. See *Life*.

PRINCE OF PEACE. See *Lord of Peace*.

PRINCE OF PRINCES

This verse from the book of Daniel was fulfilled in Jewish history, but it also awaits its ultimate fulfillment in the end time. If refers to Antiochus IV, Epiphanes, an evil Greek ruler who persecuted the Jews, as well as the Antichrist of the last days, who is described in the book of Revelation.

Antiochus tried to force the Jewish people to adopt Greek culture, even going so far as to erect an altar to the pagan Greek god Zeus in the temple. His atrocities led to rebellion by the Jews under the leadership of the Maccabees during the period between the Old and New Testaments. Antiochus died in disgrace following his defeat by these Jewish zealots.

The ultimate earthly evil force will be the Antichrist, who stands against Christ, His church, and their influence for good in the world. But this evil person will be overcome by Christ (see Revelation 14:9–11; 19:20), just as Antiochus met defeat in his time. No earthly power is able to stand against the Prince of Princes.

And through his policy also he shall cause craft [NIV: deceit] to prosper in his hand; and he shall magnify himself in his heart, and by peace shall destroy many: he shall also stand up against the **Prince of princes**; but he shall be broken without hand [NIV: yet he will be destroyed, but not by human power].
DANIEL 8:25

PRINCE OF THE KINGS OF THE EARTH

The apostle John addressed the book of Revelation to seven churches of Asia Minor, whose members were undergoing persecution by the Roman authorities. John wanted these believers to understand that he was not writing under his own authority but under the command and direction of Jesus Christ, the Prince of the Kings of the Earth.

Earthly rulers, such as the emperors of the Roman Empire, come and go. But Jesus is an eternal King, not a temporary monarch who rules for a few years and then is replaced by another. Jesus stands above and beyond all the kings of the earth.

Other titles of Jesus that are similar in meaning to this title are King of Kings (Revelation 19:16) and King over All the Earth (Zechariah 14:9). If Jesus is the world's supreme King, there is no doubt that He has the right to reign over His church and in the lives of those who claim Him as their Savior and Lord.

Grace be unto you, and peace. . .from Jesus Christ, who is the faithful witness, and the first begotten of the dead, and the **prince of the kings of the earth**.
REVELATION 1:4–5 [NASB, NIV, NRSV: **ruler of the kings of the earth**]

PROPHET. See *Great Prophet*.

PROPHET MIGHTY IN DEED AND WORD. See *Great Prophet*.

PROPHET OF NAZARETH OF GALILEE. See *Great Prophet*.

PROPHETION FOR OUR SINS

The word *propitiation* comes from an old English word, *propitiate*, meaning "to appease" or "to satisfy." Thus, the apostle John declares in this verse that God the Father sent His Son Jesus to serve as the satisfaction for our sins. This word is the key to one of the classical theories of the Atonement, or the sacrificial death of Jesus.

According to this view, God is a holy God who cannot tolerate sin. This puts us as humans in a dilemma, because we are not capable of living sinless lives, no matter how hard we try. To make matters worse, God is also a just God, who—in order to be true to His nature—must punish sin wherever He finds it. So our sin separates us from God and makes us liable to His punishment. *Hopeless* is the only word that adequately describes this situation.

But, according to John, God loved us too much to allow us to continue in this dilemma. He sent His Son, Jesus, to die to pay the penalty that He demanded from us because of our sin. Jesus was the sacrifice that covered over, or atoned, for our sin and restored the broken relationship between a holy God and sinful humanity.

Propitiation is not a word that most of us drop into casual conversation. Most people would not understand it. But aren't you glad that God knows the term and that Jesus lived out its meaning through His life and death? We as Christians can *celebrate* because Jesus came into the world to *propitiate*.

> Herein is love, not that we loved God, but that he loved us, and sent his Son to be the **propitiation for our sins**.
> 1 JOHN 4:10
> [NIV, NRSV: **atoning sacrifice for our sins**]

Jesus as Our Propitiation/Ransom

Ransom is another New Testament term that means basically the same thing as propitiation. In the Old Testament, ransom describes the price that was paid to purchase a person's freedom from slavery or from deserved punishment. In the New Testament, Jesus applies this word to Himself when he declares, "The Son of man came not to be ministered unto, but to minister, and to give his life a ransom for many" (Mark 10:45).

QUICKENING SPIRIT

This name of God the Son appears in connection with His name as the *Last Adam* (see above). Adam's act of disobedience of God brought sin and death into the world. But Jesus' perfect obedience nullified the divine curse against Adam and brought the possibility of eternal life to humankind.

As the Quickening Spirit, Jesus offers eternal life to all who accept Him as Savior and Lord.

RABBI/RABBONI

In modern society, *rabbi* is the official title of the leader of a Jewish congregation. It is similar to the title of *reverend* for a Protestant minister or *father* for a Catholic priest.

But in Jesus' time, *rabbi* was a term of respect meaning "teacher" or "master" (see *Good Master; Master* above). In John 3:2, Nicodemus's reference to Jesus as "rabbi" probably means "teacher." Nicodemus wanted to learn more about this Jewish teacher and miracle worker who was impressing the crowds in the region of Galilee.

In John 20:16, Mary Magdalene's recognition of Jesus as "Rabboni" pays homage to Him as her Master. After His resurrection, she recognized Him as such when He called her by name. *Rabboni* is the Aramaic form of *Rabbi*. Aramaic was the common language spoken in Israel during New Testament times.

Whether we call Jesus Rabbi or Rabboni, the meaning is the same: He is our Master Teacher and Guide, who deserves our utmost respect and loyalty.

And so it is written, The first man Adam was made a living soul; the last Adam was made a **quickening spirit**. 1 CORINTHIANS 15:45 [NASB, NIV, NRSV: **life-giving spirit**]

The same came to Jesus by night, and said unto him, **Rabbi**, we know that thou art a teacher come from God: for no man can do these miracles that thou doest, except God be with him. JOHN 3:2

Jesus saith unto her, Mary. She turned herself, and saith unto him, **Rabboni**; which is to say, Master. JOHN 20:16 [NRSV: **Rabbouni**]

A rabbi preaches from a scroll in a synagogue.

RABBOUNI. See *Rabbi/Rabboni.*

RADIANCE OF GOD'S GLORY. See
Brightness of God's Glory.

RANSOM. See *Propitiation for Our Sins.*

REDEEMER

> And the **Redeemer** shall come to Zion, and unto them that turn from transgression in Jacob, saith the LORD.
> ISAIAH 59:20

This verse from the prophet Isaiah refers to the coming Messiah, who will serve as a Redeemer for God's people.

In the Old Testament, God is often referred to by this name (see *Redeemer* in part 1, Names of God the Father). A kinsman redeemer in ancient Israel was a blood relative who assumed responsibility for members of his clan who were in trouble. For example, the redeemer would buy back the property of a family member who had lost it through indebtedness. Or he would purchase the freedom of an impoverished relative who had been forced to sell himself into slavery.

But Isaiah's prophecy looked toward the coming of a Redeemer of a different type. Jesus Christ the Redeemer would free God's people from their bondage to sin and death. He would do so by dying on the cross for our benefit. The purchase price that He would pay for our salvation was none other than His own precious blood.

The patriarch Job, like Isaiah, also received a glimpse of this Redeemer of the future. Out of his suffering and despair he declared, "I know that my redeemer liveth, and that he shall stand at the latter day upon the earth" (Job 19:25).

What Isaiah and Job only hoped for has now come to pass. We can rejoice with the apostle John because "the blood of Jesus Christ [God's] Son cleanseth us from all sin" (1 John 1:7).

"Blessed Redeemer," a hymn by Avis Burgeson Christiansen, expresses the praise of all believers for Jesus' work as our Redeemer.

Up Calvary's mountain, one dreadful morn,
Walked Christ my Saviour, weary and worn;
Facing for sinners death on the cross,
That He might save them from endless loss.
Blessed Redeemer! Precious Redeemer!
Seems now I see Him on Calvary's tree;
Wounded and bleeding, for sinners pleading,
Blind and unheeding—dying for me!

REFINER'S FIRE

This name of Jesus appears in the one of the final chapters of the Old Testament, in which the prophet Malachi describes the coming Messiah as a Refiner's Fire, or the hot fire that metalworkers of Bible times used to purify ore such as silver. The ore was heated in a pot until it turned to liquid and the dross or waste material rose to the surface. Then the metal-worker used a ladle to skim off the dross, leaving the pure and uncontaminated silver.

> But who may abide [NIV: endure] the day of his coming? and who shall stand when he appeareth? for he is like a **refiner's fire**, and like fullers' soap.
> MALACHI 3:2

This image of the Messiah must have been a surprise to the Jewish people of Malachi's time. They expected the Messiah to come as a conquering hero who would restore Israel to its glory days as a political kingdom. But the prophet informed them that the Messiah would come in judg-ment against Israel because of its sin and rebellion.

The name Refiner's Fire emphasizes Jesus' role as Judge. His second coming will bring judgment against all who have refused to accept Him as Savior and Lord (see 2 Peter 2:9).

An Egyptian figurine of a metalworker working a blowpipe to increase the heat in a crucible.

REFLECTION OF GOD'S GLORY. See *Brightness of God's Glory.*

RESURRECTION AND THE LIFE

Jesus used this name for Himself in His conversation with Martha, the sister of Lazarus, after Lazarus had died. She was disappointed that Jesus had not arrived at her home in Bethany in time to save her brother's life. She knew that Je-sus could perform miracles of healing, so she scolded Him, "Lord. . .if you had been here, my brother would not have died" (John 11:21 NIV).

Jesus' double-edged reply to Martha made it clear that He was the master of the living and the dead. He was capable at any time of raising Lazarus, as well as any others who had died. At the same time, He could guarantee eternal life for the living. In this sense, those who believed in Him would never die. This included Martha, as well as all believers of the future.

Jesus then proceeded to deliver on His promise. He stood before the burial chamber where the body of Lazarus had been placed, and just as God the Father had created the world with the words of His mouth (Genesis 1:1–31), Jesus the Son brought His friend back to life with a simple verbal command: "Lazarus, come forth" (John 11:43).

Note the things that are missing from this account: no incantations over the body, no lightning flash from heaven, no magical tricks to dazzle the crowd. Just three simple words from Jesus—and Lazarus walked out of the tomb. You don't have to be a genius to figure out that a person of such sensitivity and power is worthy of our loyalty and devotion. Jesus alone has the keys to life and death.

> Jesus said unto her, I am the **resurrection, and the life**: he that believeth in me, though he were dead, yet shall he live. And whosoever liveth and believeth in me shall never die.
> JOHN 11:25–26

RIGHTEOUS

The word *righteous* is used in combination with other words in the Bible to express several different names for Jesus—for example, Righteous Branch (Jeremiah 23:5), Righteous Judge (2 Timothy 4:8), and Righteous Servant (Isaiah 53:11). But this is the only place in the King James Version where Jesus is simply called the Righteous. (Note that the NIV renders this name as the Righteous One.)

Jesus can be called the Righteous or the Righteous One, because He is the only person who has ever lived who achieved perfect righteousness. Although He was *capable* of doing wrong, because of the human side of His nature (see *Flesh* above), He never gave in to temptation or stumbled into sin.

At the beginning of His ministry, Jesus was tempted by Satan to establish an earthly kingdom and to use His powers for His own self-interest. But Jesus resisted all of these temptations (see Luke 4:1–13). In the garden of Gethsemane on the night before His crucifixion, He admitted that "the flesh is weak" (Matthew 26:41). In an agonizing prayer, He asked God to deliver Him from the suffering of the cross, if possible. But He finally yielded His will to His Father's purpose and plan (see Matthew 26:37–42).

Because Jesus is the Righteous One, He calls us, His followers, to a life of righteousness. We will never achieve perfection and a sinless existence in this life, but we ought to be

> My little children, these things write I unto you, that ye sin not. And if any man sin, we have an advocate with the Father [NIV: one who speaks to the Father in our defense], Jesus Christ the **righteous**.
> 1 John 2:1
> [NIV: **Righteous One**]

growing in that direction. He has promised to guide us along this journey. "The eyes of the Lord are over the righteous," the apostle Peter declares, "and his ears are open unto their prayers" (1 Peter 3:12).

RIGHTEOUS BRANCH. See *Branch of Righteousness.*

RIGHTEOUS BRANCH OF DAVID. See *Branch of Righteousness.*

RIGHTEOUS JUDGE. See *Judge of Quick and Dead.*

RIGHTEOUS MAN. See *Just Man.*

RIGHTEOUS ONE. See *Righteous.*

RIGHTEOUS ONE, MY SERVANT. See *Righteous Servant.*

RIGHTEOUS SERVANT

The theme of service and servanthood runs throughout the scriptures. For example, several people in the Bible are referred to as "servant of God" or "God's servant" because of the loyal service they rendered for the Lord (see sidebar). But Jesus is the only person who deserves to be called God's Righteous Servant. He was the Holy and Righteous One whom the Father sent on a mission of redemption for the entire world.

This name of Jesus appears in one of the famous servant songs of the prophet Isaiah (see Isaiah 42:1–4; 49:1–6; 52:13–53:12). This Servant, the Messiah, would undergo great suffering while carrying

Jesus washes Peter's feet to teach His disciples true servanthood.

He shall see of the travail [NIV: suffering] of his soul, and shall be satisfied: by his knowledge shall my **righteous servant** justify many; for he shall bear their iniquities.
ISAIAH 53:11
[NASB, NRSV:
righteous one, my servant]

out His mission. But it would be for a divine purpose. His suffering and death would provide a means of deliverance for a human race trapped in sin.

Jesus identified Himself specifically as the Suffering Servant from God the Father, whom Isaiah had predicted. At the beginning of His public ministry, Jesus quoted Isaiah's first servant song (see Isaiah 42:1–4; Matthew 12:18–21). The implication of His words was that the mission of God's Suffering Servant was being fulfilled through His teaching and healing ministry.

Jesus saw His work as that of a humble servant. On one occasion, His disciples began to argue over who would occupy the places of honor at His side in His future glory. He gently reminded them: "Whoever wants to be first must be slave of all. For even the Son of Man did not come to be served, but to serve, and to give his life as a ransom for many" (Mark 10:44–45 NIV).

Today, the servant work of Jesus continues through His church. We who belong to Him are automatically in the serving business. The apostle Paul declares that we as Christians should think of ourselves as "a living sacrifice, holy, acceptable unto God, which is your reasonable service" (Romans 12:1).

Others Called Servants of God

The two people in the Bible who are most often called "servant of God" are Moses (see Exodus 14:31; Numbers 12:7–8; Deuteronomy 34:5; Psalm 105:26; Revelation 15:3) and David (see 2 Samuel 3:18; 1 Kings 3:6; Psalm 89:3; Luke 1:69). But the title is also applied to several other famous and not-so-famous Bible personalities, including the following:

- Abraham (Genesis 26:24)
- Ahijah (1 Kings 14:18)
- Caleb (Numbers 14:24)
- Daniel (Daniel 9:17)
- Elijah (2 Kings 9:36)
- Isaiah (Isaiah 20:3)
- Job (Job 1:8)
- Joshua (Joshua 24:29)
- Samuel (1 Samuel 3:9–10)
- Solomon (1 Kings 1:26)
- Zerubbabel (Haggai 2:23)

RISING SUN. See *Dayspring from on High.*

ROCK. See *Spiritual Rock.*

ROCK OF OFFENCE. See *Head of the Corner.*

ROD OUT OF THE STEM OF JESSE

This verse from the prophet Isaiah is a reference to the coming Messiah. We are accustomed to associations of the Messiah with King David, but Isaiah in this passage traces the Messiah back one more generation—to David's father, Jesse.

Two passages in the Bible tell us all we know about Jesse. His father was Obed, the son of Boaz and Ruth. Thus, Jesse was of mixed blood, because Ruth was a Moabite and Boaz was a Jew (see Ruth 1:4; 4:13–22). Jesse had eight sons, including David. One of the more beautiful stories in the Bible is how God, through the prophet Samuel, turned down all of Jesse's older sons for the kingship of Israel in favor of David, Jesse's youngest son. David had to be summoned from the fields, where he was watching his father's sheep, to be presented for Samuel's review (see 1 Samuel 16:1–13).

Why did Isaiah compare the coming Messiah to a Rod, or shoot, from the Stem, or stump, of Jesse? Perhaps to remind us that the Messiah sprang from a family of mixed Jewish and Gentile blood, signifying that He would be a deliverer for all people, not just the Jews. Isaiah also predicted that the nation of Judah would fall to a foreign power, thus bringing to an end the dynasty of David. But from the stump of this fallen tree, God would bring new life—the Messiah, who would reign in a spiritual sense over God's people.

Isaiah also spoke of the coming Messiah as a Root of Jesse (Isaiah 11:10). This name expresses the same idea as Rod out of the Stem of Jesse.

ROOT AND DESCENDANT OF DAVID. See *Root and Offspring of David.*

ROOT AND OFFSPRING OF DAVID

Jesus used this name for Himself in the closing verses of the final chapter of the last book of the Bible. It's as if He used His last opportunity to tell the world who He is and what His life and ministry are all about.

> And there shall come forth a **rod out of the stem of Jesse**, and a Branch shall grow out of his roots.
> Isaiah 11:1
> [NASB: **Shoot from the stem of Jesse**; NIV, NRSV: **shoot from the stump of Jesse**]

I Jesus have sent mine angel to testify unto you these things in the churches. I am the **root and the offspring of David**, and the bright and morning star.
REVELATION 22:16
[NASB, NRSV: **root and descendant of David**]

Notice the dual focus of this name—the Root of David and the Offspring of David. It summarizes His existence as the God-man, the One who is both fully human and fully divine.

Because Jesus is the divine Son, who served as the agent of creation (see *Beginning of the Creation of God* above), He is David's creator, or Root. But because he came to earth in human form, He is also David's descendant, or Offspring—the Messiah from the line of David, who reigns over the spiritual kingdom that He came to establish. Thus, Jesus is both superior to David and the rightful heir to his throne.

ROOT OF JESSE. See *Rod out of the Stem of Jesse.*

RULER IN ISRAEL. See *Governor.*

RULER OF GOD'S CREATION. See *Beginning of the Creation of God.*

RULER OF THE KINGS OF THE EARTH. See *Prince of the Kings of the Earth.*

SALVATION OF GOD. See *Horn of Salvation; Saviour.*

SAVIOUR

An angel spoke these words to shepherds in the fields outside Bethlehem on the day Jesus was born. The shepherds were awestruck and excited by the news that this newborn baby was to be a Savior for God's people (see Luke 2:8–15).

In Bible times, any person who rescued others from danger was called a savior or deliverer. For example, the judges of Israel whom God raised up to deliver His people from oppression by their enemies were called "saviours" (Nehemiah 9:27). But the only true Saviors in a spiritual sense are God the Father and God the Son, both of whom are called by this name many times throughout the Bible (see *Saviour* in part 1, Names of God the Father, and part 2, Names of God the Son).

The name that Mary and Joseph gave their firstborn Son expresses His work as Savior. *Jesus* means "God Is Salvation." From the very beginning it was clear that His purpose was to do for us what we could not do for ourselves—deliver us

I bring you good tidings [NIV: good news] of great joy, which shall be to all people. For unto you is born this day in the city of David a **Saviour**, which is Christ the Lord.
LUKE 2:10–11

from bondage to sin and death.

The phrase "all people," in the message of the angels to the shepherds, shows that Jesus was God's gift to the entire world. The universal nature of Christ's redemptive work is expressed by two other "Savior" titles in the New Testament—Saviour of All Men (1 Timothy 4:10) and Saviour of the World (1 John 4:14).

A memorial beneath the Church of the Nativity in Bethlehem, the "city of David," marks the traditional location where the "Saviour, which is Christ the Lord" was born.

Hallelujah Says It All

Philip P. Bliss wrote the hymn "Hallelujah! What a Saviour" to express his joy at the saving work of Jesus Christ.

Bearing shame and scoffing rude,
In my place condemned He stood,
Seal'd my pardon with His blood;
Hallelujah! what a Saviour!

SAVIOUR OF ALL MEN. See *Saviour*.

SAVIOUR OF THE BODY

The context of this verse from the apostle Paul makes it clear that he is not referring to a human body, but to the church as the body of Christ. Paul goes on to say, in verse 25, "Husbands, love your wives, even as Christ also loved the church, and gave himself for it."

Christ is the head of the church, and the church that He founded is so closely related to Him that it is referred to as His body several times in the New Testament (see 1 Corinthians 12:27; Ephesians 1:22–23; Colossians 1:18). Thus, the church is not a building or a lifeless institution but a living organism, dedicated to advancing the cause of the kingdom

For the husband is the head of the wife, even as Christ is the head of the church: and he is the **saviour of the body**.
EPHESIANS 5:23

of God in the world.

Christ not only died for us as individuals, but He also sacrificed Himself for His church. We bring honor and glory to Him when we work through His church to serve as witnesses to others of His love and grace.

Founded on His Life

"The Church's One Foundation," a hymn by Samuel J. Stone, describes the ultimate sacrifice that Jesus made for His church.

The church's one foundation
Is Jesus Christ her Lord;
She is His new creation,
By water and the Word:
From heaven He came and sought her
To be His holy bride,
With His own blood He bought her,
And for her life He died.

SAVIOUR OF THE WORLD. See *Saviour.*

SCEPTRE OUT OF ISRAEL

Scepters like this one held by a stauette of the Pharaoh Senusret III were used by royalty to signify power and authority. Jesus is the supreme authority—the "Scepter Out of Israel."

These words were spoken by Balaam, a pagan magician, who was hired by the king of Moab to pronounce a curse against the Israelites. But Balaam was led by the Lord to bless the Israelites instead. In this verse, Balaam even prophesied that a Sceptre out of Israel, or a strong leader, would rise up to crush the Moabites.

This verse is also considered a prophecy with a long-range fulfillment, referring to Jesus as the Savior-

Messiah, whom God would send to deliver His people.

A scepter is a short staff, similar to a walking stick, that symbolizes the power and authority of a king. In the book of Esther, King Ahasuerus of Persia extends his royal scepter for Queen Esther to touch (see Esther 5:2–3). This gives her permission to come into his presence and present her request to the king.

The imagery of a royal scepter, as applied to Jesus, symbolizes His power, authority, and universal dominion. In the book of Hebrews, God the Father declares to Jesus the Son, "Thy throne. . .is for ever and ever: a sceptre of righteousness is the sceptre of thy kingdom" (Hebrews 1:8).

SECOND MAN. See *Last Adam.*

SEED OF DAVID. See *Son of David.*

SEED OF THE WOMAN

God the Father spoke these words to the serpent, Satan, in the garden of Eden. This conversation occurred after Satan had persuaded Adam and Eve to eat the forbidden fruit in direct disobedience of God's command. This verse is known as the *protoevangelium,* a Latin word meaning "the first gospel."

It is called the first gospel because it contains the first

prediction in the Bible of the coming of Christ into the world. Jesus is depicted as the Seed of the Woman, Eve. He will wage war against Satan's forces. Satan will manage to bruise His heel—a reference to the forces that executed Jesus

There shall come a Star out of Jacob, and a **Sceptre** shall rise **out of Israel**, and shall smite [NIV: crush] the corners of Moab, and destroy all the children of Sheth. NUMBERS 24:17

And I will put enmity between thee and **the woman**, and between thy seed and **her seed**; it shall bruise [NIV: crush] thy head, and thou shalt bruise [NIV: strike] his heel. GENESIS 3:15 [NIV, NRSV: **offspring of the woman**]

This bronze relief from the Church of the Annunciation in Nazareth is a reminder of how after Adam and Eve's sin in the Garden of Eden, God had a plan to redeem the world through Eve—the "Seed of the Woman."

on the cross—but Jesus will rise triumphantly from the dead and deal a crushing blow to Satan's head. In the end time, Jesus will win the final and ultimate victory over Satan and cast him into the lake of fire (see Revelation 20:10).

The name Seed of the Woman may be a subtle reference to the virgin birth of Jesus. He was conceived in Mary's womb by the Holy Spirit, not by a human father. She was told by the angel Gabriel, "The Holy Ghost shall come upon thee, and the power of the Highest shall overshadow thee: therefore also that holy thing which shall be born of thee shall be called the Son of God" (Luke 1:35).

SERVANT. See *Righteous Servant*.

SHEPHERD. See *Good Shepherd*.

SHEPHERD OF YOUR SOULS. See *Good Shepherd*.

SHILOH

Genesis 49 contains the aging Jacob's blessings on his twelve sons, whose descendants would become the twelve tribes of Israel. This verse is part of his blessing of Judah, the tribe destined to produce the rulers of Israel.

Shiloh is a Hebrew word meaning "the one to whom it belongs." Thus, Jacob was saying that Judah would wield the royal scepter of leadership in Israel (see *Sceptre out of Israel* above) until the one to whom the scepter belonged arrived on the scene. This is a veiled reference to the coming Messiah.

Jesus is the One to whom all authority and power belong, because God has delegated jurisdiction over His people to His Son. Jesus is also deserving of all power, because He rules in justice and righteousness. Just a little power can go to an earthly ruler's head, but Jesus will never use His power for anything but the good of His church—those who devote their lives to Him and His service.

No matter what happens to us in this life, we can rest safe and secure in the arms of Shiloh—the One who holds the whole world in His hands.

SHOOT FROM THE STEM/STUMP OF JESSE. See *Rod out of the Stem of Jesse*.

> The sceptre shall not depart from Judah, nor a lawgiver [NIV: ruler's staff] from between his feet, until **Shiloh** come; and unto him shall the gathering of the people be.
> GENESIS 49:10

SIGNAL FOR THE NATIONS. See *Ensign for the Nations.*

SOMEONE TO ARBITRATE. See *Daysman.*

SON OF ABRAHAM

This is one of two names of God the Son cited in the very first verse of the New Testament (see *Son of David* below). Abraham was the father of the Jewish people. Many centuries before Jesus' time, God the Father called Abraham to leave his home and family in Mesopotamia and move to the land of Canaan. Here, God would begin to build a nation that would be His exclusive possession. He promised Abraham, "I will bless them that bless thee, and curse him that curseth thee: and in thee shall all families of the earth be blessed" (Genesis 12:3).

The book of the generation of Jesus Christ, the son of David, the **son of Abraham**.
MATTHEW 1:1

As the Son of Abraham, Jesus is the fulfillment of this promise, or covenant, that God made with Abraham. In His human lineage and by His nationality, Jesus was a Jew—the people whom God promised to bless above all the nations of the earth.

But God never intended for His promise of blessing to apply only to the Jewish people. He wanted "all families of the earth" to be brought to Him through the influence of Abraham's offspring. When the Jews forgot this part of the covenant, God sent His Son, Jesus, to remind them that He had placed no limits on His love and grace. Jesus as the Son of Abraham fulfilled God's redemptive plan by coming as a Savior for the entire world.

SON OF DAVID

Perhaps it is not accidental that the very first verse of the New Testament refers to Jesus by this name. As the Son of David, He ties together the Old and New Testaments. The genealogies of Jesus in the Gospels of Matthew and Luke make the point that Jesus, in His human lineage, was descended from David (see Matthew 1:6; Luke 3:31). Thus, Jesus fulfilled God's promise to David that one of David's descendants would always reign over His people (see 2 Samuel 7:1–16; Psalm 132:11–12).

The book of the generation of Jesus Christ, the **son of David**, the son of Abraham.
MATTHEW 1:1

During Jesus' earthly ministry, the crowds and individuals whom He healed often called Him the "son of David" (Matthew 9:27; 12:23; Mark 10:47; Luke 18:38). But Jesus never used this name of Himself. He may have avoided it because it tended to feed the expectation of the Jewish people that the Messiah would come as a political conqueror, not a spiritual Savior (see *Messiah* above).

Another name of God the Son similar in meaning to Son of David is Seed (or Offspring) of David (2 Timothy 2:8).

SON OF GOD

The centurion mentioned in this verse from Matthew's Gospel refers to the Roman military officer who presided over the execution of Jesus. He was so impressed with the miraculous signs that accompanied Jesus' death (see Matthew 27:50–53) that he declared that Jesus was none other than the Son of God. Ironically, this pagan soldier affirmed what the Jewish religious leaders refused to believe.

Son of God, as a name or title for Jesus, appears many times throughout the New Testament (see, for example, Matthew 14:33; Acts 9:20; Romans 1:4). It emphasizes His divine nature and shows that He came to earth under the authority of God the Father on a mission of redemption.

This name also highlights Jesus' close, personal relationship with God. He knew God like no other person has ever known Him, and He addressed Him often in His prayers as "Father" (John 17:1–26). He taught His disciples in a model prayer to approach God in the same way: "Our Father which art in heaven" (Matthew 6:9).

In Bible times, a son was expected to honor and obey his parents (see Exodus 20:12; Ephesians 6:1). Jesus, as God's Son, was perfectly obedient to the Father. He refused to be sidetracked from the mission on which He was sent into the world. His last words from the cross were "it is finished" (John 19:30). This was not the whimper of a dying man, but

> Now when the centurion, and they that were with him, watching Jesus, saw the earthquake, and those things that were done, they feared greatly [NIV: were terrified], saying, Truly [NIV: Surely] this was the **Son of God**.
> MATTHEW 27:54

Other Divine Sonship Titles of Jesus

- Beloved Son (Matthew 3:17)
- Only Begotten Son (John 3:16)
- Son of the Blessed (Mark 14:61)
- Son of the Father (2 John 3)
- Son of the Highest (Luke 1:32)
- Son of the Living God (Matthew 16:16)
- Son of the Most High God (Mark 5:7)

a declaration of victory over the forces of sin and death. He had accomplished the work that His Father had commissioned Him to do.

SON OF JOSEPH

After Jesus miraculously fed the five thousand (see John 6:2–11), He claimed to be the spiritual bread that had come down from heaven (see John 6:32–33). But the Jewish religious leaders rejected this claim. Instead, they attempted to discredit Jesus in the eyes of the crowd by pointing out that they knew His parents. To them, He was only the Son of Joseph, not a special messenger from God.

Jesus was the Son of Joseph, but not in the sense that these religious leaders had in mind. Jesus had no human father; He was conceived in his mother's womb by the Holy Spirit (see Luke 1:35). Technically, He was Joseph's stepson or his adopted son.

The Gospel records tell us very little about Joseph. But the few facts we do have make it clear that he was a person of sterling character. At the time that Joseph learned that Mary was pregnant, they were already engaged to be married. He prepared to break the engagement (see Matthew 1:19), but an angel assured him that Mary had not been unfaithful to him and that her baby was of divine origin (see Matthew 1:20). To Joseph's credit, he believed this explanation—one that must have seemed like a fairy tale—and married Mary (see Matthew 1:24).

Jesus grew up like any normal Jewish boy. Apparently, he learned the trade of carpentry and woodworking from Joseph (see *Carpenter* above). Mark 6:3 refers to an event, soon after Jesus launched His public ministry, in which Jesus is called a carpenter. In this verse, Mary and Jesus' four half-brothers are mentioned, but nothing is said about Joseph. This has led to speculation that Joseph may have died during Jesus' youth. If this is true, Jesus, as Mary's firstborn son, may have assumed responsibility for His family's welfare from an early age.

SON OF MAN

Jesus used this name for Himself when He responded to a man who promised to become His disciple. He wanted this would-be follower to know that serving Him as the Son of Man would require sacrifice.

And they said, Is not this Jesus, the **son of Joseph**, whose father and mother we know? how is it then that he saith [NIV: how can he now say], I came down from heaven? JOHN 6:42

And Jesus said unto him, Foxes have holes, and birds of the air have nests; but the **Son of man** hath not where [NIV: no place] to lay his head.

LUKE 9:58

Son of Man is the name that Jesus used most often when referring to Himself. It appears in the New Testament almost one hundred times, most of these in the Gospel narratives, on the lips of Jesus. A careful study of these occurrences reveals that He used the name in three different ways.

1. Sometimes He used Son of Man in a general way, almost as a substitute for the first-person pronoun "I." A good example of this usage is Jesus' response to the person in the verse above.

2. When Jesus predicted His suffering and death, He often spoke of Himself as the Son of Man. For example, He warned His disciples, "The Son of man must suffer many things, and be rejected of the elders and chief priests and scribes, and be slain, and be raised the third day" (Luke 9:22).

3. With this name or title, Jesus often referred to Himself as a person of exceptional authority and power. He made it clear that He was not acting on His own, but under the authority of God the Father. When the Pharisees criticized Him for healing on the Sabbath, He told them, "The Son of man is Lord also of the sabbath" (Mark 2:28).

Now we know *how* Jesus used the title; but the *why* is not as easy to explain. Perhaps He wanted to show His total identification with humankind. The Son of Man came to earth as a man—our brother and fellow sufferer—to deliver us from our bondage to sin.

SON OF MARY

This is the only place in the New Testament where this name of Jesus appears. It was spoken by the citizens of Nazareth, Jesus' hometown. They could not believe that the boy who had grown up in their midst could be the Messiah and Great Prophet sent from God. They knew Him only as a carpenter and the son of Mary.

Son of Mary as a title for Jesus is unusual, because a man in Bible times was usually identified by His father's name (for example, "Isaiah the son of Amoz," Isaiah 1:1). Jesus' designation as the Son of Mary in this verse lends support to the view that His father Joseph had died while Jesus was a boy (see *Son of Joseph* above).

Mary knew from the very beginning that Jesus, who was conceived in her womb by the Holy Spirit, was God's special

Is not this the carpenter, the **son of Mary**, the brother of James, and Joses, and of Juda, and Simon? and are not his sisters here with us? And they were offended [NIV: took offense] at him.

MARK 6:3

gift to the world (see Luke 1:26–38). But she apparently brought Him up like any normal boy (see Luke 2:52). Mark 6:3 shows that she had other sons and daughters, who were born by natural means after Jesus' miraculous conception. But Jesus, as her firstborn son, must have had a special place in her heart.

Mary knew about Jesus' special powers, because she told the servants at a wedding feast where the wine had run out, "Do whatever he tells you" (John 2:5 NIV). Jesus responded to her confidence in Him by turning plain water into wine—His first miracle, as reported in John's Gospel.

Did Mary realize that her firstborn was destined to be executed like a common criminal? We don't know. But the Bible does tell us that she was at the execution site when Jesus was nailed to the cross. One of the last things Jesus did before He died was to make arrangements for Mary's welfare. With the words, "Behold thy mother," He instructed His disciple John to take care of her. John reports in his own Gospel, "From that hour that disciple took her unto his own home" (John 19:27).

Mary holds the baby Jesus in this seventeenth-century painting by Sassoferrato.

Mary and the Manger

The Christmas hymn "Gentle Mary Laid Her Child," by Joseph Simpson Cook, reminds us that the Savior of mankind came into the world like an ordinary baby with a human mother.

> Gentle Mary laid her Child
> Lowly in a manger;
> There He lay, the undefiled,
> To the world a stranger:
> Such a Babe in such a place,
> Can He be the Saviour?
> Ask the saved of all the race
> Who have found His favor.

SON OF THE BLESSED. See *Son of God.*

SON OF THE FATHER. See *Son of God.*

SON OF THE HIGHEST. See *Son of God.*

SON OF THE LIVING GOD. See *Son of God.*

SON OF THE MOST HIGH GOD. See *Son of God.*

SON OVER GOD'S HOUSE. See *Son over His Own House.*

SON OVER HIS OWN HOUSE

One purpose of the book of Hebrews is to show that Jesus Christ is superior to the religious laws and regulations and the sacrificial system of the Old Testament. These verses are part of an argument by the writer of the book that Jesus is superior to Moses, the great deliverer and lawgiver of God's people in Old Testament times.

Moses was faithful in his house, or the household of God's people of faith. But he was nothing more than a servant in this house. But Jesus was a Son over His Own House, or the church that He founded by His sacrificial death. Because a son who rules *over* a household is superior to a servant *in* that house, this means that Jesus is superior to Moses.

These verses refer to a time in the wilderness when Moses' brother and sister, Aaron and Miriam, questioned his leadership over the people of Israel. God put an end to their rebellion by pointing out that Moses was His true prophet, "who is faithful in all mine house" (Numbers 12:7).

But no matter how faithful Moses had been to God, Jesus was even more so. He was God's own Son, who gave His life to set people free from their bondage to sin. All Christians are blessed by the faithfulness that Jesus demonstrated to God's redemptive plan.

SPIRITUAL ROCK

These verses from the apostle Paul reminded the Jewish people of their wilderness wandering years after their deliverance from slavery in Egypt. God guided them with a cloud, signifying His presence (see Exodus 13:21), and He gave them safe passage through the Red Sea with the Egyptian army in hot pursuit (see Exodus 14:21–27).

And Moses verily was faithful in all his house, as a servant, for a testimony of those things which were to be spoken after [NIV: testifying to what would be said in the future]; but Christ as a **son over his own house**; whose house are we, if we hold fast the confidence [NIV: hold on to our courage] and the rejoicing of the hope firm unto the end [NIV: the hope of which we boast].
HEBREWS 3:5–6
[NIV: **son over God's house**]

In the dry and barren wilderness, God also provided water for His people. It gushed from a rock when Moses struck it with his staff at God's command (see Numbers 20:8–11). Paul picked up on this rock imagery and described Jesus as the Spiritual Rock who meets the needs of God's people. Just as the rock in the desert was the source of water for the Israelites, so also Christ guides and protects those who place their trust in Him.

Was Jesus actually present with the Israelites in the wilderness? Paul declares that Christ their Spiritual Rock "followed them." Or was Paul speaking metaphorically? We can't say for sure. We know that Jesus existed with God the Father from eternity, before the world was created (see John 1:1–3). He came to earth in human form many centuries after the Israelites left Egypt. But He had the power to assume any form He desired at any time.

Maybe it's best to leave this argument to the theologians and scholars. But one thing we can say for sure is that Jesus is a modern day Spiritual Rock, who quenches our thirst and provides strength and stability for daily living. That's all we as Christians really need to know.

All our fathers were under the cloud, and all passed through the sea. . .and did all drink the same spiritual drink: for they drank of that **spiritual Rock** that followed them: and that Rock was Christ.
1 CORINTHIANS 10:1–4

En Avdat in the Wilderness of Zin. It was in the Wilderness of Zin where Moses, in his anger at the quarreling of the Israelites, struck the rock and water gushed forth and God "showed himself Holy among the people."

STANDARD FOR THE NATIONS.
See *Ensign for the Nations.*

STAR OUT OF JACOB

I shall see him, but not now: I shall behold him, but not nigh [NIV: near]: there shall come a **Star out of Jacob**, and a Sceptre shall rise out of Israel, and shall smite [NIV: crush] the corners of Moab, and destroy all the children of Sheth.

NUMBERS 24:17

This is another name assigned to the coming Messiah by Balaam, a pagan magician who blessed the Israelites (see *Sceptre out of Israel* above). The Messiah would be a Star out of Jacob, who would rule over His people with great power and authority.

The nation of Israel is sometimes referred to in the Bible as "Jacob" because it sprang from the twelve sons, or tribes, of the patriarch Jacob. A star was considered the symbol of an exceptional king. For example, Joseph had a dream in which the sun and moon and eleven stars bowed down to him (see Genesis 37:9). The eleven stars symbolized his brothers, who did eventually fall on their faces before him. This happened several years after this dream, when Joseph became a high official in Egypt (see Genesis 43:26; 44:14).

When Jesus was born in Bethlehem, a bright star appeared in the eastern sky to mark the occasion. This star guided the wise men from the east to the place in Bethlehem where He was born (Matthew 2:2–9).

The word *star* is tossed around loosely in our time. We have rock stars, movie stars, and superstars in every sport from badminton to wrestling. But the name of Jesus will live on long after all these pseudo-stars have disappeared. His eternal reign as the Star out of Jacob is assured by none other than God the Father: "And the seventh angel sounded; and there were great voices in heaven, saying, The kingdoms of this world are become the kingdoms of our Lord, and of his Christ; and he shall reign for ever and ever" (Revelation 11:15).

STONE; STONE OF STUMBLING.
See *Chief Cornerstone; Head of the Corner.*

SUN OF RIGHTEOUSNESS. See *Dayspring from on High.*

SUNRISE FROM ON HIGH. See *Dayspring from on High.*

SURE FOUNDATION. See *Foundation.*

SURETY OF A BETTER TESTAMENT.
See *Mediator of the New Testament.*

TEACHER. See *Master; Teacher Come from God.*

TEACHER COME FROM GOD

This name of Jesus was spoken by Nicodemus, a wealthy and respected Pharisee who wanted to learn more about Jesus and His teachings. He had probably heard about Jesus from others in the region of Galilee. To his credit, Nicodemus did not judge Jesus based on hearsay. He sought to talk with Him face-to-face before deciding what to make of this teacher and miracle worker from Nazareth.

The Gospels contain many references to Jesus' ministry as a teacher. In this role, He communicated God's message to individuals, such as Nicodemus, as well as to large groups of people (see Mark 4:1). He was also a patient teacher with His disciples, who were slow to understand His mission of redemptive suffering (see Luke 24:45–47).

Jesus was an effective Teacher Come from God because of His teaching style. He did not focus on abstract theories, but on down-to-earth truths that the common people could understand. He used familiar objects from everyday life—birds, flowers, sheep, salt, bread, water, light—to connect with the life experiences of His audience. He told stories, or parables, to illustrate divine truths He wanted the people to understand and act upon.

> The same came to Jesus by night, and said unto him, Rabbi, we know that thou art a **teacher come from God**: for no man can do these miracles that thou doest, except God be with him. JOHN 3:2

Some Subjects on Which Jesus Taught
- Eternal life (Matthew 22:9–10; John 7:37–38)
- Faith (Matthew 14:27, 31; Luke 17:6, 19)
- Forgiveness (Mark 11:25–26; Luke 17:3–4)
- Holiness (Matthew 5:8; Luke 1:74–75)
- Kingdom of God (Matthew 13:11–50; Luke 22:29–30)
- Love (Matthew 18:15; John 13:34–35)
- Money (Mark 12:43–44; John 6:27)
- Prayer (Matthew 6:9–13; John 14:13–14)
- Service (Matthew 20:28; Luke 22:27)
- Wisdom (Mark 4:12; John 6:45)

But the most impressive thing about Jesus' teaching is that it was stamped with the power of God the Father. Jesus did not quote learned rabbis from the past to authenticate His words, as was the custom among the religious teachers of His day. He made it clear that He spoke under direct commission from God Himself. The people were "amazed at his teaching, because his message had authority" (Luke 4:32 NIV).

Good teachers work with their students to be sure they understand what they've learned.

TREASURE OF ALL NATIONS. See *Desire of All Nations.*

TRIED STONE. See *Chief Cornerstone.*

TRUE. See *Faithful and True.*

TRUE BREAD FROM HEAVEN. See *Bread.*

TRUE GOD. See *God.*

TRUE LIGHT. See *Light.*

TRUE VINE. See *Vine.*

TRUE WITNESS. See *Faithful and True Witness.*

TRUTH

Jesus used this name for Himself in a conversation with His disciple Thomas. This is the only place in the New Testament where Jesus is referred to as the Truth.

> Jesus saith unto him, I am the way, the **truth**, and the life: no man cometh unto the Father, but by me. JOHN 14:6

We usually use the word *truth* in referring to words or speech. For example, we might pay a compliment to a friend by saying, "She always tells the truth." This use of the word certainly applies to Jesus. He always spoke the truth to His disciples and to others, even when they had a hard time accepting it. This was especially the case with His statements about His coming death (see Matthew 16:21–22).

But beyond speaking the truth, Jesus *acted out* the truth in His life and ministry. And even more importantly, He *was* and *is* the Truth, because He is the ultimate reality in the universe. This is the sense in which Jesus referred to Himself as the Truth in His conversation with Thomas.

We live in a world in which it is sometimes hard to nail down the truth. Our materialistic society tries to convince us that money and possessions are the essence of truth and the way to the good life. Some people say that learning or knowledge is the ticket to the truth. Others believe that each person has to find truth for himself by constructing it from his own life experiences. What is truth for one person may not be truth for another, these people say, because there is no such thing as absolute truth.

These modern theories remind us of Pilate, the Roman governor who pronounced the death sentence against Jesus. When Jesus told him that He had come into the world to "bear witness unto the truth" (John 18:37), Pilate asked sarcastically, "What is truth?" (John 18:38). The Truth stood so close to Pilate that he could touch it, but he missed it because of his unbelief.

What a tragedy! And what an accurate picture of a sinful and unbelieving world—the arena into which we as Christians are sent to bear witness of the Truth (see Mark 16:15).

Jesus as the Truth
- "Then they that were in the ship came and worshipped him, saying, Of a truth thou art the Son of God" (Matthew 14:33).
- "Ye shall know the truth, and the truth shall make you free" (John 8:32).
- "And if I say the truth, why do ye not believe me?" (John 8:46).
- "When he, the Spirit of truth, is come, he will guide you into all truth" (John 16:13).

UMPIRE. See *Daysman*.

UNSPEAKABLE GIFT. See *Gift of God*.

VINE

I am the **vine**, ye are the branches: He that abideth [NIV: remains] in me, and I in him, the same bringeth forth much fruit: for without me [NIV: apart from me] ye can do nothing.
JOHN 15:5.

Vineyards of antiquity were common at the time of Christ. The image of the vine stretching out across the ground with multiple branches bearing fruit was something the disciples could easily relate to.

Jesus spoke these words to His disciples during the Last Supper, which He ate with them on the night of His arrest. He knew they would need to be firmly attached to Him as the Vine in order to weather the crisis of His forthcoming execution and death.

The imagery that Jesus used was that of a grapevine. This domestic vine has one main stem with several smaller shoots or runners branching off in all directions. These smaller branches owe their lives to the main stem. They could not live apart from the big vine that is rooted in the ground. In the same way, Jesus' disciples were to stay attached to Him as their Lord and Savior. He as the Vine would sustain and nourish them so they would bear "much fruit" in the days ahead.

The fruit that Jesus mentions probably refers to the witness that they would bear for Him after His resurrection and ascension to God the Father. Most of these disciples, His "branches," abandoned Jesus when He was arrested and executed on the cross (see Matthew 26:56). But after His

resurrection, they regained their courage and continued the work that Jesus had trained them to do (see Acts 1:13–14; 2:42–43).

In the Old Testament, the nation of Israel was often referred to as a vine (see Psalm 80:8; Isaiah 5:2). But the people fell into sin and idolatry, becoming an empty vine that bore no fruit for the Lord (see Hosea 10:1). Jesus, therefore, has become the True Vine (see John 15:1) whom God has sent to bring salvation to His people.

WAY

This is one of only three places in the Gospels where Thomas is mentioned apart from a mere listing of the twelve disciples (see John 11:16; 20:24–29). The context of these two verses shows that Thomas was puzzled by Jesus' statement that He would leave His disciples soon after His death, resurrection, and ascension (see John 14:1–4).

Thomas wanted to know how he and the other disciples could find their way to Jesus after He left. Jesus replied in spiritual terms, assuring him that He was the only Way to their eternal reward, and that Thomas didn't need to know all the details about this destination or how to get there.

This conversation between Jesus and Thomas provides a valuable lesson for modern Christians. Sometimes our curiosity about heaven takes our eyes off the One who has promised to take us there. We wonder where heaven will be. What will our resurrected bodies look like? Will we know our family members and friends? Will heaven's streets be paved with literal gold?

The truth is that we don't know the answers to any of these questions. But we do have a grasp of the most important thing: Jesus is the only Way to that wonderful place. He knows the way there, and we know Him as the Way. So we can relax, put away our road maps, and leave the driving to Him.

Thomas saith unto him, Lord, we know not whither thou goest [NIV: we don't know where you are going]; and how can we know the way? Jesus saith unto him, I am the **way**, the truth, and the life: no man cometh unto the Father, but by me.
JOHN 14:5–6

WEALTH OF ALL NATIONS. See *Desire of All Nations.*

WISDOM OF GOD. See *Only Wise God.*

WITNESS. See *Faithful and True Witness.*

WONDERFUL COUNSELOR. See *Counsellor*.

WORD

In the beginning was the **Word**, and the **Word** was with God, and the **Word** was God.
JOHN 1:1

The prologue of John's Gospel (John 1:1–18), of which this verse is a part, focuses on Jesus as the eternal Son, who existed with God the Father before the creation of the world.

This verse is an obvious reference to the first three words of the book of Genesis. Just as God was "in the beginning" (Genesis 1:1), so Jesus existed "in the beginning" (John 1:1) as the eternal Word. This Word, who assumed human form to make His dwelling among human beings on earth (see John 1:14), is comparable to the words that God used to speak the universe into being (see Genesis 1:3).

Words are the primary units of language that enable humans to communicate with one another. In the same way, Jesus reveals the will and mind of God the Father to earthbound mortals.

The description of Jesus as the Word is unique to the apostle John's writings. In his first epistle, John declares, "There are three that bear record in heaven, the Father, the Word, and the Holy Ghost: and these three are one" (1 John 5:7). This leaves little doubt that John thought of Jesus as the Word who was the second person of the Trinity.

The German monk, Martin Luther, translated the Bible into his native German so others could understand Jesus as "the Word" in their own language.

John continues this imagery in the book of Revelation. He describes Jesus as victorious over all His enemies in the end time: "He is dressed in a robe dipped in blood, and his name is the Word of God" (Revelation 19:13 NIV).

WORD OF GOD. See *Word*.

WORD OF LIFE. See *Life*.

YOUNG MAN EXALTED FROM AMONG THE PEOPLE. See *One Chosen out of the People*.

PART 3

Names of God the Holy Spirit

The Holy Spirit has fewer names than God the Father and God the Son in the Bible. You will find twenty-six names assigned to the Spirit in this section. But this does not mean that He is less important than the first two Persons of the Trinity.

The Holy Spirit is God's agent who convicts people of sin and leads them to the Father in repentance and confession. He empowers God's people for the task of witnessing, leads them to recognize the truth, and brings honor and glory to Jesus the Son. The Spirit inspired biblical writers to record God's revelation of the scriptures, and He also illuminates our minds to understand the message of the Bible.

ADVOCATE. See *Comforter.*

BREATH OF THE ALMIGHTY

This name of the Holy Spirit comes from the long speech that the young man Elihu addressed to Job. He spoke after Job's three friends—Eliphaz, Bildad, and Zophar (see Job 2:11)—had ended their speeches.

Elihu stated that he owed his life to the Breath of God. This is a reference to God's creation of the first man in the Garden of Eden. The Lord "breathed into his nostrils the breath of life; and man became a living soul" (Genesis 2:7). It was God's own breath that brought Adam to life. Even today, our ability to breathe life-giving oxygen into the lungs is evidence of God's care of the physical world through the agency of His Spirit.

The Holy Spirit, or the Breath of God, also energizes Christians in a spiritual sense. Just before His ascension to His Father, Jesus empowered His followers for the task of carrying on His work by breathing on them and charging them to "receive the Holy Spirit" (John 20:22 NIV). This is the same life-giving Spirit that enables Christians in our time to witness to others about God's transforming power.

> The Spirit of God hath made me, and the **breath of the Almighty** hath given me life.
> JOB 33:4

The Breath of the Spirit

In his hymn "Breathe on Me," Edwin Hatch expresses the prayer of every believer for divine power from the Father through His Spirit.

Holy Spirit, breathe on me,
Fill me with power divine;
Kindle a flame of love and zeal
Within this heart of mine.
Breathe on me, breathe on me,
Holy Spirit, breathe on me;
Take thou my heart, cleanse every part,
Holy Spirit, breathe on me.

COMFORTER

Jesus spoke these words to His disciples after He told them that His death was drawing near (see John 13:33). He would no longer be with them in a physical sense, but He was not leaving them alone. He would send a Comforter, the Holy

Spirit, to fill the void caused by His own return to the Father in heaven after His resurrection.

Notice that Jesus referred to the Holy Spirit as "another" Comforter. The Greek word He used means "another of the same kind." This implies that Jesus Himself was the other or first Comforter of His disciples and He was sending another like Himself to serve as His stand-in. So close and personal would be the presence of the Holy Spirit that it would seem as if Jesus had never left.

The Greek word behind Comforter is *parakletos*, meaning "one called alongside." This is the same word translated as "Advocate," one of the names of God the Son (see 1 John 2:1; see also, *Advocate* in part 2, Names of God the Son). In addition to "Comforter" and "Advocate" as rendered by the King James Version, this word is translated as "Counselor," "Companion," "Guide," "Helper," "Instructor," or "Teacher" by other English versions of the Bible.

When Jesus promised that the Comforter will come "alongside" us, He meant that the Holy Spirit would help us in our times of need. If we are lost and stumbling, He will serve as our Guide. If we are discouraged, He will lift us up. If we are confused, He will bring wisdom and understanding. If we are mired in grief, He will sustain us with His presence. The Comforter will be there for us when we need Him most.

COUNSELOR. See *Comforter*.

ETERNAL SPIRIT

The Gospels make it clear that the Holy Spirit guided and empowered Jesus throughout His public ministry. For example, Jesus was led by the Spirit into the region of Galilee, where He began to teach and heal (see Luke 4:14). He cast demons out of people "by the spirit of God" (Matthew 12:28). And this verse from the book of Hebrews shows that the Holy Spirit—described here as the Eternal Spirit—gave Jesus the determination and strength to offer His life as a sacrifice to atone for our sins.

This is the only place in the Bible where the phrase "Eternal Spirit" appears. It clearly identifies the Holy Spirit as a divine being. Only the three persons of the Trinity—Father, Son, and Holy Spirit—are eternal. Everything else is created matter.

> And I will pray the Father, and he shall give you another **Comforter**, that he may abide with you for ever.
> JOHN 14:16
> [NASB: **Helper**; NIV: **Counselor**; NRSV: **Advocate**]

> How much more shall the blood of Christ, who through the **eternal Spirit** offered himself without spot to God, purge [NIV: cleanse] your conscience from dead works [NIV: from acts that lead to death] to serve [NIV: so that we may serve] the living God?
> HEBREWS 9:14

The eternality of the Holy Spirit is evident in the very first book of the Bible. As God began to mold and shape the universe, "the Spirit of God moved upon the face of the waters" (Genesis 1:2). Thus, the Spirit of God existed with God before time began and participated with Him in the creation of the world. The Bible makes it clear that Jesus was also involved with His Father in the Creation (see John 1:1–3). So Creation was an activity in which all three Persons of the Godhead played an active role.

The Creative Work of God's Spirit

- "The spirit of God hath made me, and the breath of the Almighty hath given me life" (Job 33:4).
- "By the word of the LORD were the heavens made; and all the host of them by the breath of his mouth" (Psalm 33:6).
- "Thou sendest forth thy spirit, they are created: and thou renewest the face of the earth" (Psalm 104:30).

FREE SPIRIT

> Create in me a clean heart, O God, and renew a right spirit within me. . . . Restore unto me the joy of thy salvation; and uphold me with thy **free spirit**.
> PSALM 51:10, 12
> [NASB, NIV, NRSV: **willing spirit**]

David's prayer for forgiveness in Psalm 51 is one of the most eloquent prayers in the Bible. He had plotted the murder of Uriah, the husband of Bathsheba, to cover up his sin of adultery, which had resulted in her pregnancy (see 2 Samuel 11:1–17). David's great sin had separated him from God. He prayed for the restoration of this relationship ("a right spirit") through a movement of God's Spirit, which he described as God's Free Spirit.

The Holy Spirit of God might be described as "free" in two distinct senses.

He is free because His presence is offered freely by God the Father to those who accept His Son Jesus as Savior and Lord. We can't buy God's grace and forgiveness (see Acts 8:18–20; Ephesians 2:8). But He offers it willingly to those who repent of their sins and commit themselves to His lordship over their lives.

The Holy Spirit is also free in the sense that He is not bound by our expectations. God is sovereign; He does not have to wait for our permission before He acts in His world. Sometimes, His actions take us by surprise. For example, it took a while for the early church to realize that the gospel was meant for all people, not just the Jews. The famous vision of the apostle Peter on the roof of Simon the tanner convinced him that he "should not call any man common or unclean" (Acts 10:28).

This insight came to Peter from the Holy Spirit, who brought many Gentiles to saving faith in Jesus Christ. The work of God's Free Spirit is evident throughout the book of Acts. So powerful is the Spirit's work in this New Testament book that it is often called "The Acts of the Holy Spirit" rather than "The Acts of the Apostles."

We should be grateful that God's Free Spirit is not limited by time or circumstances. He kept on working until He convicted us of our sin, drove us to our knees in repentance, and brought us into God's kingdom.

Peter encountered the Free Spirit that is not bound by expectations when he was told to eat the "unclean" animals at Simon the Tanner's house, as shown in this painting from the St. Peter's Monastery in Jaffa.

Free as the Wind

This is how Jesus described the work of the Holy Spirit as God's Free Spirit to Nicodemus: "The wind bloweth where it listeth, and thou hearest the sound thereof, but canst not tell whence it cometh, and whither it goeth: so is every one that is born of the Spirit" (John 3:8).

GOOD SPIRIT

This verse describes the provision of God for the Israelites in the wilderness after their release from slavery in Egypt. These words were spoken by Levites in Nehemiah's time who led the people to renew the covenant with God the Father. They described the Holy Spirit as God's Good Spirit.

Because the very essence of God is goodness, He showered His people with goodness during the perilous years of their wandering in the wilderness. He led them by His presence in a cloud and fire, encouraged them with His promise of a land of their own, and instructed them in how to live,

> Thou gavest also thy **good spirit** to instruct them, and withheldest not [NIV: did not withhold] thy manna from their mouth, and gavest them water for their thirst.
> NEHEMIAH 9:20

through the laws that He delivered to Moses. Through His Good Spirit, God provided many good things for His people.

God is still the God of goodness who provides abundantly for us through His Spirit. He expects us to exemplify this spirit of goodness to others. The apostle Paul told the believers at Rome: "I. . .am persuaded of you, my brethren, that ye also are full of goodness, filled with all knowledge, able also to admonish one another" (Romans 15:14).

HELPER. See *Comforter*.

HOLY GHOST

This farewell speech of the apostle Paul to the elders of the church at Ephesus is one of many places in the King James Version of the Bible where the Holy Spirit is referred to as the Holy Ghost.

When the KJV was first published in England in 1611, *ghost* was a word that meant the spirit, or immaterial part of a person, in contrast to the physical or visible body. In modern times, the word *ghost* refers to the shadowy, supernatural appearance of a dead person. All modern translations render the KJV's "Holy Ghost" as "Holy Spirit."

HOLY ONE

The name Holy One is applied to God the Father and Jesus the Son (see *Holy One* in part 1, Names of God the Father; and part 2, Names of God the Son). In this verse, the apostle John also refers to the Holy Spirit by this name.

John makes it clear in this verse that the specific role of the Holy Spirit as the Holy One is to safeguard Christians from erroneous thinking about the nature of Jesus. Some false teachers in John's time were attesting that Jesus was the divine Son of God, but denying that He had come to earth in human form. To them, He only *seemed* to be human. In his second epistle, the apostle John also declares that Jesus was both fully human and fully divine (see 2 John 7) .

The word *unction* in this verse from 1 John means "anointing." Thus, John declares that the Holy One anoints or fills believers with the truth about Jesus. We know "all things"—or the only thing we really need to know—about Jesus and His nature as the God-man who came into the world as the Mediator between God and man.

Take heed therefore unto yourselves, and to all the flock, over the which the **Holy Ghost** hath made you overseers, to feed the church of God, which he hath purchased with his own blood.
Acts 20:28
[NASB, NIV, NRSV: **Holy Spirit**]

But ye have an unction [NIV: anointing] from the **Holy One**, and ye know all things [NIV: all of you know the truth].
1 John 2:20

HOLY SPIRIT OF GOD

These words from the apostle Paul to the believers at Ephesus emphasize several important truths about the Holy Spirit.

It is clear from this verse that the Holy Spirit can be grieved or pained by the sinful actions of Christians. This shows that the Holy Spirit is not a vague, ethereal force, but a person. Only a person can experience emotions such as grief and sorrow. Thus, we should speak of the Spirit not as "it" but as "He." He is as much a person as God the Father and Jesus the Son.

This verse also emphasizes the *sealing* work of the Holy Spirit. A seal symbolizes ownership and security. The seal of the Holy Spirit upon us as Christians marks us as God's property until the day of our total and final redemption in the end time (see Romans 8:23).

If some actions by Christians grieve the Holy Spirit, it follows that certain acts and attitudes bring Him joy and pleasure. These include the fruit of the Spirit in the apostle Paul's famous list in Galatians 5:22–23 (see sidebar). Paul contrasts these positive attributes with works of the flesh that he lists in Galatians 5:19–21. The fruit that we bear as Christians should issue from the influence of the divine Spirit in our lives rather than from our fleshly human nature.

> Let no corrupt communication [NIV: unwholesome talk] proceed out of your mouth, but that which is good. . .that it may minister grace unto the hearers. And grieve not the **holy Spirit of God**, whereby ye are sealed unto the day of redemption.
> EPHESIANS 4:29–30

Paul's List of the Fruits of the Spirit (Galatians 5:22–23)

- Love
- Joy
- Peace
- Longsuffering
- Gentleness
- Goodness
- Faith
- Meekness
- Temperance

HOLY SPIRIT OF PROMISE

This is the only place in the Bible where the Holy Spirit is called by this name. The apostle Paul used it in his long greeting to the church at Ephesus—the congregation that he founded and where he spent more than two years (see Acts 19:1–12). Paul wanted these Ephesian Christians to realize what a treasure they had received in the Holy Spirit of Promise.

This is an appropriate name for the Spirit, because of the revelation given to the prophet Joel about six hundred years before Paul's time. God promised through Joel that He would pour out His Spirit "upon all flesh. . .and also upon the servants and upon the handmaids in those days will I pour out my spirit" (Joel 2:28–29).

God's Spirit was active among God's people in Old Testament times, but the Spirit seemed to be given only to select leaders for accomplishing specific tasks (see *Spirit that Was upon Moses* below). God's promise through Joel was that in the future He would place His Spirit as a constant presence in all His people.

Seals, like this ancient Sumerian seal, were used to authenticate the authority of the one who used it. Today, God uses the Holy Spirit as His seal, authenticating that we belong to Him.

During Jesus' earthly ministry, He renewed this promise of God the Father. Jesus told His disciples that He would send the Spirit as a *Comforter* (see above) to them after He had ascended to the Father. His Spirit would fill them with power so they could continue His work through the church after He was gone (see John 14:16, 26; Acts 1:8).

Both these promises of the coming of the Spirit—from Joel and Jesus—were fulfilled on the Day of Pentecost. The sound of a "rushing mighty wind" and the settling of "cloven tongues as of fire" on each of the apostles left no doubt that they had been filled with the Holy Spirit (see Acts 2:2–3). This gave them confidence and power and turned them into bold witnesses for Jesus Christ.

The Holy Spirit is also the Spirit of Promise because of what He provides for Christians of all generations. Paul declares in this verse that all believers are sealed by the Spirit.

This "sealing" is a reference to the process by which documents were authenticated in Bible times. A king would stamp a decree or official proclamation with his royal seal to show that it had been issued under his authority. This order was to be obeyed because it came from the highest authority in the land.

Our sealing by the Holy Spirit at our conversion shows that we belong to Jesus Christ. We have His irrevocable promise that He will abide with us forever—in this life and the life beyond. When the Spirit stamps us with His seal, we are safe and secure in God's love.

NEW SPIRIT

Just as Jeremiah is known as the prophet of the new covenant (see Jeremiah 31:31–34; see also, *Husband* in part 1, Names of God the Father; and *Mediator of the New Testament* in part 2, Names of God the Son), so, too, Ezekiel might be called the prophet of the New Spirit. This name of the Holy Spirit is unique to him, and he uses it three times in his book (see also Ezekiel 11:19; 18:31).

> A new heart also will I give you, and a **new spirit** will I put within you: and I will take away the stony heart out of your flesh, and I will give you an heart of flesh.
> EZEKIEL 36:26

The word *new* does not mean that God would give His people the Holy Spirit for the first time at some time in the future. The Holy Spirit was active with God the Father in the Creation and among selected people in Old Testament times. *New Spirit* refers to the spiritual redemption that God would provide for His people through His love and grace. God's Spirit would bind believers to Him in a new covenant sealed with the blood of Jesus Christ.

POWER OF THE HIGHEST

These words of assurance were spoken to Mary, the mother of Jesus, by the angel Gabriel. Although Mary was a virgin, she would give birth to the Son of God. His conception would occur through the action of the Holy Spirit, whom Gabriel described as the Power of the Highest.

No other word describes the work of God's Spirit as well as *power*. Throughout the Bible, this is the dominant feature of His miraculous work.

For example, Saul, as the first king of Israel, learned

And the angel answered and said unto her, The Holy Ghost shall come upon thee, and the **power of the Highest** shall overshadow thee: therefore also that holy thing which shall be born of thee shall be called the Son of God.

LUKE 1:35

[NASB, NIV, NRSV: **power of the Most High**]

firsthand about the overwhelming power of the Holy Spirit. Insanely jealous of David, he sent several assassins to kill him. But the Spirit of God came upon them, causing them to utter prophecies instead of carrying out the king's orders.

Finally, Saul himself went to murder David, but the same thing happened to him (see 1 Samuel 19:19–24). He fell into a prophetic trance, and the people asked, "Is Saul also among the prophets?" (1 Samuel 19:24). King Saul was the most powerful man in Israel, but he was no match for the Holy Spirit and His power. God's Spirit protected David, who had been selected by the Lord to succeed Saul as king.

In the New Testament, when Jesus prepared to ascend to His Father, He told His disciples, "Ye shall receive power, after that the Holy Ghost is come upon you: and ye shall be witnesses unto me both in Jerusalem, and in all Judea, and in

Painting from the Church of the Annunciation in Nazareth depicting the angel Gabriel informing Mary that the Power of the Highest will overshadow her.

Samaria, and unto the uttermost part of the earth" (Acts 1:8).

As Jesus promised, the Holy Spirit empowered His disciples and other early Christians to carry out the Great Commission. The initial outpouring of the Holy Spirit occurred on the Day of Pentecost (see sidebar), transforming the followers of Jesus into bold witnesses for Him. Their zeal in preaching the gospel is described throughout the book of Acts. From the Jews to the Samaritans to the Gentiles, the good news about Jesus spread like a roaring forest fire until it reached the very center of the Roman Empire, the capital city of Rome (see Acts 28:14–31).

But the Holy Spirit has not restricted His work to that long-ago time. He is still at work in our day and age through those who follow Jesus as Lord and Savior. God the Father will do His work through us as Christians: "Not by might, not by power, but by my spirit, saith the LORD of hosts" (Zechariah 4:6).

Holy Spirit Power at Pentecost (Acts 2:1–4)

"And when the day of Pentecost was fully come, they were all with one accord in one place. And suddenly there came a sound from heaven as of a rushing mighty wind, and it filled all the house where they were sitting.

"And there appeared unto them cloven tongues like as of fire, and it sat upon each of them. And they were all filled with the Holy Ghost, and began to speak with other tongues, as the Spirit gave them utterance."

POWER OF THE MOST HIGH. See *Power of the Highest*.

PROMISED HOLY SPIRIT. See *Holy Spirit of Promise*.

SEVEN SPIRITS

This reference to the Holy Spirit as Seven Spirits is puzzling to many Bible students. We know from the apostle Paul's writings that the Holy Spirit is one. He declared to the believers at Corinth, "By one Spirit are we all baptized into one body" (1 Corinthians 12:13). So how could the apostle John

> John to the seven churches which are in Asia: Grace be unto you, and peace, from him which is, and which was, and which is to come; and from the **seven Spirits** which are before his throne; and from Jesus Christ, who is the faithful witness.
> REVELATION 1:4–5

in these verses from Revelation claim that the Holy Spirit is seven in number?

The best explanation is that John used the number seven to emphasize the fullness and completeness of the Holy Spirit. Seven was considered the perfect number in Bible times, and it appears often throughout the Bible to symbolize wholeness and perfection (see Deuteronomy 16:15; Matthew 18:21–22). John uses the number in this sense many times throughout Revelation: seven candlesticks (1:12), seven stars (1:16), seven seals (5:1), seven horns (5:6), and seven eyes (5:6).

SPIRIT OF ADOPTION

In this verse, the apostle Paul compares our situation before we become believers to the new status we enjoy after our conversion. The old life is comparable to that of a slave in bondage, with no rights or privileges. But after coming to new life in Christ, we have all the advantages of sonship as children of God the Father.

> For ye have not received the spirit of bondage again to fear; but ye have received the **Spirit of adoption**, whereby we cry, Abba, Father.
> ROMANS 8:15
> [NIV: **Spirit of sonship**]

Paul uses the concept of adoption to emphasize our new status with God. We were once children of sin, but God delivered us from our bondage and adopted us as His own. So close is our relationship to God as our adoptive Father that we can call Him "Abba," an Aramaic word equivalent to our modern "Daddy" or "Papa" (see *Abba, Father* in part 1, Names of God the Father).

The Holy Spirit has a vital role in this adoption process. His presence in our lives assures us that we belong to God. The Spirit will never let us forget that we enjoy a position of dignity and honor with Him in the family of God the Father and Jesus the Son.

SPIRIT OF BURNING.

See *Spirit of Judgment/Spirit of Burning.*

Adoption brings diverse people together into a unified family.

SPIRIT OF CHRIST

This is one of those verses in the King James Version that is made even more impressive by a modern translation. The New International Version renders it like this: "You, however, are controlled not by the sinful nature but by the Spirit, if the Spirit of God lives in you. And if anyone does not have the Spirit of Christ, he does not belong to Christ."

The first dramatic truth emphasized by this verse is that the Holy Spirit is both the Spirit of God and the Spirit of Christ. This is a bold affirmation that Jesus was one with the Father, yet distinct from Him at the same time. Our minds have a hard time taking in this concept, but this is the clear teaching of the Bible.

The apostle Paul also declares in this verse that the Holy Spirit is a gift of God's grace that transforms us when we accept Jesus as Savior and Lord. Paul even goes so far as to say that the presence of the Holy Spirit in our lives is proof of our salvation, showing that we "belong to Christ."

This name for the Holy Spirit—Spirit of Christ—also shows that He was closely connected with Jesus' earthly ministry and that He continues to empower the church to continue Jesus' work in our time. The Holy Spirit enabled the prophets to foresee the coming of Jesus into the world (see 1 Peter 1:10–11). The Spirit unites the church, Jesus' body, to Him as the head of the church (see 1 Corinthians 12:12–13). The Holy Spirit causes us as Christians to grow more and more like the Lord whom we serve (see 2 Corinthians 3:18).

Two similar names that Paul uses for the Holy Spirit are Spirit of God's Son (Galatians 4:6) and Spirit of Jesus Christ (Philippians 1:19).

SPIRIT OF COMPASSION. See *Spirit of Grace and Supplications.*

SPIRIT OF COUNSEL AND MIGHT

The prophet Isaiah in this passage looks more than six hundred years into the future and predicts the coming of the Messiah. This great leader among God's people would be filled with God's Spirit, to whom the prophet refers as the Spirit of Counsel and Might.

All of us have known people who love to give us their

> But ye are not in the flesh, but in the Spirit, if so be that the Spirit of God dwell in you. Now if any man have not the **Spirit of Christ**, he is none of his.
> ROMANS 8:9

And the spirit of the LORD shall rest upon him, the spirit of wisdom and understanding, the **spirit of counsel and might**, the spirit of knowledge and of the fear of the LORD.
ISAIAH 11:2
[NASB: **spirit of counsel and strength**; NIV: **Spirit of counsel and of power**]

Sixth-century fresco of the Apostle Paul discovered in a cave in the hills overlooking the harbor of Ephesus. The early Church recognized that Paul's life exemplified someone who lived by the Spirit of Faith.

advice and counsel—at no charge! And we know others who are people of action. But how many people do you know who can tell you what to do and then fill you with the strength to accomplish their advice? People like this are a rarity, but Isaiah declares that work like this is just a routine "day at the office" for the Holy Spirit.

The Holy Spirit knows what we should do to bring our lives into line with God's will. He warns us about the dangers of temptation. But He also gives us the strength to resist temptation. When we do stumble and fall, He assures us of our restored relationship with God, when we confess our sins before God the Father and Jesus the Son.

Counsel *and* might. This unusual combination of skills is just one more proof of God's love for His people.

SPIRIT OF FAITH

This is the only place in the New Testament where the Holy Spirit is called the Spirit of Faith. It is no accident that it appears in the writings of the apostle Paul, who has more to say about faith than any other New Testament writer (see sidebar).

To understand this verse from 2 Corinthians, we need to consider Paul's famous statement in the book of Ephesians about the centrality of faith: "For by grace are ye saved through faith; and that not of yourselves: it is the gift of God: not of works, lest any man should boast" (Ephesians 2:8–9).

Notice that Paul does not say that we are saved *by* faith, but *through* faith. It is Christ's sacrifice on the cross that saves us; we claim this sacrifice for ourselves by placing our faith in Him as our Savior and Lord. Faith is our human response to His sacrifice, which we must exercise before we can experience forgiveness for our sins and find new life in Jesus Christ.

If human faith is an essential element of the salvation process, how do we have such faith? Paul's answer is that saving faith is a work of the Holy Spirit—the Spirit of Faith. He alone can convict us of sin and lead us to declare our faith in Jesus Christ as our Savior. Without the movement of the Holy Spirit to kindle faith in our hearts and minds, we would remain hopelessly lost in our sin.

> We having the same **spirit of faith**, according as it is written, I believed, and therefore have I spoken; we also believe, and therefore speak.
> 2 CORINTHIANS 4:13

Paul: The Apostle of Faith

- "Therefore being justified by faith, we have peace with God through our Lord Jesus Christ" (Romans 5:1).
- "I am crucified with Christ: nevertheless I live; yet not I, but Christ liveth in me: and the life which I now live in the flesh I live by the faith of the Son of God, who loved me, and gave himself for me" (Galatians 2:20).
- "I have fought a good fight, I have finished my course, I have kept the faith" (2 Timothy 4:7).

SPIRIT OF FIRE. See *Spirit of Judgment/Spirit of Burning.*

SPIRIT OF GLORY

The apostle Peter may have been thinking back to the time when Jesus told His disciples what to do when they were persecuted for following Him. They were to "take no thought how or what ye shall speak: for it shall be given you in that same hour what ye shall speak. For it is not ye that speak, but the Spirit of your Father which speaketh in you" (Matthew 10:19–20).

In effect, Jesus told them not to retaliate against or resist their persecutors, but to trust the Holy Spirit—the Spirit of

> If ye be reproached [NIV: insulted] for the name of Christ, happy [NIV: blessed] are ye; for the **spirit of glory** and of God resteth upon you: on their part he is evil spoken of, but on your part he is glorified.

Glory—to take care of them and give them the words to say in rebuttal. The same Spirit that guided Jesus throughout His ministry would also abide with the disciples, strengthening them to serve as Jesus' bold witnesses.

The Spirit of Glory does not desert us during our times of persecution. He honors us for our sacrificial suffering in God's service, just as He gloried Jesus by raising Him from the dead (see 1 Peter 3:18).

SPIRIT OF GOD

These verses describe Jesus' baptism by John the Baptist at the beginning of His public ministry—an event reported by all three Synoptic Gospels (see also Mark 1:9–11; Luke 3:21–22).

But Matthew's Gospel is the only one of the three that calls the Holy Spirit who descended upon Jesus the Spirit of God. This is a common name for the Spirit in the Old Testament (see 1 Samuel 11:6; Job 33:4), but it appears only a few times in the New Testament (see Romans 8:9; 1 Corinthians 2:11).

Perhaps Matthew used this name for the Holy Spirit because he wanted to emphasize that Jesus was empowered directly by God Himself when God sent His Spirit upon His Son. Matthew's Gospel is also known for its portrayal of Jesus as the fulfillment of Old Testament prophecy. And the coming of the Spirit upon Jesus at His baptism fulfilled Isaiah's prophecy about the Messiah that "the spirit of the Lord shall rest upon him" (Isaiah 11:2).

One of the most interesting things about this passage is Matthew's description of God's Holy Spirit "descending like a dove" and alighting on Jesus. As a spirit being, the Holy Spirit is invisible. The only other time in the Bible when the Spirit appeared in visible form was on the Day of Pentecost, when He appeared to the apostles as "cloven tongues like as of fire" and settled on "each of them" (Acts 2:3).

Was the visible appearance of the Holy Spirit on this occasion God's way of assuring Jesus of His power and presence? Possibly. But Jesus had been conscious of His unique mission from an early age (see Luke 2:48–50).

Did the Holy Spirit actually look like a dove, or was Matthew using symbolic language? Matthew says the Spirit descended "like a dove," but Luke's account says the

And Jesus, when he was baptized, went up straightway out of the water: and, lo, the heavens were opened unto him, and he saw the **Spirit of God** descending like a dove, and lighting upon him. And lo a voice from heaven, saying, This is my beloved Son, in whom I am well pleased.
Matthew 3:16–17

Spirit came down "in a bodily shape like a dove upon him" (Luke 3:22).

Maybe we're trying a little too hard to make sense of the details in this passage and missing the real message that Matthew was trying to get across. Here's the double-edge bottom line: (1) God was pleased to send His Son into the world as His personal representative on a mission of redemption. (2) This mission was so important that God empowered Jesus with His own Spirit for the task.

Relief from the Church of the Annunciation in Nazareth depicting the Spirit of God descending on Jesus in the form of a dove after His baptism by John the Baptizer.

Names that Associate the Spirit with God

- "For it is not ye that speak, but the **Spirit of your Father** which speaketh in you" (Matthew 10:20).
- "Forasmuch as ye are manifestly declared to be the epistle of Christ ministered by us, written not with ink, but with the **Spirit of the living God**" (2 Corinthians 3:3).
- "And when they were come up out of the water, the **Spirit of the Lord** caught away Philip, that the eunuch saw him no more: and he went on his way rejoicing" (Acts 8:39).
- "The **Spirit of the LORD God** is upon me; because the LORD hath anointed me to preach good tidings unto the meek; he hath sent me to bind up the brokenhearted, to proclaim liberty to the captives, and the opening of the prison to them that are bound" (Isaiah 61:1).

SPIRIT OF GOD'S SON. See *Spirit of Christ*.

SPIRIT OF GRACE. See *Spirit of Grace and Supplications*.

SPIRIT OF GRACE AND SUPPLICATIONS

The prophet Zechariah in this verse looks into the future to the coming of the Messiah, the one "whom they pierced"—

a clear reference to the crucifixion of Jesus. Along with the Messiah, God the Father would also send the Holy Spirit, whom Zechariah describes as the Spirit of Grace and Supplications.

The Holy Spirit is the Spirit of Grace because He convicts people of their sin and leads them to place their faith in Jesus Christ (see John 16:8–11). No one can earn God's grace or purchase His indwelling Spirit. He gives His grace and His Spirit generously to those who confess His Son Jesus as Savior and Lord.

Supplication is a distinct form of prayer in which a person is keenly aware of his sin and he cries out to God for forgiveness. Jesus commended the unrighteous publican or tax collector because he prayed, "God be merciful to me a sinner" (Luke 18:13). The Holy Spirit is the Spirit of Supplications because He leads us to drop our self-righteous pride and throw ourselves on the mercy and grace of God for forgiveness and restoration.

> And I will pour upon the house of David, and upon the inhabitants of Jerusalem, the **spirit of grace and of supplications**: and they shall look upon me whom they have pierced, and they shall mourn for him, as one mourneth for his only son. ZECHARIAH 12:10 [NRSV: **spirit of compassion and supplication**]

SPIRIT OF HIS SON. See *Spirit of Christ*.

SPIRIT OF HOLINESS. See *Holy Spirit of God*.

SPIRIT OF JESUS CHRIST. See *Spirit of Christ*.

SPIRIT OF JUDGMENT/SPIRIT OF BURNING

This verse from the prophet Isaiah emphasizes the Holy Spirit's work as Judge. His twin titles—Spirit of Judgment and Spirit of Burning—show that He is active with God the Father and Jesus the Son in exercising divine judgment against sin and rebellion.

Isaiah speaks in this verse about the Spirit's judgment against the sinful nation of Judah, but the three Persons of the Trinity have the authority to exercise judgment against sin wherever it is found.

The name Spirit of Burning depicts divine judgment as a fire. Most of us think of fire in negative terms because of the destruction it can cause. But fire can also purify, as it does when ore is heated to separate useless dross from a precious metal such as silver. We as Christians should pray for the Spirit of Burning to convict us of our sin, refine our lives,

> When the Lord shall have washed away the filth of the daughters of Zion, and shall have purged the blood of Jerusalem from the midst thereof by the **spirit of judgment**, and by the **spirit of burning**. ISAIAH 4:4 [NIV: **spirit of judgment and spirit of fire**]

and shape us into instruments of usefulness in God's service.

These names of God the Holy Spirit are similar to names by which God the Father and God the Son are known. God is called a Consuming Fire (Hebrews 12:29), and Jesus is described as a Refiner's Fire (Malachi 3:2).

Judgment throne at the ancient site of Dan in northern Israel.

SPIRIT OF KNOWLEDGE AND THE FEAR OF THE LORD

These two names of God the Holy Spirit are among six that the prophet Isaiah uses in this one verse. This in itself is unusual, but another striking feature of the verse is that the prophet groups these names together into three sets of two names each. Perhaps he thought of these sets of two as names that were closely related to each other.

So how do the Spirit of Knowledge and the Spirit of

And the spirit of the LORD shall rest upon him, the spirit of wisdom and understanding, the spirit of counsel and might, the **spirit of knowledge and of the fear of the LORD**. ISAIAH 11:2

the Fear of the Lord relate? Isaiah may have had in mind a well-known verse from the book of Proverbs: "The fear of the LORD is the beginning of knowledge" (Proverbs 1:7 NIV). In the Bible "fear of the Lord" means respect or reverence for God. Thus, this proverb declares that a healthy respect for God is the most important attitude for a person to have as he accumulates the knowledge he needs in order to be happy and successful in life.

Through His Spirit, God plants in our hearts a reverence for Him that leads us to honor God in our lives. This is the foundation on which we build knowledge and understanding through the continuing influence of His Spirit.

This is what happened with the prophet Daniel in the Old Testament. When he was a young man, He was taken into captivity after his native Judah fell to the Babylonian army. Trained for service as an administrator in the Babylonian government, he managed to remain faithful to God while rendering service to a pagan king. Even his captors recognized that "an excellent spirit, and knowledge, and understanding. . .were found in the same Daniel" (Daniel 5:12).

SPIRIT OF LIFE

For the law of the **Spirit of life** in Christ Jesus hath made me free from the law of sin and death.
ROMANS 8:2

This statement of the apostle Paul reminds us of another of his famous declarations about the Holy Spirit in 2 Corinthians 3:17: "Where the Spirit of the Lord is, there is liberty." By the "law of the Spirit of life" in Romans, Paul means the principle by which the Holy Spirit operates.

Life in the Spirit gives us the power to live free from the law, or principle, of sin and death. This does not mean that Christians will never experience death, because physical death is the lot of every human being. Paul means that those who have accepted Jesus Christ as Savior and Lord are no longer in bondage to sin and death. Just as Jesus defeated death, He has promised that all believers will enjoy eternal life with Him.

As the Spirit of Life, the Holy Spirit shares this name with Jesus (see *Life* and *Resurrection and the Life* in part 2, Names of God the Son). Those who have Jesus and the Holy Spirit in their lives are not held hostage by the threat of death.

Tapestry from the school of Raphael in Brussels illustrating the Spirit of Life culminating in the resurrection of Jesus.

Life for the Church

In his hymn "O Spirit of the Living God," Henry H. Tweedy prays that the Holy Spirit would continue to empower the church for its work in the world.

O Spirit of the living God,
Thou light and fire divine,
Descend upon thy church once more,
And make it truly thine.
Fill it with love and joy and power,
With righteousness and peace;
Till Christ shall dwell in human hearts,
And sin and sorrow cease.

SPIRIT OF MIGHT. See *Spirit of Counsel and Might*.

SPIRIT OF POWER. See *Spirit of Counsel and Might*.

SPIRIT OF PROPHECY

The apostle John, author of the book of Revelation, fell in awe before an angel at the throne of God. The angel told John not to worship him but to worship God and His Son, Jesus Christ. The angel went on to identify the Holy Spirit, who bore witness of Jesus as the Spirit of Prophecy.

The coming Messiah was often spoken of by the prophets of the Old Testament. This insight did not come to them

Mosaic above the chapel entrance of the Cave of the Apocalypse on the island of Patmos depicting John's dictation of his vision recorded in the book of Revelation.

through the power of their intellect but by direct revelation of God through the agency of His Holy Spirit.

These inspired prophecies were not restricted to the Old Testament. When Simeon saw the infant Jesus in the temple, He declared that He was the long-awaited Messiah whom God had finally sent to His people. This truth was revealed to Simeon by the Holy Spirit (see Luke 2:25–27).

SPIRIT OF REVELATION. See *Spirit of Wisdom and Revelation.*

SPIRIT OF SONSHIP. See *Spirit of Adoption.*

SPIRIT OF STRENGTH. See *Spirit of Counsel and Might.*

SPIRIT OF SUPPLICATION. See *Spirit of Grace and Supplications.*

SPIRIT OF THE FATHER. See *Spirit of God.*

SPIRIT OF THE FEAR OF THE LORD. See *Spirit of Knowledge and the Fear of the Lord.*

SPIRIT OF THE LIVING GOD. See *Spirit of God.*

SPIRIT OF THE LORD. See *Spirit of God.*

SPIRIT OF THE LORD GOD. See *Spirit of God.*

SPIRIT OF TRUTH

This is one of three places in the Gospel of John where Jesus refers to the Holy Spirit by this name (see also John 14:16–17; 15:26–27). In all three cases, He was explaining to His disciples that He would soon be leaving them to return to the Father. But they would continue to feel His presence through the operation of the Spirit of Truth in their lives.

One dimension of truth is "accordance with fact." In other words, do the facts support a specific statement or claim, proving it to be true? But the word *truth* can also refer

> And I fell at his feet to worship him. And he said unto me, See thou do it not: I am thy fellowservant, and of thy brethren that have the testimony of Jesus: worship God: for the testimony of Jesus is the **spirit of prophecy**. REVELATION 19:10

> Howbeit when he, the **Spirit of truth**, is come, he will guide you into all truth: for he shall not speak of himself; but whatsoever he shall hear, that shall he speak: and he will shew you things to come. JOHN 16:13

to something that is enduring or authentic, in contrast to something that does not last or is artificial or of little value.

The second meaning of *truth* is what Jesus had in mind when He spoke of the Holy Spirit as the Spirit of Truth. His disciples would discover that the Spirit was enduring and dependable. He would never leave them or forsake them. When all else crumbled and faded away, the Spirit would continue to empower their lives.

In John 15, Jesus tells His disciples that the Spirit of Truth would also help them bear witness of Him "because ye have been with me from the beginning" (John 15:27). The memory of Jesus' physical presence would eventually grow dim in their minds. But the Holy Spirit would help them recall His life and teachings and pass these truths on to others. This is exactly what happened in the book of Acts as the apostles bore witness about Jesus to people who had not seen Him in the flesh.

But even the disciples would not live forever. To preserve a record of Jesus' life, they recorded, under the inspiration of the Holy Spirit, what they remembered about Jesus. They also repeated these stories to other early Christians, who faithfully wrote down these eyewitness accounts. These records were passed on to future generations through the written Gospels of the New Testament. All believers are beneficiaries of their faithful witness.

Jesus was right. The Spirit of Truth is eternal. He is still revealing the truth about Jesus almost two thousand years after His death, resurrection, and ascension. Though we have not seen Jesus in the physical sense, we feel His presence through the work of His Spirit.

SPIRIT OF UNDERSTANDING. See *Spirit of Wisdom and Revelation.*

SPIRIT OF WISDOM AND REVELATION

This name of the Holy Spirit—Spirit of Wisdom and Revelation—from the apostle Paul is striking because of its combination of three important ingredients of the spiritual life: wisdom, revelation, and knowledge.

Revelation is the process by which God makes Himself known to man. Our human minds would know nothing about God unless He had chosen to reveal Himself to us. He has done this supremely through the written scriptures.

The writings that make up the Bible were revealed by God. But He inspired human beings through the activity of His Spirit to understand these divine messages and to write them down. "No prophecy of Scripture came about by the prophet's own interpretation," the apostle Peter declares. "For prophecy never had its origin in the will of man, but men spoke from God as they were carried along by the Holy Spirit" (2 Peter 1:20–21 NIV).

Through the inspired scriptures, we gain knowledge about God—His nature as Creator, Sustainer, and Redeemer. But the Spirit teaches us more than factual information about God. We come to know Him in a personal sense as the God who loved us enough to send His own Son, Jesus Christ, to save us from our sins.

Finally, wisdom is one of the ministries of the Holy Spirit in our lives. Wisdom is the ability to apply the facts to practical situations. Knowing the truth, and applying and living the truth, are two different things. The Holy Spirit gives us the wisdom to honor God in the way we live out our faith in the real world.

Another name of the Holy Spirit that is similar to Spirit of Wisdom and Revelation is Spirit of Wisdom and Understanding (Isaiah 11:2). In addition to inspiring human beings to write down God's revelation in the Bible, the Holy Spirit works with us as we read these writings. He opens our understanding so we can comprehend and apply God's message to our lives. With the Holy Spirit as our Helper and Guide, the Bible is always as fresh and meaningful as the nightly television newscast.

SPIRIT THAT WAS UPON MOSES

During the exodus from Egypt, the Israelites often frustrated Moses, their leader who had been selected by the Lord. Finally, Moses grew tired of their constant bickering and the burden of solo leadership. He needed others to help him with the task of hearing complaints and settling disputes. "I am not able to bear all this people alone," he told the Lord, "because it is too heavy for me" (Numbers 11:14).

God responded by instructing Moses to select seventy elders with leadership skills from among the tribal leaders of

> That the God of our Lord Jesus Christ, the Father of glory, may give unto you the **spirit of wisdom and revelation** in the knowledge of him.
> EPHESIANS 1:17

> And the LORD came down in a cloud, and spake unto him, and took of the **spirit that was upon him [Moses]**, and gave it unto the seventy elders: and it came to pass, that, when the spirit rested upon them, they prophesied, and did not cease.
>
> NUMBERS 11:25

the people. Then He empowered them for their assignment as Moses' assistants by filling them with the Spirit that was upon Moses. The same Spirit of God that enabled Moses to bear the responsibility of leadership among God's people would strengthen the elders for their work under Moses' supervision.

This account shows that leadership and the Holy Spirit go together like a portrait in a picture frame. God never selects a person for a job without giving him the power through His Spirit to accomplish the task He has called him to do. The Bible is filled with examples of people whom God filled with His Spirit after calling them to serve as leaders of His people (see sidebar).

If God has called you to some important leadership task, you can rest assured that His Spirit will make you equal to the challenge.

Biblical Leaders Who Were Empowered by God's Spirit

- Balaam (Numbers 24:2)
- Joshua (Numbers 27:18; Deuteronomy 34:9)
- Othniel (Judges 3:9–10)
- Gideon (Judges 6:34–35)
- Jephthah (Judges 11:29)
- Samson (Judges 13:24–25; 14:6, 19; 15:14)
- Saul, king of Israel (1 Samuel 10:10; 11:6–7)
- David (1 Samuel 16:13; 2 Samuel 23:1–2)
- Amasai (1 Chronicles 12:18)
- Azariah (2 Chronicles 15:1)
- Zechariah (2 Chronicles 24:20)
- Ezekiel (Ezekiel 2:2; 8:3)
- Micah (Micah 3:8)
- Jesus (Luke 4:14)
- Philip (Acts 8:29)
- Paul and Barnabas (Acts 13:2, 4)

WILLING SPIRIT. See *Free Spirit.*

Scripture references in **bold** indicate the background passages for major articles on divine names included in the book. For example, Genesis 3:15 contains a prophecy about Jesus the Messiah as the *Seed of the Woman*. See the article on this name of Jesus on p. 185. Numbers in *italics* indicate book page numbers.

Collection of the Israel Museum, Jerusalem and Courtesy of the Israel Antiquities Authority, Exhibited at the Israel Museum, Jerusalem: Page 21

Corbis/Alinari Archives: Page 179

Corbis/Araldo de Luca: Page 169

Corbis/Benjamin Lowy: Page 111

Corbis/Bettmann: Pages 85, 126, 159

Corbis/Leonard de Selva: Page 128

Corbis/Pascal Deloche/Godong: Page 139

Corbis/Paul Almasy: Page 148

Corbis/Ron Nickel/Design Pics: Page 104

Corbis/Stefano Bianchetti: Pages 107, 157

Corbis/The Corcoran Gallery of Art: Page 67

Corbis/The Gallery Collection: Pages 191, 200

Design Direct: Pages 24, 37, 62, 108, 141, 153

Dr. James C. Martin: Pages 22, 23, 27, 29, 34, 35, 38, 40, 42, 45, 47, 50, 51, 56, 57, 59, 60, 61, 63, 64, 72, 76, 79, 118, 121, 129, 133, 137, 163, 165, 177, 183, 184, 185, 193, 198, 205, 208, 210, 214, 217, 219, 221, 222

Dr. James C. Martin/Illustrated by Timothy Ladwig: Page 168

Dr. James C. Martin/Photographed with permission from The British Museum: Pages 31, 33, 54

iStockphoto: Pages 5, 7, 11, 15, 16, 52, 66, 74, 81, 90, 93, 94, 99, 103, 115, 124, 149, 175, 196, 201, 212

NASA/Hubble Space Telescope/NGC 2207 & IC 2163: Page 19

The British Museum: Page 18

Ellen SHAY

212-661-7659

THE
ToppFast™
DIET PLAN

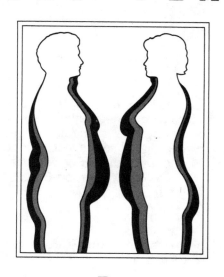

By
FRANK R. TOPPO, M.D.
&
ALAN T. SCHRAMM, Ph.D.

TOPPMED, INC.

Library of Congress Catalogue Card No.: 84-72769
ISBN: 0-932209-00-9

Printed in the United States of America
First Printing: December 1984
Second Printing: October 1986

This book is dedicated to the memory of Mario "Spanky" Toppo – our teacher, our best friend..... our son.

Sharen and Frank Toppo

To Fred, April and Kathryn.

Alan T. Schramm, Ph.D.

ABOUT THE AUTHORS

A graduate of Boston University School of Medicine, Dr. Frank R. Toppo is Co-Director of the Orange County Risk Factor Obesity (RFO) Medical Group in Orange, California. The RFO Medical Group has fasted in excess of 6,000 patients.

Alan T. Schramm received his Ph.D. in Psychology from United States International University, San Diego, California and has been working as a Clinical Psychologist specializing in treatment for addictive behaviors since 1968. In addition to his clinical practice at the Lake Forest Psychological Clinic, Lake Forest, California, Dr. Schramm is also associated with the Orange County RFO Medical Group in Orange, California. He is an enthusiastic weekend aviator, scuba diver and creative diet menu cook.

TABLE OF CONTENTS

Appendices

PREFACE
By Frank R. Toppo, MD.

Although I am opposed to people fasting without medical supervision, the time has come for those of us in medicine to realize that people are going to attempt protein-sparing modified fasting—that is, eating only a diet supplement—on their own, whether we like it or not. Therefore we must alert the public to the potential dangers of such fasting, insist that they visit their doctors, and make available safe, inexpensive supplements.

I personally became interested in obesity as a medical student. While working in the Emergency Room, I overheard a conversation between a Resident Physician and a medical student who was having difficulty drawing a patient's blood. He asked the Resident to assist him. After the Resident declined a trip upstairs at 3:00 AM simply to draw someone's blood, he instructed the medical student to find Toppo to draw the blood. When the student asked, "Who is Toppo?" the Resident replied, "He's the fat guy from California." Well (after questioning the Resident about the legitimacy of his birth), I immediately relayed the conversation to Sharen, my wife. She tactfully suggested I look in a full-length mirror and then weigh myself. I did both, and guess what? That Resident was right. During my medical education, I ballooned from a

1

mere 190 pounds (of lean, mean, fighting machine) to a robust 247 roly-poly pounds.

The following day I began the first of several "diets." You know—high protein/low carbohydrate. I even attempted running, but one minute into my first effort I found myself clutching a lamp post gasping for air. I almost got myself arrested by two of Boston's finest because they just knew that this fat guy holding onto a lamp post at 5:30 in the morning had to be taking drugs.

After failing several other diets and becoming frustrated and guilty because of my inability to lose weight, I moved back to California, to continue my education. At a welcome home party, after being razzed about my weight gain, I was approached by Dr. Jim Vanderhoof who is one of the kind physicians who put up the necessary monies for this poor boy to go to medical school. Dr. Van told me about an exciting new protein-sparing modified fast program he was directing at the University.

Dr. Van gave me a drawer full of literature concerning the program, and after reading all I could get my hands on, I started the program. The regimen consisted of taking five packets of powder mixed in cold water along with some potassium each day. To my amazement, I discovered not only did I feel great, but the fat was literally melting off. I lost a total of fifty-seven pounds in just six short weeks. At the end of this six-week period, I returned to my normal eating habits and promptly regained twenty pounds.

In addition to my personal experiences with weight loss, my professional training as a physician was forcing me to confront obesity.

At the Long Beach Veterans Hospital, I did three rotations in the Medical Intensive Care Unit. Late one night I was looking at all those unfortunates lying there with tubes either going into or coming out of every bodily orifice and suddenly I was struck by the observation that all of these people had two things in common: first, they were all smokers, and secondly, they were all obese!! At that moment, I knew what I would do in medicine—treat obesity effectively and derail the ever increasing train of humanity that ends up in Medical Intensive Care Units everywhere in the world.

After completing my medical training, I immediately began treating obesity. There have been many highs and lows for me since going into private practice. The highs have resulted from successful *people*—people who have lost incredible amounts of weight and are no longer on insulin or blood pressure medications; people whose personalities have undergone dramatic changes, people who have become more confident and outgoing since losing their weight. It has been joyous to be a part of their success. The lows I have experienced have motivated me to create a new and improved protein powder, namely, TOPP-FAST™. When I began to comment on various side effects from which people were suffering while on the protein-sparing fast, my remarks fell on deaf ears. Therefore, I decided to stop talking about how to improve various products and just do it!

I do not want anyone to read this book while sitting by the fireplace eating buttered popcorn. I want you to sit in an uncomfortable chair. I want you to underline what you consider to be important words or phrases. In others words, I want you to *study* this book . . . it just may be the most important book you have ever read.

3

By Dr. Alan T. Schramm

Why did we feel the need to write another diet book? Basically, we got fed up with the annual onslaught of "Who's Who Diet Books" that preached only so much nonsense. At our clinic, we developed and utilized fasting and weight maintenance procedures that have worked for thousands of patients. We thought it was important to let you know about our findings. Obesity is a killer disease. We want you to be thin. We want you to succeed. We know that you can take off excess weight and we know that with an earnest effort and the tools you learn here you can keep that weight off.

Good Luck, Healthy Dieting,

FRANK R. TOPPO, M.D.

ALAN T. SCHRAMM, Ph.D.

THE MEDICAL SIDE

Frank R. Toppo, M. D.

CHAPTER I

WHY ANOTHER DIET PROGRAM?

I have been invited to speak about obesity and its treatment by various radio and television talk shows. The initial idea of developing a safe product which people could use to manage themselves while fasting came to me after the following conversation, which took place in 1981, in El Toro, California, between a lady, whom we will call Mrs. Smith, and me.

Nurse:	"Frank, there is a lady on line three who insists on speaking to you."
Me:	"Hello, this is Frank Toppo."
Mrs. Smith:	"Hi, my name is Sheila Smith. Are you the doctor who was on the radio on Sunday?"
Me:	"Yes, ma'am."
Mrs. Smith:	"Is it true what you said about people who are 20% overweight dying earlier and having those other diseases high blood pressure, diabetes, heart disease, gall bladder disease, just to mention a few."
Me:	"Yes, it sure is."

Mrs. Smith:	"According to the charts, I am about 150 pounds overweight. Your nurse told me that neither MediCal or Medi-Care pay for your program. Is that true, and if so, how come?"
Me:	"It is true that the government-funded insurance plans do not cover our program. As to why, I guess the government does not yet believe in preventive medicine."
Mrs. Smith:	"Do you ever put people on your program for free?"
Me:	"Oh sure, we have had several people on what we call scholar-ships, but for obvious financial reasons the number of people on scholarships at any one time is limited. If you leave your name and number we will put you on the list."
Mrs. Smith:	"Let me ask you a question, Dr. Toppo. I am on MediCal and cannot afford the program. Even though I'm poor, don't I have the right to be healthy, too?"

Of course, Mrs. Smith deserved to be healthy. Moreover, I felt I had no business discussing a cure for people like her without trying to make a product available that was safe and inexpensive for her to use in a self-managed program of weight reduction.

CHAPTER II

WHAT IS OBESITY?

Obesity is not a social blunder like belching inadvertently at the dinner table. Obesity is a killer disease. If you are 20% or more above ideal body weight, you are at increased risk of dying and/or of having various nasty diseases. Look at this mortality chart:

MEN		WOMEN	
PERCENT OVER- WEIGHT	PERCENT INCREASED MORTALITY	PERCENT OVER- WEIGHT	PERCENT INCREASED MORTALITY
20%	25%	20%	21%
30%	42%	30%	30%

These statistics mean that if you are a man and are 20% or more above ideal body weight, you are at a 25% increased risk of dying compared to your counterpart who is not obese. A man 30% overweight has a 42% increased risk of dying compared to his counterpart of normal body weight.

Moreover, people 20% or more above ideal body weight are also at increased risk for having various diseases including but not limited to the following:

INCREASED RISK OF DISEASE

	Men	Women
Heart Disease	43%	51%
Cerebral Hemorrhage	53%	29%
Cancer	16%	13%
Diabetes	133%	83%
Digestive System Diseases	68%	39%
(Gall Stones, Cirrhosis,		
etc.)		

Unfortunately, I do not have any statistics concerning osteoarthritis. However, this disease is common in obese people and affects hips and knees in particular. Finally, obesity also seems to be implicated in certain kinds of cancers.

In addition to the physical risks of obesity the psychological and social consequences are numerous, too. I always tell our patients that we fat people are born no more crazy than thin people. In other words, our mothers didn't sit us on the potty any longer than our skinny brothers and sisters. What may have happened is that unkind, uncaring, cruel people have caused us to build up defense mechanisms that make us a little different. Just recently a sobbing, young female patient of ours told me that she stays awake late at night just so she can eat after her husband goes to bed. In order to avoid being chastised by her thin husband, this young lady actually waits for him to go to sleep in order to eat! Sounds rather bizarre? Not so. There are many more people with the same story. If Johnny Carson only knew how many are watching his show just so they can eat, he would take even more time off! In fact, I have heard this story of "midnight foraging" at least one hundred times. The majority of these people were embarrassed to

9

tell me their stories about clandestine binges because they felt they were the only ones in the world exhibiting such behavior. Indeed, the old saying that "fat people are happy people" was not coined by a person with a weight problem.

Have you ever noticed how overweight people are portrayed by the advertising industry? The distinguished man in a three-piece suit with hair graying around the temples is selling expensive wines or thanking some brokerage firm for making him a multi-millionaire. He's successful, he's rich, he's *thin*!! What about the guy selling kitchen cleanser? He's a dishwasher, he's ignorant, and he is *overweight*!! We are portrayed as overweight, incompetent clowns.

Does this stereotyping from Tinseltown advertising carry over to the real world? You bet it does! A study done at an East Coast university revealed that females who happened to be 40 pounds or more overweight, had a 50 percent less chance of being admitted to a major college in the United States than her counterpart with the same qualifications who happened to be of ideal body weight.

The overweight also have less of a chance of being hired or; if hired, they start at lower wages than those of ideal body weight. Finally, the obese have fewer opportunities for promotion even when they get a chubby foot in the door. Alas, all of us who are overweight have medical, psychological, and social problems directly related to that ugly word—obesity.

CHAPTER III

WHAT WE PHYSICIANS KNOW ABOUT NUTRITION . . . ALSO KNOWN AS THE WORLD'S SHORTEST CHAPTER

"I was taught in medical school that a balanced diet was when you are standing with a beer in each hand" . . . Merton Vanderhoof, M.D., Co-founder, Orange county RFO Medical Group.

Actually, medical schools are beginning to add nutrition courses to their standard curricula. Traditionally, however, this subject has been sorely neglected, and most present day physicians are not well versed in nutrition or obesity.

CHAPTER IV

WHAT PHYSICIANS KNOW ABOUT
OBESITY . . . ALSO KNOWN AS
THE SECOND SHORTEST CHAPTER

I was asked by the staff at a Newport Beach, California hospital to participate in a panel discussion concerning the treatment of obesity. I represented the supplemented fasting approach.

After I had explained to approximately *100* physicians the seriousness of obesity, my brother Bob overheard the following comment made by a physician leaving the seminar; "Aw, just tell the fat bastards to stop eating so much."

CHAPTER V

SO IT'S YOUR GLANDS?

There are two chances that your weight problem is due to your "gland problem," and those two chances are "slim" and "none." Obesity caused by a "glandular condition" is extremely uncommon. There are two reasons we are overweight; we have eaten too much and we have exercised too little. Nevertheless, it is helpful to know about some endocrine or glandular problems. Also, there are some unsafe "hormone treatments" for obesity that you *MUST* be aware of for your own well being.

For simplification, I have utilized the outline format.

Endocrine Disorders and Obesity

1. Thyroid Disease—the thyroid gland is located in your neck. It produces a hormone called Thyroxine (T4). If your blood is checked for the amount of T4 and it is found to be low (normally less than 5.5), you are said to be *hypothyroid*. Hypothyroid people suffer from lethargy, constipation, changes in or absence of menstruation, and mental dullness. Moreover, many complain of always being cold and tiring easily. Also, food seems bland and tasteless to them, partly because their senses of taste and smell are greatly impaired. Therefore, hypothyroidism is a rather rare cause of obesity.

2. Cushings Syndrome

a. People with this disorder have a problem with the adrenal glands which sit atop our kidneys. These glands produce an excess of *adrenocortical hormones* in Cushings Syndrome.

b. These people tend to have a round face and a heavy protuberant abdomen.

c. In reality a substantial degree of weight gain is rather unusual for people with Cushings Syndrome. These excess hormones actually cause a decrease in the amount of muscle and bone; therefore, we see people with very thin arms and legs and with large abdomens.

3. Tumors of the Hypothalamus

a. The hypothalamus is a part of our brain.

b. In conjunction with being obese, people with these tumors commonly suffer disturbances in mood, sleep and body temperature regulation.

4. Tumors of the Pancreas

a. The pancreas, located approximately across the upper part of our abdomen, makes insulin.

b. Some tumors of the pancreas (insulinomas) cause an overproduction of the hormone insulin. Insulin not only increases a person's appetite, it also increases the storage of energy by the body in the form of fat.

5. Laurence-Moon-Biedl Syndrome

a. An inherited disorder consisting of unexplained childhood obesity, mental retardation, polydactyly (six or more fingers per hand), hypogonadism (very small testicles) and eye problems (even blindness).

b. Particularly in Switzerland there is a high correlation with consanguinity, which is a nice way to say, first cousins are making babies.

6. Prader-Willi Syndrome

A disorder in infancy, consisting of swallowing difficulty, delayed onset of walking, weakness, childhood obesity, childhood diabetes, mental retardation, and a characteristic facial appearance.

7. Pseudohypoparathyroidism

a. The parathyroid glands (4) are located on and behind the thyroid gland. They secrete parathyroid hormone.

b. The explanation of this disorder is beyond the scope of this discussion, but clinically, these people are all short, stocky obese people with round faces, and cataracts are common. Also, these people are mentally retarded.

CHAPTER VI

TREATMENT OF OBESITY WITH HORMONES AND OTHER CONCOCTIONS

A. *Human Chorionic Gonadotropin* (HCG).

1. In 1954, an Italian physician, Dr. Simeons, discovered that there was a high incidence of decreased levels of Growth Hormone (G.H.) in obese people. Growth hormone is secreted by a gland in our brain (pituitary). HCG is secreted by the placenta during the first sixty days of pregnancy and ultimately passed in the urine. HCG and G.H. are both made up of alpha and beta chains. The alpha chains in HCG and G.H. are identical; however, the beta chains are extremely different. What Dr. Simeons did was to isolate the HCG hormones from the urine of pregnant women and inject it into people. In addition he placed these same patients on a 500 calories per day diet. HCG has been proven to be absolutely useless in the treatment of obesity, however, people do lose weight on 500 calories per day.

2. However, there are some potential side effects to HCG injections. Namely, adults may experience some degree of stimulation of the ovaries or testes. Also, there is a fear of producing precocious puberty (example: a four-year old girl with pubic hair, breast tissue, and menstrating) in children. I think the moral of this story is, "Never let

an Italian physician shoot the urine from a pregnant woman into your rear end."

B. Thyroid Hormones

1. Weight loss through treatment with thyroid hormones in large amounts is restricted to the period during which the hormones are taken. When the hormones are discontinued, people tend to gain weight rapidly..

2. The weight loss seen during treatment with large doses of thyroid hormones consists of little body fat. With prolonged treatment, there may be a loss of muscle and bone with resulting weakness.

3. Large doses of thyroid hormone also causes diminished intestinal absorption and an increased urinary excretion of calcium which together may deplete the bone of calcium.

4. High dosages of thyroid may cause various problems such as high blood pressure, a rapid or irregular heart beat, changes on the electrocardiogram, and even a heart attack!!

C. Growth Hormone

1. Growth hormone (G.H.) is secreted by a portion of our brain (pituitary).

2. In theory, G.H. should be useful for treating obesity because it depletes body fat and increases energy expenditure without reducing body nitrogen stores (muscle).

3. Unfortunately, since we presently must grind up pituitary glands of deceased persons for the majority of G.H., the unavailability makes even a trial of G.H. unlikely in the treatment of obesity.

D. Appetite Suppressants

Treatment of obesity with "diet pills" (e.g., amphetamines) has no place in the practice of medicine.

E. Dietary Treatment of Obesity

1. Over-the-counter products—most of these contain either phenylpropanolamine or caffeine.

a. *Phenylpropanolamine* is a sympathomometic or a stimulant type of drug like amphetamines—although not so strong. It can cause your blood pressure to go up and your heart to beat faster. Therefore, people with high blood pressure or heart problems should not be taking this drug. Phenylpropanolamine also interacts with several different medications that might be prescribed by your doctor. Therefore, he or she should be notified if you decide to try one of the preparations which contain this drug.

b. Caffeine is rapidly absorbed in the gut and distributed throughout the body within one hour. In medicine, the biological effect of a drug is measured as a half-life. In other words, how long after absorption, does it take for one-half of a certain drug to be inactivated. A cup of brewed coffee contains 85 mg. of caffine. Three hours after ingestion, 42.5 mg. of the original 85 mg. of caffeine are still biologically active. In six hours, 21.25 mg. of the original caffeine are still biologically active. Therefore, the half-life of caffeine is three hours. As you can figure out, that 8:00 a.m. wake-up cup of coffee which gave you 85 mg. of caffeine continues to be biologically active at 8:00 p.m. (5.25 mg. caffeine). The physiological effects of caffeine include diuresis (increased urination), stimulation of the central nervous system (brain) with subsequent insomnia and nervousness, and stimulation of heart muscle followed by abnormal heart beat. In 1976, the *New England Journal of Medicine* suggested causal association between coffee drinking and a heart attack. Most recently, heavy coffee drinkers are reported to run an increased risk of developing cancer of the pancreas.

    c. Average caffeine contents:

1. Ground coffee (per cup)   85 mg.
2. Instant coffee (per cup)   60 mg.
3. Decaffeinated coffee (per cup)   3 mg.
4. Tea (per cup)   30-50 mg.
5. Cocoa (per cup)   6-42 mg.
6. Cola (per 8 oz. glass)   32 mg.
7. Excedrine, Anacin (per tablet)   32 mg.
8. Dristan, Sinarest (per tablet)   30 mg.
9. No-Doz, Vivarin   100-200 mg.

    d. Over-the-counter diet pills which contain phenylpropanolamine *and* caffeine:

1. Dietac—75 mg. of phenylpropanolamine
2. Dexatrim—75 mg. of phenylpropanolamine and 200 mg. of caffeine.
3. Hungrex Plus—25 mg. of phenylpropanolamine and 66 mg. of caffeine
4. Diet-Gard—25 mg. of phenylpropanolamine
5. Permathene—25 mg. of phenylpropanolamine and 140 mg. of caffeine.

2. Starch Blockers

    a. The latest thing? Don't count on it. This product was described in the medical literature 50 years ago.

    b. These pills presumably inhibit the action of *alpha amylase* which breaks down starch to dextrines and maltose. Therefore, starch is said to pass to the lower part of the bowel without being absorbed. I have been unable to find one clinical study done on people to verify this claim. On the contrary, a recent article in the *New England Journal of Medicine* concluded that "starch blocker tablets do not inhibit the digestion and absorption of starch calories in human beings" (December 2, 1982).

c. This so-called "starch blocker" is an extract found in legumes, particularly red kidney beans. The problem is these raw beans contain three anti-nutritional ingredients: phytates which inhibit mineral absorption of the gut; hemagglutinins which cause our blood to "clump"; and protease inhibitors which interfere with the digestion and absorption of protein!

d. I might add that chickens fed a diet which included starch blockers for only four weeks showed a forty-one percent increase in the size of the pancreas. Sounds as if the old pancreas is working overtime, doesn't it?

e. The bottom line is that we, particularly in the Western World, have become overweight from eating *too much fat, not starches*!! Therefore, do you really want to put something in your mouth that will do nothing for your obesity, but *may* cause you other health problems? Enough about starch blockers as magical cures.

3. Liquid Protein

These will be covered in more detail in Chapter VIII, Physiology of Fasting. Briefly, the protein was produced from the hoofs and hides of animals; therefore, it could not be used by humans. We call it an incomplete protein. Also, its use resulted in severely low potassium levels in the blood.

4. Balanced Diets (ex: Weight Watchers, TOPS)

My momma taught me never to try to make my own candle burn brighter by blowing everyone else's candle out. What I am trying to say is, these are both basically good programs, but they have an extremely low overall success rate. It has been our experience that people need a break from making food choices before they can learn about the caloric value of food. Also, the weight loss on these programs is slow compared to fasting standards. If you are twenty pounds overweight, a one or two pound weight loss per week sounds alright, but what if you are 100 pounds overweight? Also, planning menus days in advance is a bit tough in our fast-paced and changing lifestyle.

5. Low Carbohydrate/High Protein Diets

The initial rapid weight loss experienced on these programs is secondary to the breakdown of stored glycogen in liver and muscle tissue. Glycogen is sugar with a great deal of water connected to it. When glycogen is broken down to sugar, this water is released and eventually passed into the urine. Unfortunately, when people eat carbohydrate again, glycogen is formed and the water weight people have lost is now regained. Furthermore, to counteract the *ketosis* (fat breakdown = ketone bodies), many of these programs out of necessity are high in red meat content. Since red meats are high in fats, dramatic increases in blood fats may occur. It has long been recognized by many in the medical community that high levels of cholesterol are associated with an increased risk of "hardening of the arteries" or arteriosclorosis and therefore, an increased risk for cardiovascular disease such as heart attack and stroke.

6. Beverly Hills Diet

a. As a little fella I was also taught that, "If you can't say anything good about something, don't say anything at all."

b. Actually, I was told recently that the Beverly Hills diet really does work. It seems that the people spend so much money on Rodeo Drive in Beverly Hills that they cannot afford to buy any food.

    7. Pritikin Plan

       a. A diet consisting of lower fat and protein intake.

       b. The scientific community appears divided in its assessment of this program. Some consider it nutritionally sound; others describe the program as "restrictive, austere, and dreary."

       c. The American Medical Association questions the safety and effectiveness of this plan. The Association thinks this diet may reduce resistance to infection and prevent wound healing. Also, the lowered intake of calcium and iron may be inappropriate for pregnant women and other women of childbearing age.

F. Surgical Treatment of Obesity

    1. Jaw Wiring or Braces

    As soon as the braces are removed and the people can again chew, they become obese again. They have learned nothing besides how difficult it is to vomit when their mouths are wired shut.

    2. Intestinal Bypass

       a. Potentially very dangerous. This procedure hooks one part of the bowel to another part further along the intestinal tract, bypassing part of the small bowel.

       b. Side effects include intra-operative death, protein malabsorption with subsequent fatty infiltration of the liver and liver damage. Also, severe electrolyte, particularly potassium imbalances, which results from the severe diarrhea common after this surgery.

       c. We have heard from some physicians, who attempt to justify such surgery, that their patient was not stable enough to undergo such a radical thing like going on a fast. Radical? What the hell do you call putting someone under general anesthesia for a couple of hours while you cut them open from stem to stern and then rearrange their plumbing?

3. Gastric Stapling

a. Again the procedure here is to put people under general anesthesia and again cut them open, stem to stern, but this time a large portion of the stomach is actually stapled off, leaving only a small pouch for a stomach. The logic here is that people cannot eat as much because they have a smaller stomach.

b. It appears that this procedure is only a temporary measure because as these people eat more, and over a period of time, the small pouch becomes large again and people regain their weight.

c. Recent literature suggests a problem with the nerves (peripheral neuropathy) in the legs of the patients who have undergone this surgery.

After reading this chapter, we realize no magic potions, no shots, no starch blocker, and no surgeon's scalpel will cure our weight problem. Nevertheless, humans were given reasoning ability, which we can use to take charge of our own lives. Let's solve this weight problem together, logically and safely.

CHAPTER VII

HISTORY OF PROTEIN
SPARING MODIFIED FASTING

In the 1960's Dr. Victor Vertes, Chief of Medicine at Mt. Sinai Hospital in Cleveland, Ohio, observed that people 20% or more above ideal body weight were at an increased risk of having various diseases and even of dying than were people of ideal body weight.

Dr. Vertes and his colleagues decided to do something about it; they began a protein-sparing modified fast program. Simply stated, *protein sparing* means that proper amounts of protein, fat and carbohydrate are consumed daily so that the body does not "eat-up" its own stored protein in the form of muscle.

In addition to weight loss, Dr. Vertes' fasting patients began to have wonderful results with respect to other medical conditions. Adult onset diabetics no longer needed daily insulin injections. People who had previously had high blood pressure no longer needed medication. Others with large amounts of fats in their blood showed dramatic decreases in blood cholesterol and triglyceride levels. Best of all, they were losing large amounts of weight, quickly and safely.

This program was replicated across the country, at medical schools and in the private medical sector. Initially, everyone involved was excited to see these fantastic results. Then reality set in. These same patients who had done so well on the fast were now returning to their doctors just as obese, just as carbohydrate intolerant (diabetic), and just as hypertensive (high blood pressure). What to do? Well, some practitioners initiated programs of behavior modification. Behavior modification. Such a term. Such crap! We were telling patients to eat on small plates, put their fork down between bites, always eat at the dining room table at the same time each day and God forbid you should never eat while watching television! Well, we had about as much success with this sort of nonsense as we did before.

The point is: taking the weight off is no problem; keeping the weight off is. In fact, maintaining the weight loss is the most critical part of the process both medically and psychologically.

CHAPTER VIII

PHYSIOLOGY OF FASTING

When you begin the fast, the amount of glucose or sugar in your blood decreases. Your body senses this decrease in blood sugar and various hormones, such as glucagon and adrenalin, are released causing stored sugar or glycogen to be released from the liver and muscle tissue. Indeed the initial large weight loss on the popular "low-carbohydrate diets" is almost exclusively from the water loss incurred when the stored sugar, which contains large amounts of water, is broken down. It takes about eighteen hours for the stored sugar in our bodies to be used up.

Once the body has used its stored sugar, it will begin breaking down *adipose tissue* or fat, using this fat as its new energy source. Burning of fat as an energy source results in *ketone-bodies* in the blood. I am sure you have read other diet books which tell you that your body is in a *state of ketosis*. Well, being in a ketotic state is both good news and bad news. The good news about ketones is that they are a natural appetite suppressant. They also give us a feeling of well-being. The bad news is, if we do not supplement our diet with either carbohydrates or protein, we will burn up more and more fat tissue and we will become more and more ketotic. A ketotic state is characterized by nausea, listlessness and even mental confusion. Have you ever heard of someone being in a "diabetic coma"? Such comas are, caused in part by too many ketone bodies in their blood.

Also, ketones inside the kidney compete with the excretion of uric acid. People with gout have elevated uric acid levels in their blood and therefore a gout attack, usually a very tender big toe, may be precipitated. Also, people with high blood uric acid levels can develop a kidney stone which is not only painful, but may be dangerous.

Again, if we continue "pure fasting" or "improper fasting," our bodies will next begin breaking down our own body proteins. Muscle, simply stated, is protein. Our bodies will actually begin breaking down its own muscle. Protein is converted, principally by the liver, into sugar (glucose), and this sugar is now used by the various body tissues as its energy source. Now, I can just hear some of you saying, "Well, big deal, I never wanted big muscular arms and legs anyway." Remember this, not only are the muscles in your arms and legs broken down, but so are heart muscle, spleen, and kidneys!! This is one reason why many unfortunate people died on the old liquid protein diet.

Perhaps a discussion of protein will clarify the problems these liquid protein diets created.

Several sources of protein are available to us from either plants or animals. Protein is either complete or incomplete. To be complete, proteins must contain adequate proportions of what are called *essential amino acids*. Amino acids are the building blocks of protein. These essential amino acids must be supplied to us by our diet because we cannot manufacture them.

The liquid protein diet garnered its protein from *collagen*, the protein found in the hides and hoofs of animals. Collagen, an incomplete protein, is essentially useless to us. The people taking this substance, which has been taken out of the marketplace by the FDA, were eating up their own muscles—heart, kidney and spleen included.

The only complete protein in the plant world is the protein found in soy. That is not to say that all vegetarians are at a health risk because they do not eat meat. Various combinations of incomplete proteins can produce a complete protein. In other words, what one protein needs, another protein has. An example of this combining property of protein is corn and dry beans. Both are incomplete proteins but when eaten together produce a complete protein. The same is true when cheese and macaroni, milk and cereal and blackeyed peas and corn bread are combined. These pairs of foods all produce a complete protein.

However, complete proteins are not all the same. Believe it or not, there are people in this world who have gone to four years of college, four years of medical school and up to 4-5 years of postgraduate work so that they can feed laboratory rats different types of protein. These dedicated human beings feed these rats protein for about two weeks and then calculate a ratio between the amount of protein consumed and the amount of weight the rats gained. This is called the Protein Efficiency Ratio (PER).

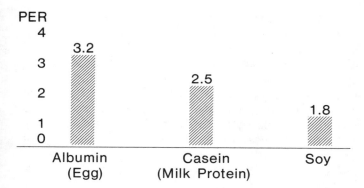

PER

	3.2	2.5	1.8
Albumin (Egg)	Casein (Milk Protein)	Soy	

As you can see, egg albumin has the highest PER and would, therefore, be the logical choice to use as a protein source. However, egg albumin is extremely expensive and must be meticulously monitored for Salmonella contamination because Salmonella infection of the gut will cause a potentially deadly diarrhea.

Finally, we will talk about potassium. Potassium is what we in medicine call an intracellular cation, that is, a substance which is mainly within each cell in our bodies. Its presence is necessary for muscle contractions and conduction of impulses in every nerve.

In the absence of kidney disease, the normal adult male passes between 60 and 80 MEq (milequivalents) of potassium per day in his urine. Therefore, this must be replaced or low blood potassium or hypokalemia occurs. This low blood potassium can be deadly!!! Initially, people with low potassium levels complain of tiredness and muscle cramping. Although the muscle cramping can affect any muscle, most people complain of a kind of "charlie-horse" in the muscles of the legs or a cramping of the toes.

If the potassium levels are allowed to continue to decline, heart beat irregularities may occur. This also is one of the reasons people died on the liquid protein diet—irregular heart beat secondary to low blood potassium.

There are approximately 70 MEq of potassium in our supplement. No matter which supplement you may be using, if you notice tiredness and muscle cramping—beat feet to your doctor and have your blood potassium checked!

Here is a list of food high in potassium. *This is not to be used instead of seeing your doctor*!

Foods Containing at Least 9 MEq of Potassium

Food	Amount	MEq
Banana, raw	1 med.	14.2
Beans, baked (no pork)	1 cup	12.8
Beef, lean, cooked	4 ozs.	10.7
Cantaloupe or honeydew	½ whole, med.	24.8
Chicken, cooked		
a) White meat	4 ozs.	12.8
b) Dark meat	4 ozs.	9.3
Fish		
a) Cod, broiled	4 ozs.	11.8
b) Haddock, fried	4 ozs.	10.0
c) Halibut, broiled	4 ozs.	15.2
Milk		
a) Whole 3.7%	1 cup	9.0
b) Skim	1 cup	9.0
c) Evaporated, unsweetened	1 cup	19.6
Orange	1 med.	9.0
Orange Juice	1 cup	12.8

Pork
  a) All cuts, lean
     cooked   4 ozs.   11.3
  b) Ham, cured, cooked   4 ozs.   9.4
Potatoes
  a) Peeled, boiled,
     unsalted   1 med.   9.0
  b) French fried, unsalted   10 pieces   12.5
  c) Mashed, milk added   1 cup   13.0
Pumpkin, canned   1 cup   14.0
Spinach, cooked   1 cup   15.0
Tomato Juice (canned)   1 cup   14.0
Turkey, roasted   4 ozs.   10.6
Veal, all cuts, cooked   3 ozs.   10.9
Watermelon, 1/6 medium
size melon   1-4"x8"   23.7
Yogurt   1 cup   9.0

CHAPTER IX

VITAMINS—ALL YOU EVER WANTED TO KNOW, BUT WERE AFRAID TO ASK

No diet book should be without a chapter on vitamins. Admittedly, I have gone a bit overboard on this chapter. However, the more I prepared for the chapter, the more I discovered how little I knew about vitamins. Also, I was absolutely fascinated with the interactions of various medications we physicians prescribe for people and what these medications *may* do to some vitamins.

I have broken this chapter down into three parts. The first part concerns itself with the *fat soluble vitamins*. To simplify the process let's say fats and liquids must be supplied by either the gallbladder or pancreas in order for these vitamins to be absorbed. The second part deals with *water soluble vitamins*. These vitamins do not require fats to be present in order to be absorbed from the gut. In part three I review common and some rather uncommon medications which may inhibit either the action or absorption of various vitamins.

I. Fat Soluble Vitamins
   A. Vitamin A—(Retinol)
      1. Functions of Vitamin A
         a. Necessary for night vision.
         b. Necessary for normal bone formation.

  c. Necessary for maintenance of various specialized tissues such as the mucous membranes of the eyes, the respiratory system, the gastrointestinal system, the reproductive system including ureters, bladder, and urethra, and also the lining of gland ducts (e.g., oil ducts of the skin).

  d. Recent studies have suggested that Vitamin A may protect against development of cancer of the lung, even in those of us who smoke.

2. Dietary Sources of Vitamin A

  a. Dairy products, eggs, vegetables.

  b. As with the other fat-soluable vitamins (D, E and K), large amounts (25-200 micrograms) of Vitamin A are stored in the liver. Signs of deficiency develop only after long periods of dietary deprivation.

  c. Fresh-water fish.

  d. Liver oils such as cod liver oil.

3. Signs of Vitamin A deficiency

  a. Retardation of bone growth in children.

  b. Night blindness.

  c. Persistent "goosebumps" of the skin, particularly on the sides of the arms and top of the thighs.

4. Causes of Vitamin A deficiency

  a. Inadequate diet—usually seen in children living in underdeveloped countries.

  b. Diseases of the pancreas gland (e.g., cystic fibrosis).

  c. Other malabsorption syndromes (e.g., celiac disease—disease of the intes-

tines).
   d. Severe liver disease.
   e. Laxatives.
   f. Irradiation (high dose X-rays used in treatment of bowel cancer, etc.).
   g. Excessive use of Vitamins E or D.
5. Actute toxicity from taking too much Vitamin A.
   a. Headaches usually with blurred vision.
   b. Dizziness.
   c. Vomiting.
   d. Diarrhea.
6. Chronic toxicity from taking too much Vitamin A over a long period of time (e.g., to "prevent colds" or for treatment of acne).
   a. Skin is mostly affected (e.g., itching, thick skin, etc.).
   b. Thinning hair or patchy balding.
   c. Painful swollen bones.
   d. Loss of appetite—no this is *not* a recommended treatment for obesity!
   e. Enlarged liver.
   f. Increased pressures in the brain followed by headaches and blurred vision.
B. Vitamin D
   1. Functions of Vitamin D
      In conjunction with Parathyroid Hormone, Vitamin D facilitates the absorption of calcium from the gut and kidneys for mineralization of bone.
   2. Dietary Sources of Vitamin D
      a. Foods in developed countries are Vitamin D fortified.
      b. D3 (cholecalciferol) is produced in the skin by sunlight, from cholesterol.

Therefore, people living in cloudy climates or working indoors may become deficient. Particularly susceptible are the elderly or disabled shut-ins.

   c. Sources of Vitamin D:
     1. Eggs, butter, milk and cheese.
     2. Liver oils are very rich in Vitamin D (and Vitamin A).

3. Signs of Vitamin D deficiency
   a. Rickets—soft, yielding bones (e.g., bowlegs, pigeon-breast, etc.).
   b. In adulthood—weak, brittle bones.

4. Causes of Vitamin D deficiency
   a. Sometimes people of low socioeconomic levels eat foods not fortified by Vitamin D because these foods are expensive.
   b. People who are not exposed to sunlight because of climate, indoor employment or shut-ins.
   c. Fad diets (e.g., macrobiotics).
   d. Liver or gallbladder disease because there is a decrease in absorption of the fat soluble Vitamins (A, D, E and K).
   e. People with kidney disease because the kidney converts "inactive Vitamin D" to "active Vitamin D."
   f. People with seizure disorders (epileptics) who are being treated with anticonvulsant medication.

5. Toxicity from taking too much Vitamin D
   a. Nausea, vomiting and/or diarrhea.
   b. With extreme overdosage, high blood calcium levels result from the increased absorption of calcium from the gut and depletion of bone calcium with subse-

quent possibility of the development of kidney stones and "weak bones" which are easily broken.

C. Vitamin K
  1. Functions of Vitamin K
     a. Vitamin K enables the blood to clot. People deficient in Vitamin K are "bleeders."
  2. Sources of Vitamin K
     a. The most important type of Vitamin K (K2) is produced by bacteria which is present in the bowel.
     b. Green leafy vegetables contain large amounts of Vitamin K.
     c. Seeds, tubers, and fruits are second highest source of the vitamin.
     d. Eggs and milk also contain amounts of Vitamin K.
  3. Signs of Vitamin K deficiency
     a. Easy bruisability.
     b. Difficulty in stopping bleeding (e.g., following blood drawing, trauma, or surgery).
  4. Causes of Vitamin K deficiency
     a. Liver, gallbladder or pancreas disease—again because of the decreased amount of fat and/or lipids delivered to the intestine necessary for the absorption of the fat soluble Vitamin K. (Vitamins A, D, and E are also fat soluble.)
     b. Certain antibiotics which decrease the amount of bacteria which produce Vitamin K in the bowel.
     c. The newborn infant may be deficient in this vitamin if the mother is deficient.

d. Some breast-fed infants have decreased stores of Vitamin K as opposed to infants fed with cow's milk. This point may be of great significance if the child is also being treated with an antibiotic (reference above paragraph 2).

e. Persons with certain diseases of the gut such as ulcerative colitis which impair absorption.

f. Persons who have undergone a colostomy.

g. People taking Dicumerol, a medication which inhibits Vitamin K.

h. Products utilized in protein-sparing modified fasts that are without Vitamin K. (Note: Our product contains 100 mcg.)

D. Vitamin E (Tocopherol)
1. Functions of Vitamin E
a. Acts as an antioxidant to prevent highly unsaturated fatty acids from becoming hard, tough deposits in various body tissues (e.g., fat, liver, etc.) when exposed to oxygen at the cellular level. For the life of me I do not know why I put the preceding sentence in this book. The next time you are at the neighborhood pub and someone mentions Vitamin E—nail them with the antioxidant effect of Vitamin E. Believe me, it's a conversation stopper.

b. May have some effect on red blood cell survival.

c. Does *not*, I say again does *not*, when consumed by the male species create a sexual superman as reported in many of the national tabloids. How do I know this to be true? Well you're just going to have to trust me on this one.

2. Dietary sources of Vitamin E
   a. Seed oils are richest sources—wheat germ, liver, corn, peanut, cottonseed and soybean.
   b. Liver and eggs.
   c. Fresh greens and many other vegetables.

3. Signs of Vitamin E deficiency
   a. Anemia—particularly in children and infants.
   b. Loss of male fertility in *rats* only !!! (So if you have a boy rat who doesn't seem interested in girl rats, give him a little Vitamin E.)

4. Causes of Vitamin E deficiency
   a. Low birth weight infants fed with artificial formulas *may* develop anemia.
   b. Low ratio of Vitamin E to polyunsaturated fatty acids. This means if a person is fed a formula consisting of a large amount of polyunsaturated fat and a very small amount of Vitamin E, the person will be depleted of Vitamin E. For those of you who are interested, the formula is: for each gram of polyunsaturated fatty acids taken per day, the daily requirement for Vitamin E is increased by 0.6 mg.

5. Toxicity from taking too much Vitamin E Severe influenza—extreme fatigability and malaise. This has been observed in

those persons taking 800 I.U. or more per day (1 mg. of synthetic alpha-tocopherol equals 1. I.U.).

II. Water Soluble Vitamins
  A. Vitamin C (Ascorbic Acid)
    1. Functions of Vitamin C
      a. Necessary for proper bone formation.
      b. Prevention of scurvy.
      c. Prevention of anemia.
      d. Maintains the strength of the walls of blood vessels and prevents abnormal bleeding into the skin, joints, and muscle.
      e. Necessary for healthy gums.
      f. Necessary for wound healing (e.g., following trauma, surgery, burns).
      g. This vitamin may have a connection with the production of steroids by the adrenal glands which are located atop our kidneys.
    2. Dietary sources of Vitamin C
      a. Citrus fruits and their juices.
      b. Strawberries and cantaloupes.
      c. Raw or minimally cooked vegetables, especially tomatoes, potatoes, cabbage, turnip greens, peppers, broccoli, and brussel sprouts. Note: Prolonged standing at room temperature, blanching, overcooking or washing may drastically reduce the Vitamin C content in the above foods.
    3. Signs of Vitamin C deficiency (mainly signs of scurvy)
      a. Poorly formed, painful bones and joints.
      b. Bleeding from the gums or into joints, muscle and skin. Bleeding into the

skin gives an appearance of purple bruises particularly around the neck and arms.

c. Poor wound healing.

d. Anemia.

e. In infants, particularly those who are bottle fed, loss of weight, loss of appetite, listlessness, increasing irritability and later the assuming of a "pitched frog position." These babies will lie still on their backs with their legs spread open giving the appearance of a frog. They assume this position in order to relieve the tension on muscles and tendons and therefore minimize their pain.

f. In adolescents and adults there is increasing fatigue and a decreased exercise tolerance.

g. Increase number of colds? Unfortunately double-blind studies have failed to prove that people taking large doses (one gram per day) of Vitamin C have fewer common colds, but interestingly these people tend to miss work less when they have colds as opposed to those taking no supplemental Vitamin C.

4. Causes of Vitamin C deficiency

a. Long periods (about 45 days) of dietary deprivation.

b. Smoking (cigarettes) decreases Vitamin C levels.

c. Aspirin blocks the affects of Vitamin C on blood clotting (platelets). Therefore, everyone being treated with aspirin for

rheumatoid arthritis should be taking
supplemental Vitamin C.
d. Birth control pills have been shown to
decrease Vitamin C levels.
5. Toxicity from taking too much Vitamin C
a. Massive doses of Vitamin C may cause
the formation of kidney and/or bladder
stones.
b. Pregnant guinea pigs given megadosis
of Vitamin C produce offspring who
have an inordinately high requirements
for the vitamin. (No human correlation
to the best of my knowledge has been
made.)
B. Vitamin B1 (Thiamin Hydrochloride)
1. Function of Vitamin B1
a. Functions at the cellular level in the
metabolism of certain amino acids
(building blocks of protein) and sugars.
b. Is crucial in the prevention of pyruvic
acid build-up which is thought to be a
toxin, particularly to nerve tissue.
c. There is a daily need for this vitamin
since total body stores of Vitamin B1
are minimal.
2. Dietary sources of Vitamin B1
a. Organ meats (heart, kidney, liver), pork,
lean meats, sausage, eggs, yeast,
green leafy vegetables, berries, nuts,
legumes; *whole* or *enriched* cereals.
b. The process of milling of grain and rice
(e.g., white flour and polished white
rice) removes B1 from these food
stuffs.
3. Signs of Vitamin B1 deficiency
a. Beriberi—there are two types of

beriberi, but basically, these persons become extremely weak and cannot stand from a squatting position without help.

1. Dry Beriberi—affects the peripheral nerves and muscles (numbness and tingling of the legs, painful calf muscles, shrinking with weakness of the leg and arm muscles, decreased reflexes and mental depression).

2. Wet Beriberi—same signs and symptoms as Dry Beriberi plus fluid is accumulated in the legs so that if a thumb is pressed firmly against the front of the ankle it will leave a large dent or indentation.

b. Wernicke's syndrome—mental confusion, difficulty or inability to walk and problems focusing or moving the eyes. This is seen almost exclusively in chronic alcoholics. At one time the State of Massachusetts was actually contemplating requiring B1 (thiamine) to be added to brands of cheap wines. (For those of you who have had the privilege of training at Boston City Hospital as I did, you can appreciate the benefits of "fortifying" the cheap brew with B1.)

4. Causes of Vitamin B1 deficiency
   a. Conditions of increased metabolism (hyperthyroidism, exercise, fever, pregnancy, and mothers who are breast-feeding.)
   b. Severe bowel disease (decreased absorption in the small bowel, severe

diarrhea).

    c. Lower socio-economic groups (elderly and the poor).

    d. Chronic alcoholics.

    e. Fad diet—persons on very high carbohydrate diets (0.5 mg of B1 are needed each day for every one thousand calories consumed).

C. B2 (Riboflavin)

  1. Functions of B2

    a. Assists in the transport of oxygen from the blood into each cell.

    b. Important in the metabolism of fatty acids.

  2. Dietary sources of B2

    a. Organ meats (heart, kidney, liver), meat, eggs, and liver sausage.

    b. Milk, cheese, whole grain products, legumes, green leafy vegetables.

  3. Signs of B2 deficiency

    a. Chapping of the corners of the mouth. This normally begins as a thickening of the skin at the corners of the mouth and progresses to small sores to cracks or fissures.

    b. The tongue may take on a red-blue color.

    c. Conjunctivitis or reddening of the white part of your eyes (similar to what one sees in the mirror Sunday morning after drinking that cheap wine Saturday night—which happens to lack which vitamin that may cause Wernicke's syndrome?).

    d. And itchy, scaling condition of the scrotum in males and vulva in females.

e. Greasy, scaling lesions that begin at the lower corners of the nose and may extend over the cheeks.

4. Causes of Vitamin B2 (Riboflavin) deficiency
   a. Chronic alcoholism.
   b. Poor diet.
   c. Persons who excrete large amounts of urine because of a disease state or because they are on a low-sodium, protein sparing modified fast and therefore their kidneys cannot concentrate the urine?
   d. Persons with low amounts of hydrochloric acid in their stomachs (e.g., stomach cancer).
   e. Persons with increased metabolic demands (particularly protein) such as hyperthyroidism, pregnancy, lactating females, fever, etc.

D. Niacin
   1. Functions of Niacin
      a. Niacin, like Riboflavin (B2) is important in the "breathing" process of each cell. But, unlike B2, Niacin is involved in the electron transport system (for energy) and not in the oxygen delivery into each cell.
      b. Also, as in the case with B2, Niacin is involved in fat and pigment metabolism.
      c. Niacin *may* play a role in lowering the amount of fats (triglycerides) in the blood.
      d. In large doses, Niacin can cause extreme vasodilation (increase size of blood vessels) and can be very helpful

in older people who have decreased blood flow to their brains.

2. Dietary sources of Niacin
   a. Liver, beef and pork.
   b. Whole grain cereals, yeast, fruits and most vegetables.
   c. Niacin also may, in part, be manufactured by the bacteria present in our intestines much like which vitamin?

3. Signs of Niacin deficiency
   a. Niacin deficiency causes a disease known as Pellegra which means "rough skin." If you were to ask your family physician about Pellegra he or she would immediately tell you of the three D's, and they are:
      1. Dermatitis—which roughly means inflammation of the skin. Initially, the skin becomes red and thickened. Later, fluid accumulates just below the superficial layer of the skin. This is most apparent in the areas most exposed to sunlight, although these same skin changes occur on the tongue and indeed the tongue may become so swollen that swallowing may be impaired.
      2. Diarrhea—due to changes in the inner lining of the bowel.
      3. Dementia—this is what we see in grandmas and grandpas as they get older and also in those unfortunate souls who have fried their brains with alcohol. Coldly stated, these people act as if they don't have both paddles in the water (e.g., forgetful,

intellectually one-step behind, etc.).
4. Causes of Niacin deficiency
   a. Not uncommon in underdeveloped countries secondary to inadequate intake of this vitamin.
   b. Chronic alcoholism, various diseases of the intestine, etc.
   c. As in the case with most vitamins, there is a need greater than the daily RDA requirements in people with hyperthyroidism, those who are pregnant or lactating (breast-feeding), and those with infections.
   d. Fad diets (e.g., those on diets consisting primarily of corn which is very low in both Niacin and its precursor Tryptophan).
E. Pantothenic Acid
   1. Functions of Pantothenic Acid
      a. Essential for the metabolism of carbohydrates and fats.
      b. Necessary for the synthesis (manufacture) of fatty acids and sterols (male and female hormones, cholesterol, etc.).
   2. Dietary sources of Pantothenic Acid
      a. Meat and liver.
      b. Dairy products, eggs, broccoli, most fruits, and molasses.
      c. Small amounts may be produced by the bacteria in our intestines, much like that of which two other vitamins?
   3. Signs of Panthothenic Acid deficiency
      a. Tiredness, muscle cramps, numbness (particularly hands and feet) and the "burning feet" syndrome which was

experienced by prisoners of war in World War II.
b. Personality changes—particularly irritability, quarrelsomeness, restlessness, and insomnia.
c. Heartburn, nausea, abdominal cramps and flatulence, or as my youngest son would say, "It gives you the toots."
4. Causes of Pantothenic Acid deficiency
Because this vitamin is present in all living tissues, it is difficult to imagine a deficiency occurring solely due to dietary deprivation. However, there are various "vitamin antagonists" which can cause lowered levels of this vitamin in our bodies.
F. Pyridoxine (B6)
1. Functions of B6 (Pyridoxine)
a. Important factor in protein metabolism, in the manufacture of skin pigment, in the metabolism of unsaturated fatty acids and cholesterol.
b. Necessary for the preservation of nerve tissue and in the production of antibodies which fight infection.
c. *May* play a role in proper bone development.
2. Dietary sources of Vitamin B6 (Pyridoxine)
Widely available in both animal and vegetables (meat—particularly liver and kidney, milk, whole grain cereals and numerous other vegetables).
3. Signs of Vitamin B6 deficiency
a. Convulsive seizures, irritability and anemia in infants.
b. Seborrhea, inflammation of the eyelids,

redness around the nose and cheeks.
- c. Low white blood cell count (lymphopenia).
- d. Polyneuritis—painful extremities, particularly the feet. This is because there is an "inflammation" of the nerves caused by the deficiency itself.
- e. *Some* types of kidney stones.
4. Causes of B6 (Pyridoxine) deficiency
   - a. Exclusively dietary deprivation *extremely* rare if not impossible.
   - b. Person with bowel problems (malabsorption).
   - c. Excessive, chronic alcohol abuse.
   - d. Treatment with isonicotinic acid hydrazide (INH) or tuberculosis.
   - e. Oral contraceptives—indeed the depression which may accompany the use of birth control pills responds dramatically to B6 (Pyridoxine).
   - f. Those persons being treated with L-dopa for Parkinson's disease.

G. Folic Acid
   1. Functions of Folic Acid
      - a. Important for the manufacturing of several amino acids (the building blocks of protein); to include RNA and DNA which, simply stated, are responsible for passing on to our offspring our individual human traits such as skin and eye color, stature, and intelligence or lack of.
      - b. Prevents certain anemias such as megaloblastic anemia.
   2. Dietary sources of Folic Acid
      - a. Richest sources are vegetables such

as asparagus, lima beans, lentils and dark green edible leaves.
  b. Kidney and liver are also good sources.
  c. To a lesser extent, cereals, meat and fruits.
3. Signs of Folic Acid deficiency
  a. Primarily anemia (macrocytic).
  b. Inflammation of the tongue, inflammation of the mouth, and diarrhea.
4. Causes of Folic Acid deficiency
  a. Various diseases of the bowel (Sprue or other diarrheal and malabsorption conditions).
  b. Certain leukemias ("cancer of the blood" or lymph nodes).
  c. Certain cancers.
  d. Anticonvulsants (drugs used by epileptics—conversely, high doses of Folic Acid can increase the metabolism of various antiseizure medications and thereby decrease their effectiveness).
  e. Drugs used for prevention or cure of malaria.
  f. Birth control pills.
  g. Chronic alcohol abuse.
  h. Pregnancy, because of an increased need for the vitamin.
  i. Deficiency of Vitamin C which converts folacin to the more active folinic acid.
  j. Persons fasting—this is why there is much more Folic Acid given to you each day on our program than the RDA recommends.
H. Vitamin B12 (Cyanocobalamin)
  1. Functions

a. Intimately linked to folate metabolism and therefore is important in the normal production of red blood cells.
b. Prevents the degeneration of the "covering" of nerves.
c. Important in the manufacturing of DNA and RNA—remember this had to do with our genes.

2. Dietary sources of Vitamin B12:
   Meat products, kidney, liver and fish.

3. Signs of Vitamin B12 deficiency
   a. Anemia—the life span of a red blood cell is about 120 days. In Vitamin B12 deficiency that same red blood cell will "live" between 40 and 60 days only.
   b. There is a degeneration of the central nervous system secondary to a demyelination (loss of the covering of the nerves) process which causes a loss of the sense of position (with the patient's eyes closed he cannot tell in which direction his toes have been moved) and sense of touch.
   c. Initially, the tongue becomes pale and shiny, but later may become red and very painful.

4. Causes of Vitamin B12 deficiency
   a. Strict vegetarians—of note is the fact that enormous quantities (100 mg) of Vitamin B12 are stored in the liver. So it would take months of total dietary deprivation before signs of Vitamin B12 deficiency are seen.
   b. Those people with stomach cancer or those who have had either part or all of

their stomachs removed (gastrectomy). This is because the stomach produces a substance which causes the absorption of Vitamin B12.

    c. Fish tapeworm and bacterial overgrowth because both interfere with the absorption of Vitamin B12.

    d. Diseases of the intestine.

    e. Small bowel bypass for treatment of obesity.

I. Biotin

  1. Function of Biotin

  A necessary co-factor or "activator" of several enzymes.

  2. Dietary sources of Biotin

  Biotin is present in several foods, but sufficient quantities are manufactured by the bacteria in our intestines, much like which vitamins?

  3. Signs of Biotin deficiency

  "Peeling" of the skin, *hair loss*, pain, loss of appetite, nausea and problems with nerves (neuropathy).

  4. Causes of Biotin deficiency

    a. Egg white contains a substance called "avidin" which binds with Biotin in the gut thereby making its absorption impossible. Over the years, we have seen several patients on protein sparing modified fasts lose their hair temporarily. To the best of my knowledge they have all responded to Biotin therapy.

    b. Antibiotics which destroy the bacteria in the intestine which produce Biotin.

III. Drugs Which Cause Vitamin Deficiencies

A. Folic Acid
   1. Anticonvulsants used in the treatment of epilepsy
      a. Phenytoin.
      b. Primidone.
      c. Phenobaritone.
   2. Oral contraceptives used for birth control
   3. Methotrexate used in the treatment of psoriasis and other diseases (some types of cancer)
   4. Pyrimethamine used in the treatment of malaria
   5. Aspirin used in doses sufficient for the treatment of rheumatoid arthritis
B. B12 (Cyanocobalamin)
   Metformin and phenformin, both of which have been used in the treatment of diabetes since the mid-1950's
C. B6 (Pyridoxine)
   1. INH (Isoniazide) used in the treatment of tuberculosis.
   2. Hydralazine used in the treatment of high blood pressure (hypertension).
   3. Penicillamine which is used to remove copper from the body in patients with Wilsons' Disease.
   4. Large doses of Pyridoxine (B6) can inhibit the action of L-dopa, a drug used in the treatment of Parkinsons' Disease.
D. Niacin
   INH which, again, is used in the treatment of tuberculosis.
E. Vitamin C (Ascorbic Acid)
   1. Aspirin in doses sufficient for the treatment of rheumatoid arthritis.

2. Indomethacin is an anti-inflammatory agent used in the treatment of arthritis (rhematoid, gout, osteo, etc.).
3. Oral contraceptives used for birth control.

F. Vitamin D
1. Anticonvulsants used in the treatment of epilepsy.
2. Diphosphonates which are a class of drugs used in a disease of the bone called Paget's Disease.

G. Vitamin K
1. Coumarin anticoagulants are drugs which are used as "blood thinners" in people who have suffered a blood clot in their legs or lungs, etc.
2. Cholestyramine is a drug used in people with high blood cholesterol levels and also in patients with billiary cirrhosis.

The following represents a list of substances which may inhibit the absorption, metabolism, action or increase the excretion of various vitamins and iron. Some of these medications have been explained in more detail in the proceeding text. If you are taking any of these medications, consider increasing your intake of specific vitamin(s) that may be affected.

Substance	A	D	E	K	Folacin	Niacin	B-2	B-1	B-6	B-12	Biotin	C
Alcohol	X				X			X	X	X		
ACTH, Acthan, Cortico-tropin	X				X				X			X
Actino-mycin D												
Aldomet					X					X		
Amphojel	X	X						X				

Substance	A	D	E	K	Folacin	Niacin	B-2	B-1	B-6	B-12	Biotin	C
Amytal (Amobarbital)	X				X			X		X		
Aristocort (Triamcinolone)	X								X			X
Aspirin			X		X			X				X
Atromid-S (Clofibate)	X								X			
Azo Gantonol (Sulfamethoxazole & Phenazopyridine)				X	X	X	X	X	X	X	X	
Azulfidine (Sulfasalozine)			X		X							
Benemid (Probenecid)							X					
Butazolidin (Phenylbutazone)					X							
Castor Oil	X	X	X	X								
Chloromycetin (Chloramphenicol)						X	X		X			
Cholestyramine (Questran)	X	X		X	X					X		
Cigarettes												X
Colchicine	X				X					X		
Decadron (Dexamethasone)					X				X			X
Diethystilbestrol		X					X					
Dilantin (Phenytoin)		X	X									
Dyazide					X					X		
Gantolol (Sulfamethoxazole)			X		X	X	X	X	X	X	X	X
Gantrisin (Sulfasoxazole)			X		X	X	X	X	X	X	X	X
Gelusil	X							X				
Hydrochlorothiazide								X				
Indocin (Indomethacin)												X

Substance	A	D	E	K	Folacin	Niacin	B-2	B-1	B-6	B-12	Biotin	C
INH (Isoniazide)					X				X	X		
K-Ceil, K-Lor, K-Lyte, Kaochlor, Klorvess (Potassium Choride)										X		
Larodopa (Levodopa)										X		
Maalox	X								X			
Metformin										X		
Methobrexate	X				X					X		
Mineral Oil	X	X	X	X								
Mylanta	X							X				
Mysoline (Primidone)					X							
Neomycin	X	X		X						X		
Ortho-Novum					X				X			
Penicillamine									X			
Phenformin										X		
Phenobarbitol	X	X				X				X		
Prednisone	X		X		X				X			
Premarin	X				X			X	X	X		
Septra (Trimethoprin)			X		X	X	X	X	X	X	X	X
Ser-Ap-E's (Reserpine w/Hydrochlorothiazide)									X			
Solu-Cortef (Hydrocortisone)	X				X				X			
Stelazine (Trifluroperazine)									X			
Tetracycline/Teracyn					X	X						
Triamterene										X		

FOOD AND NUTRITION BOARD, NATIONAL ACADEMY OF SCIENCES-NATIONAL RESEARCH RECOMMENDED DAILY DIETARY ALLOWANCES, Revised 1974

Designed for the maintenance of good nutrition of practically all healthy people in the U.S.A.

Fat-Soluble Vitamins				Water-Soluble Vitamins						
Vitamin A Activity (RE)	(IU)	Vitamin D (IU)	Vitamin E Activity (IU)	Ascorbic Acid (mg)	Folacin (mg)	Niacin (mg)	Riboflavin (mg)	Thiamine (mg)	Vitamin B (mg)	Vitamin B12 (mg)
420	1,400	400	4	35	50	5	0.4	0.3	0.3	0.3
400	2,000	400	5	35	50	8	0.6	0.5	0.4	0.3
400	2,000	400	7	40	100	9	0.8	0.7	0.6	1.0
500	2,500	400	9	40	200	12	1.1	0.9	1.5	
700	3,300	400	10	40	300	16	1.2	1.2	1.2	2.0
1,000	5,000	400	12	45	400	18	1.5	1.4	1.6	3.0
1,000	5,000	400	15	45	400	20	1.8	1.5	2.0	3.0
1,000	5,000	400	15	45	400	20	1.8	1.5	2.0	3.0
1,000	5,000		15	45	400	18	1.6	1.4	2.0	3.0
1,000	5,000		15	45	400	16	1.5	1.2	2.0	3.0
800	4,000	400	12	45	400	16	1.3	1.2	1.6	3.0
800	4,000	400	12	45	400	14	1.4	1.1	2.0	3.0
800	4,000	400	12	45	400	14	1.4	1.1	2.0	3.0
800	4,000		12	45	400	13	1.2	1.0	2.0	3.0
800	4,000		12	45	400	12	1.1	1.0	2.0	3.0
1,000	5,000	400	15	60	800	+ 2	+0.3	+0.3	2.5	4.0
1,200	6,000	400	15	80	600	+ 4	+0.5	+0.3	2.5	4.0

CHAPTER X

IS FASTING SAFE FOR EVERYONE?

Absolutely not!! I have read the labels of various products used in modified fasting and they all list various diseases that exclude certain participants. However, these lists are merely disclaimers so that if someone becomes ill while taking their product, the manufacturer's liability is diminished. Well, we are not only going to tell you which health problems are exclusionary, we are going to tell what can happen to you and why if you decide to forego our demands that you consult your personal physician before going onto a fasting program.

People who absolutely, positively should *not* be on our, or any other, protein-sparing modified fasting program are:

1. Pregnant or lactating women. Both pregnant and breast-feeding ladies should be on relatively high caloric diets. Also, the vitamin intake in most of these fasting supplements is only RDA minimal requirement and, therefore, suboptimal for these women. TOPPFAST™ however, contains a rather unique vitamin mix as discussed in the Vitamin Chapter.

2. Anyone suffering a heart attack within the past year is excluded from fasting. That is not to say that these people should not be on a diet. If a heart attack victim is obese, he or she should be on a restricted diet (example: low calories, low choles-

terol, low sodium diet, like the American Heart Association's). There currently is no data available to suggest that it is potentially life threatening for these patients to fast. However, prudence dictates that it is probably best that these people are given a one year stabilizing period before attempting the fast.

3. People who have suffered a stroke (cerebral vascular accident), or who suffer from TIA's (transient ischemic attacks), should not be on the fast. TIA's are, for the most part, caused by hardening of the arteries in the brain. From time to time there is an insufficient amount of blood in the brain and these people may pass out or simply sit in a stupor for a few seconds or longer. While fasting a person's blood pressure drops rather dramatically thereby increasing the risk of a TIA in those people who are susceptible.

4. Active liver disease (example: cirrhosis, hepatitis): Persons whose livers are damaged or are being damaged do not, among other things, process ingested protein properly. These people may, for example, need to be on a diet consisting of high carbohydrate and low protein, and must not fast.

5. Kidney Disease: One of the first things that can happen in people with kidney damage is impairment of the ability of the kidney to clear potassium from the blood and into the urine. When this happens, the amount of potassium in the blood increases. This increased blood potassium (hyperkalemia) can be very dangerous. Namely, it (high blood potassium) can cause your heart to stop and that's about as serious a complication as you can have.

6. Alcohol or drug addiction within the last two years: Again, the reason is that there may have

been liver or other vital organ damage caused by either the alcohol or drug abuse.

7. Unstable chest pain (angina): Unstable chest pain *may* signify an upcoming cardiac event (heart attack) and the patient should therefore be examined (e.g., treadmill, cardiac cath., etc.) and should not be on the fast.

8. Abnormal heartbeat: This will be covered in more depth in the "Getting Ready To Fast" chapter.

9. People less than eighteen years old: There is an excellent chance that those under the age of 18 have not completed their growth spurt. What would a program of restricted caloric intake like ours do to a young person's growth spurt? I don't know and neither does anyone else, and guess what? None of us want to find out either!

10. People being treated with a "water pill" (diuretic) for the control of high blood pressure. These people must absolutely visit their personal physicians for several reasons, most of which have to do with the amount of potassium in the blood. Most water pills cause the kidney to excrete large amounts of potassium into the urine from the blood. Low blood potassium levels can cause the heart to beat irregularly and, therefore, may be life threatening. Other water pills (e.g., Aldactazide, Dyazide, Aldactone, Midamore, Moduretic, etc.) are potassium sparing. In other words, they cause the kidney to hold on to potassium and thereby can cause the amount of potassium in the blood to increase. Remember what can happen when the blood potassium gets too high? That's right, your heart stops! Seems as if you're damned if you do, but damned if you don't. Not really. I will explain in Chapter 12 about your doctor monitoring patients taking water pills.

11. People being treated with *Lithium*: Lithium is a medication used in depression/manic-depression states. This medication severely depletes the body of salt (sodium) by increasing the amount of salt which is cleared from the blood to the urine by the kidney.

12. People who have had a blood clot either in their legs or their lungs. This is considered to be a relative contraindication. In other words, it could be argued that anyone who has a history of clots should not participate in any program which might make their blood more viscous or thicken (hemo-concentration) and thereby predispose them to develop another clot.

13. People who have high uric acid levels (hyperuricemia) or gout must have their blood checked for uric acid levels before going on the fast and also after fasting for one week. As we discussed in Chapter VIII, the Physiology of Fasting, because of the mild ketosis, uric acid, which competes with ketone bodies for excretion in the urine, *may* increase while fasting. To reiterate, it is not our intention to precipitate either a gout attack or a uric acid kidney stone.

14. People who are being treated for an abnormal heart beat with digitalis. The effect of digitalis is dependent on the amount of blood potassium. If potassium levels decrease, digitalis can *cause* an abnormal, dangerous heart beat.

15. If a person is taking 20 mg. or more per day of *Prednisone*, or its equivalent, they should not be on the fast. Prednisone, and related corticosteroids, at certain doses can cause the breakdown of muscle. These people *may* need to be on a higher protein diet.

16. If a person has had a bleeding peptic ulcer within the past six months, he also should not be on the fast.

17. People who are being treated with insulin.

18. People who are bulimic.

CHAPTER XI

MEDICALLY MONITORED PROTEIN-SPARING MODIFIED FASTING

I have been in the fasting business since June of 1981. I have several thousand patient weeks under my belt—no pun intended. I have seen too many people leave our program because of the expense. I have also seen these patients end up with an over-the-counter preparation that, in my opinion, is neither nutritionally nor medically acceptable.

In our supplement I have added ingredients which are either not available in present products or are, in my opinion, present in quantities that are suboptimal. Many of these ingredients have either been added or increased purely because of my observations of my patients and are, therefore, anecdotal. That is to say, I did not, because of the enormous costs, draw blood and check levels of various substances. I simply observed various side effects and then read about each and its potential causes. I then treated the patients for whatever nutritional deficiency that could cause the side effect.

Let me give you a few examples. We receive at least part of our supply of Biotin, Vitamin K, Niacin and Pantothenic acid from germs within our intestines. These germs feed off the bulk manufactured by various processes following the consumption of *solid food*! As you will soon see, the amount of fecal material produced while on the fast is minimal.

Mentioned in the "Vitamin" chapter, one side effect we have noticed after fasting thousands of patients is temporary hair loss. Biotin is a B-vitamin. A deficiency in this vitamin results in hair loss, a scaly skin rash, muscle weakness and possibly a breakdown in your body's defense system. Simply stated, persons who were Biotin-deficient may not be able to fight off infection effectively. This is why I have added such a large amount (0.3 mg. per day) in TOPPFAST™. Another side effect, anemia, could, either be linked to deficiencies in Vitamin K (decreased red blood cell survival time), Folic acid (inability of the bone marrow to produce new red blood cells) or even B12 (deficiency causes a decrease in red blood cell survival time from 120 days to about 50 days). When people become anemic on our program, I have treated them with combinations of the above vitamins. I have built these vitamins, in what I feel to be the *proper* amounts, into the supplement.

There is also twice the recommended daily requirement of iron in TOPPFAST™. The extra iron was added to prevent the occurrence of iron deficiency anemia that I have seen in some of our patients. The increased amount of iron will turn stools extremely dark—almost black. (By the way, you will be having about one bowel movement or so per week while on the fast, but this does vary from person to person.)

Another well recognized side effect of fasting is easy bruisability. Well, I am here to tell you that bruising is not common when you give larger than RDA recommended doses of Vitamin C each day.

One of the manifestations of Vitamin C deficiency is a decreased strength in the walls of the blood vessel. This results in bleeding under the skin which looks like purple patches.

As you will notice on the packaging, there is a lot of Vitamin A in our supplement. I have noticed that the persisent goosebumps on the sides of the arms and tops of the thighs are decreased with relatively high doses of Vitamin A.

Several hundred women are actually responsible for what makes TOPPFAST™ truly revolutionary. Women who are fasting claim that their menstrual periods are much milder. That is, there is much less cramping, and headaches, but when these same women begin to eat again, their periods again become painful. I would, therefore, prescribe a drug which inhibits a substance (prostaglandin) which is thought to cause all those unpleasant side effects many women experience during their periods. Also, as mentioned above, one of the potential side effects of fasting is temporary hair loss. Initially when women would complain of this phenomenon, I would tell them that at least they would be skinny while they were going bald. I have to admit that as Father Time catches up with me and I am now beginning to lose my hair, I don't find that statement quite so humorous. As previously mentioned, I would treat these people with high dose Biotin and the majority of people would respond to treatment, but some people did not respond. Their hair grew back *only* when they began eating again. Also, there has been a recognized phenomenon seen in many fasting patients that is referred to as a plateau. This is when a person who has been on the fast faithfully, but still needs to lose additional weight, simply stops losing weight. This plateau phenomenon was well discussed in the *Obesity/Bariatric Journal* in 1982. The recommended treatment for the patient who has reached a plateau is the same for the above two problems—linoleic acid which is an essential polyunsaturated fatty acid. Linoleic acid is necessary for the production of prostaglandin which causes the menstrual cramping. One of the side effects of linoleic acid deficiency is hair loss. Those persons who did not respond to Biotin therapy did respond to linoleic acid replacement. When linoleic acid was given to patients who had plateaued, their weight loss increased! In September 1982, it was reported in the *British Medical Journal* that "low dietary intake of linoleic acid predisposes to myocardial infarction"—or a heart attack! I personally am not aware of any other supplement currently available in the open marketplace that has the equivalent amount of linoleic acid that TOPPFAST™ contains. Check the ingredients for either corn or safflower oil which is how linoleic is added to the powder. Be informed, be aware—your life just may depend on it!!!

It has been one of my duties at the clinics to closely monitor the blood potassium levels. When I notice a significant change in blood potassium levels, I immediately notify each patient. In the range of 95% of the patients I have called concerning potassium changes admit to non-compliance. In other words, they do not take the liquid potassium because it tastes bad. So I have put the potassium into the supplement. You do not have to think about taking your daily potassium because, by taking five servings of TOPPFAST™ each day, you will be getting what's considered to be a physio-logically safe dose.

I want to communicate to the public and to the manufacturers of diet products, that fasting patients need *more* vitamins and trace elements than non-fasting persons. Manufacturers cannot merely put a little protein, carbohydrate, fat and the basic RDA vitamin requirements together and *safely fast* people with the resulting product.

CHAPTER XII

GETTING READY TO FAST

The first thing you are to do *before* starting the fast is *go see your personal physician*!!! We must first exclude all the nasty diseases that would exclude you from participating in the fast (reference Chapter X).

Your doctor should first do a thorough physical exam. Secondly, an electrocardiogram should be done to exclude a recent heart attack or a Q-T interval of 0.44 or greater (your doctor will understand this Q-T interval business but, suffice it to say, this Q-T interval prolongation syndrome, is an exclusionary condition). Also, an EKG (electrocardiogram) will identify extra, possibly abnormal heart beats, such as premature ventricular contractions (PVC's). Six or more unifocal PVC's per minute and a 24-hour continuous EKG (Holter Monitor) should be done in order to exclude potentially lethal abnormal heartbeats. If your doctor discovers PVC's that are what we in medicine call multifocal (meaning there are at least two places in your heart which are causing your heart to beat abnormally), you should, *not* be on the fast and a 24-hour EKG tracing should be done. By the way, this 24-hour EKG (Holter Monitor) is just a little tape recorder that is strapped onto your belt for a day, and it records the electrical activity of your heart.

Next, you need to get your blood drawn while you are in a fasting state. This means you must do without food or beverage from 11:00 p.m. until your blood is drawn the next morning.

Lab tests done should include an SMA-20, CBC and T-4. The following is a list of what these tests are and their significance to you.

1. Sodium. This value is the amount of salt that is present in your blood (serum). Unless you are taking a water pill (diuretic) or you have an exotic disease (example: Inappropriate ADH secretion), this value should remain rather constant throughout the fast.

2. Potassium

    a. As previously stated, potassium is an intracellular cation which is essential for muscle and nerve function. Unless you are on a water pill, are vomiting or have diarrhea, are bulimic or have another rather exotic disease such as Bartters Syndrome or Aldosteronism, there should be adequate amounts of potassium in the supplement for you. Remember, both low blood potassium (hypokalemia) and high blood potassium (hyperkalemia) may be lethal.

    b. I know that there are those of you reading this saying, "What if 70 MEq of potassium a day is more than I need?" Well, if you have normal kidneys, you will simply pass the extra potassium in your urine. Later on I will tell you which lab is done to check to make sure that your kidneys are all right.

    c. Clinical findings in persons with high blood potassium (hyperkalemia) are:
        1. Muscle weakness
        2. Diminished sensations (soft touch, pin prick, position and vibratory)

3. Diminished reflexes (example: knee jerk)
4. Sensation of numbness, prickling or tingling
5. Changes on the electrocardiogram (tall T waves, prolonged PR interval, and a widened QRS)
6. Abnormal heart beat (AV, SA and IV blocks)
7. Decreased cardiac output
8. Alkaline urine

d. Clinical findings in persons with low blood potassium (hypokalemia) are:
1. Muscle weakness and/or cramping
2. Decreased blood pressure (hypotension)
3. Metabolic alkalosis
4. Acid urine
5. Changes in the electrocardiogram (broad, flattened T waves, U waves)
6. Abnormal heart beat—namely extra (ectopic) beats and rapid heart beat (tachycardias)
7. Altered consciousness—drowsiness, apathy, lethargy, confusion or depression

3. Chloride (CL). Unless you are on a water pill or have vomiting or diarrhea, this value should remain fairly stable.

4. Bicarbonate (CO_2)

a. This value is important since it is an indication of how acid or alkaline your blood is. After being on the fast for five days, if bicarbonate decreases to a value of 17 or less, you are either not consuming the five servings per day or you need *more* than five servings per day. If the latter is the case you should drink two glasses of skim milk in addition to your five servings each day.

b. Remember when we talked about ketone bodies in the blood? Well, when people are on the fast and their blood bicarbonate decreases, it means that they are more *acidotic*, because they are breaking down too much fat tissue. Therefore, they have too many ketones running around in their blood, competing in the kidney for excretion into the urine. As you now know, too much of this uric acid in your blood can cause gout or a kidney stone.

c. I want all of you to go to your local pharmacy and buy a bottle of LABSTIX. This bottle will contain 100 plastic strips which have five colored little pieces of paper attached. We are most interested in the second piece of paper in from the end of the plastic stick. These are to be used to check your urine for ketones. Never check your first urine of the day since it is more concentrated and therefore may show a false elevation of ketones. Meanwhile, soak the five pieces of paper in urine. This process is easy for men; however, women have to catch a little of their urine in a container first and then dipstick it. However, some of you women may feel that you are good enough shots . . . well, whatever. After soaking the dipstick in urine, if the color on the second piece of paper matches color with either "trace" or "small" on the LABSTIX bottle, everything is all right. However, if the color of the paper matches with the color indicated to be "moderate" on the bottle, probably your urine is concentrated because you are not drinking enough water. To correct this condition increase the amount of fluids you drink each day. If your urine dipstick matches with the color indicated "large," you must do two things. First, you must increase the amount of fluids you drink by at least one quart. After increasing your water intake for a few days, if your urine still checks out to be "large" in ketones we must consider increasing your caloric intake by mixing your supplement with eight ounces of skim milk, instead of with water or diet soda.

5. Blood sugar or Glucose

A blood test should be done in order to find out the amount of sugar you have in your blood.

a. If your blood sugar is too high (diabetes) it will decrease dramatically while on the fast. If you are on insulin or an oral hypoglycemic agent, talk with your doctor about the dosages of each. Remember, if you happen to be a juvenile diabetic, you should not be on the fast.

b. If your blood sugar is too low (hypoglycemia) it is imperative that you space out your supplement equally. You might take one supplement at 8:00 a.m., the second at 11:00 a.m., the third at 2:00 p.m., the fourth at 5:00 p.m., and the fifth supplement at 8:00 p.m. If you take two servings of supplement at one time, your blood sugar may rise quickly. When the pancreas senses the increase in blood sugar, it secretes a large amount of insulin which, in turn, rapidly decreases blood sugar. This swing from an elevated to a diminished blood sugar is not healthy. People experiencing these swings complain of headache, shakiness, irritability, hunger, blurred vision, sweating, and even of rapid heart beat—all signs of hypoglycemia.

6. Liver Function Tests (SGOT, SGPT, LDH, Alkaline Phosphatase)

Liver function tests are done in order to rule out liver diseases such as hepatitis and cirrhosis. If you have liver disease you should not be on the fast. After being on the fast for five days, test values for liver enzymes may increase a bit. This increase is an expected phenomenon: it does not mean you have a liver disease.

7. Uric Acid

This test is done to make sure you do not have gout or are not at risk for having a gout attack. This test, along with the others, must be repeated in five days. If results remain elevated, increase the amount of fluids you are consuming each day and then buy a bottle of LABSTIX. Next, follow the directions outlined in number 4, Bicarbonate (CO_2). If, after following these steps, your uric acid is still elevated, your doctor will have to give you a medicine to prevent a gout attack while you are on the diet.

8. Protein/Albumin

These two tests give us an indication of your state of nutrition. Also it gives us another look at how well your liver works.

9. Cholesterol/Triglycerides

Roughly, these tell us how much fat you have in your blood. Triglycerides will decrease dramatically while you are fasting. Cholesterol levels will also decrease but not as dramatically as triglyceride levels. As previously stated, high blood cholesterol levels have long been recognized by most of the medical community to be a risk factor associated with heart disease.

10. Calcium/Phosphorous

Both are minerals that we measure in the blood. High calcium levels increase the risk of developing a kidney stone. The ratio between calcium and phosphorous can sometimes help to determine the cause of elevated calcium levels. Neither of these values would change significantly while a person is on the fast.

11. Complete blood count (CBC) with indices.

a. A CBC tells us how many red and white blood cells you have. Also, if you are anemic, we can narrow down the potential causes of the anemia.

b. Your hematocrit (HCT), which is a percentage of red blood cells, is a part of the CBC. If it is low, you are considered anemic. As Co-Medical Director of the Orange County RFO Medical Group, I saw many people become anemic while on the fast. It was this "fasting anemia" which began my research into what I feel to be the building of a better mouse trap (e.g., a new supplement). With the exception of menstruating females, your hematocrit should not decrease significantly while on the fast.

12. Thyroxine (T4). Thyroxine is a hormone secreted by the thyroid gland.

a. If there is too much thyroxine in the blood, a person is considered to be hyperthyroid. These people complain of diarrhea, nervousness, insomnia, and of being warm when others around them consider the surroundings to be comfortable. Their pulse tends to be fast and their knee jerk reflex tends to be brisk.

b. A low thyroxine level indicates a person is hypothyroid. These people complain of always being tired and cold. They also may be constipated and have difficulty concentrating; and body temperature and pulse rate are frequently subnormal. Finally, their knee reflex is either diminished or absent.

13. Blood Urea Nitrogen (BUN)

BUN is a by product of protein metabolism and, therefore, affords us some measure of a persons daily protein consumption. It is also helpful in determining whether a person is dehydrated. You see if a person has not consumed a proper quantity of fluids and becomes dehydrated, BUN will increase in the blood. Also, BUN INCREASES IF A PERSON HAS KIDNEY DAMAGE.

14. Creatinine

a. Creatinine, simply stated, is a by-product of muscle metabolism. Therefore, a 250-pound construction worker will have more creatinine than a 120-pound woman who lives a rather sedentary life style because the construction worker has more muscle tissue.

b. Creatinine, because it is neither secreted nor absorbed by the kidneys, is a good indicator of kidney function. If your kidneys are malfunctioning, your blood creatinine as well as BUN will be increased. If the creatinine in the blood is elevated to greater than 1.5, a 24-hour urine collection must be done to calculate your *creatinine clearance*. The elevated value is a sensitive indicator of kidney function. Of course, if your creatinine clearance reveals kidney damage, you should *not* be on the fast.

If your physical exam, EKG and blood test results are all within normal limits, you are ready to begin the fast!

CHAPTER XIII

BEGINNING THE FAST

There are some basic rules you must follow while on the program. First, you must take at least five servings per day if you are on the full fast. If you are eating one meal a day, take only three servings each day. In both cases, space the servings out every two or three hours. Mix the powder in either ice-cold water or diet soda. Add 6 to 8 ounces of liquid depending on the consistency you prefer. Second, drink at least ten eight-ounce glasses of distilled water each day. Distilled water has minimal amounts of salt in it compared to tap water or bottled water. Do not drink caffeinated coffee or regular or herbal tea while on the fast because both of these drinks contain substances which act as a diuretic. In other words, these substances cause you to make more urine. Speaking of diuretics or water pills, at the Orange County RFO Medical Group, all our patients stop their water pills when they begin the fast. The reason is that while on the fast you will be in a state of natural diuresis, a medical way to say that you will urinate a lot. If you continue to take water pills, depending on which water pill you are taking, your potassium levels can either decrease or increase tremendously. (Now do you see why I want you to visit your doctor?)

While on the fast you *may* have a few side effects. Most problems have been covered. However, there are some conditions we need to talk about. You will get bad breath. I'm talking here about breath that's been known to stop speeding trucks at fifty paces. You are allowed to chew five pieces of sugarless gum each day, but watch out for gum which contains sorbitol. Too much sorbitol can give you wicked diarrhea.

While fasting, stand up slowly or you may get light headed. If you get light headed even when you stand up slowly, get your blood pressure and pulse checked. If your blood pressure has dropped significantly—more than 15 points—and your pulse has increased significantly—more than 10 per minute—you are hypotensive and need fluids and some salt. Weight Watchers makes boullion cubes which are inexpensive and easy to prepare. Simply heat a cup of water and drop in a cube. After drinking the boullion, drink two ten-ounce glasses of water.

I would prefer that you do minimal amounts of exercise for the first five days that you are fasting. After that, you can build up your exercise program— slowly! Also, no jacuzzies, saunas, or steam baths for at least the first five days! I can just hear all the moans and groans from the Californians. The reason is when you first begin the fast, you lose tremendous amounts of fluids and you become what we in medicine refer to as volume depleted. This means that there is a decreased amount of fluid in your veins and arteries, because while fasting you have passed the excess fluid into your urine. When we get into a jacuzzi, sauna or a steam bath, our bodies react by *vasodilating* or increasing the size of our blood vessels in our skin. This vasodilation transiently decreases our already decreased blood pressure and we can pass out. What do you think would happen to you if you passed out in a jacuzzi alone?

After five days of fasting, return to your doctor. Have him or her check your blood pressure and pulse and compare these readings with the readings done prior to starting the fast. Also, have your physician repeat the SMA-20 blood test and again make comparisons.

The only problem we have encountered in our experience with fasters is occasional patient non-compliance. For example, some people think that if they can lose five pounds in five days taking five servings of TOPPFAST™ each day—just think how they could lose taking four servings each day! First of all, by shorting yourself one serving each day (120 calories), you are increasing your weight loss by about 1/6 of a pound over a five day period. You will learn how to make this computation later on in the book, but for now, trust me; it's only about 1/6 of a pound difference per week. Also, if you decrease your intake to less than five servings each day you are now not getting enough protein, fat, carbohydrate, vitamins, trace minerals and most importantly, potassium. And what can happen if you do not get enough potassium? That's right—blood potassium levels can decrease and a dangerous abnormal heart beat may follow. If you are not eating and are, therefore, consuming only TOPPFAST™ —*TAKE ALL FIVE SERVINGS EACH DAY!!!!*

If you run out of supplement or it is unavailable for a day use this Emergency Diet.

EMERGENCY DIET

In lieu of *each* serving of TOPPFAST™:

A. 12 oz. skim milk, *or*

B. *2 oz. chicken or turkey or* lean meat (prepared without fat)
   plus 4 oz. orange *or* pineapple *or* grapefruit juice
   or 2 oz. regular coke *or* gingerale,
   or

C. ½ cup cottage cheese
   plus 4 oz. orange *or* pineapple *or* grapefruit juice
   or 2 oz. regular coke *or* gingerale,
   or

D. 1 egg
   plus 4 oz. orange *or* pineapple *or* grapefruit juice
   or 2 oz. regular coke *or* gingerale

MEDICATIONS

If the following medications are needed, they may be taken for minor complaints. If the symptoms continue, your family physician should be notified.

HEADACHE or Mild Pain elsewhere:
   2—Tylenol—up to four times per day
   1—Darvocet N—up to three times per day
   1—Darvon (plain not compound)—up to three times per day
COLDS:
   Nose drops (unless hypertensive) use as label directs

Dimacol—for cough
Antihistamines—up to two per day
CONSTIPATION which is causing discomfort:
Milk of Magnesia—2 tablespoons for two consecutive nights
Dulcolax suppository
Glycerine suppository
Maalox—four tablespoons
DIARRHEA:
Kaopectate—as directed on label
INDIGESTION OR HEARTBURN:
Mylanta
Maalox
Gelusil ⎤ Two tablespoons up to six times per day
Riopan
GAS:
Di-Gel—as directed on label
Metumucil Powder—as directed on label
HEMORRHOIDS:
Tucks
Nupercainal Ointment
Sitz Bath
STOOL SOFTENER:
Colase 100 mg.—up to two per day
ANTIBIOTICS:
NO Tetracycline
NO Cholramphenicol
NO Clindomycin (Cleocin)
NONE OF THE FOLLOWING ARE TO BE TAKEN WHEN ON THE FAST:
Tranquilizers
Sleeping Pills
Aspirin
Diuretics
Emetics

Enemas
Cortisone, Prednisone or related drugs
Alcohol
Caffienated Coffee
Regular or Herbal Tea
Cocaine
Marijuana
Digitalis

HERE IS A QUICK SUMMARY OF STEPS TO FOLLOW BEFORE AND DURING YOUR FAST:

1. Before you start the fast go to your physician and have the following done:
   A. Physical exam
   B. EKG
   C. SMA-20, CBC, T-4
2. While fasting follow these rules:
   A. Consume five servings per day, space the feedings 2-3 hours apart.
   B. Mix the supplement in either ice cold water or diet soda.
   C. In addition to the fluid used to mix the supplement, drink eight ten-ounces glasses of distilled water each day.
   D. Dipstick your urine for ketones at about 11:00 a.m. or later each day for the first few days on the fast.
3. After five days of fasting do the following:
   See your physician and have your blood pressure, pulse and an SMA-20 repeated. If there have been any significant changes in either your vital signs (blood pressure, pulse or SMA-20) your physician may want to see you again.

DR. SCHRAMM:
During your five days on the fast you will lose a lot of weight. Most of this weight is from the large

amounts of water lost while your body adjusts to a fasting state. After this initial water loss, your weight loss should be more predictable. This loss can actually be predicted by doing a few simple math computations. Men burn about twelve calories per pound each day, women about eleven calories per pound each day. See chart:

CALORIES NEEDED TO MAINTAIN A WEIGHT

Male	Female
250 pounds	200 pounds
×12 calories/pound	×11 calories/pound
3,000 calories needed each day to maintain 250 pounds	2,200 calories needed each day to maintain 200 pounds

In order to lose one pound of fat, you must deficit 3,500 calories less than your basal metabolic rate (BMR) calories. Let's go back to our 250-pound man who needs 3,000 calories (250 × 12) each day to maintain his 250 pounds. In one week this 250-pound man will, in order to maintain his present weight, consume 21,000 calories (3,000 calories × 7 days). In order for this man to lose one pound in a week, he would either have to eat 3,500 less calories (21,000 − 3,500 = 17,500) or expend 3,500 exercise calories or a combination of decreasing caloric intake while increasing exercise (example: 2,000 calories + 1,500 exercise calories = 3,500 calories).

There are 120 calories in each serving of TOPP-FAST™. You will be taking at least five servings each day, or 600 calories (5 × 120 = 600 calories). We are now armed with all the ammunition we need to figure out approximately how much weight you should lose. As you now are aware, a 250-pound man needs 3,000 calories (250 pounds × 12 calories/pound) to maintain his 250 pounds. If he were taking TOPPFAST™ only, how many pounds could he expect to lose in one week? Well, let's see if we can figure it out.

250-pound man consuming 5 servings (600 calories) of TOPPFAST™ each day:

250	pounds
X12	calories/pound/day
3,000	calories/day to maintain
—600	calories-amount of calories per day in TOPPFAST™
2,400	deficited calories each day
X5	number of days in each week
12,000	total amount of calories deficited in one week

Now all we have to do is divide the total amount of calories deficited in one week (12,000 calories) by the amount of calories you need to deficit in order to lose one pound (3,500).

3.4 pounds loss

$$3,500 \overline{\smash{\big)}\ 12,000}$$

In other words, a 250-pound man who consumes 600 calories in the form of TOPPFAST™ could expect to lose 3.4 pounds in five days.

Now I want you to figure out how much weight a 220-pound woman should lose if she is on TOPPFAST™. Remember, multiply by eleven for women. After you have figured it out, refer to the answer later in this chapter.

There are four factors that can cause weight lose fluctuations due to water retention and you should take them into consideration when you figure your own weight loss computation:

1. *Carbohydrates*—Carbohydrates act like magnets for water, and at 8 pounds per gallon of water weight, large weight fluctuations can take place if you eat carbohydrates while you are on the fast.

2. *Salt*—Both table salt and sodium used in processed foods can cause an increase in fluid in the body and again cause varied fluctuations in your weight. While five diet sodas are the usual maximum while you are fasting, if you are losing at a rate slower than predicted by your own computations you might consider cutting back on the diet drinks. Distilled water tends to be better than tap water because it doesn't have sodium in it. If your tap water comes from a water softener it will be very high in sodium and you should switch to distilled water.

3. *Changes in Physical Activity*—Muscle requires more water to metabolize protein for energy so increases or decreases in exercise or physical activity can cause temporary water fluctuations. Of course, it is better to continue the exercise and understand that your weight will vary.

4. *Hormonal*—Both men and women can have periodic hormonal changes that cause the body to retain water. These are extremely individualized and often change from month to month.

Whenever your actual weight loss differs from your expected weight loss, you need to be able to understand the role that the above four factors have on weekly and even daily weight changes. These factors are equally important later on as you learn to balance your eating and exercising to maintain your weight.

Expected weight loss for 220-pound female consuming 5 servings (600) calories each day:

```
  220- pounds
  X11  calories/pound/day
─────
2,420  calories/day
 —600  calories-amount of calories per day in
       TOPPFAST™
─────
1,820  amount of deficited calories each day
   X5
─────
9,100  total amount of calories deficited in one
       week
```

$$\begin{array}{r}\underline{2.6 \text{ pound loss}} \\ 3,500 \overline{\smash{\big)}\,9,100}\end{array}$$

Again, a 220-pound woman can expect to lose 2.6 pounds in five days.

THE PSYCHOLOGICAL SIDE
Alan T. Schramm, Ph.D.

CHAPTER XIV

WHY ARE WE OBESE?

That's an easy question to answer. People who are obese eat more calories than they expend. Period. The body is the ultimate calorie counter and, believe me, it doesn't miss a single calorie, whether it's in a sliver of carrot cake or a dribble of booze. What goes in is counted.

How has obesity become the number one health hazard since 1900? Three reasons become obvious as we look at the changes that have taken place in the United States since the turn of the century.

First, our diet has changed radically. Forget any of the other nonsense you've heard. We eat about 30% more fat in our diets than we did in 1900. Why would this be the basis of the problem of obesity? Because there are more calories in fat than there are in proteins and carbohydrates. Fats contain 9 calories per gram. Proteins and carbohydrates have only 4 calories per gram. How often have you heard that it was the carbohydrates that were causing the problem? Not so.

As our diets increased in fat, mostly due to our own industriousness, so have the calories in our diets. A chicken in 1900 had only 10% fat. Today's chicken contains up to 20% fat, and it may not have even touched the ground at our modern and efficient chicken farms.

Second, food is cheaper. The production and preparation of food for the average family in 1900 cost over a third of their income. Today it is less than 15%. With today's smaller families and abundance of food available it is far less a burden to provide food for our tables. Food is out there, it's everywhere. It's fattening food, prepared food. Every corner of every street seems to have a fast food joint or a convenience food market vying for our business. And we give it to them. We meet our friends for breakfast. We have luncheon meetings and we take our wives to dinner. Sunday morning means brunch with the Elwell's, Wednesday evenings it's ON TV at the Landerman's house. We are a food oriented society, and we love every minute of it. An important point that we will cover later in the book is the fact that we probably won't change the living style we adhere to now. And that's okay.

The third reason that we differ from our turn-of-the-century ancestors is related to the amount of calories that we expend. Since weight is put on the body by ingesting calories in excess of the ones required to "fuel" the body, it stands to reason that calories can also be "used up" or expended when the body is functioning at an energy level above that required to roll one's eyeballs.

In 1900, people used their bodies more. There weren't any cars. There weren't any elevators. People walked to school, to work, to church and to the market. It's estimated by the Department of Agriculture that it took a woman about 2 hours to prepare a dinner for her family of six people in 1900. No frozen foods. No microwave ovens. No electric can openers, mixers, frypans or food processors. She had to chop the wood, dress the chicken, milk the cow, and bake the bread. And if she ran out of salt, sugar, or flour, she ran down the stairs, up the street and probably to one or two different shops to fetch them.

The estimate is that a 120-pound woman in 1900 required about 2,000 calories each day to maintain her body weight with all of the physical activity she was required to perform. Today, that same 120-pound woman, with her less active lifestyle needs only about 1,300 calories each day to maintain her size 9 Gucci figure. You needn't be a mathematician to figure out that it's a lot easier to weigh 120 when you're eating 2,000 calories each day as opposed to 1,300 calories a day.

Americans always seem to want to blame their overweight condition on anything other than the fact that they eat more calories than their body expends. They love to blame the genes passed down to them from their fat Aunt Wanda. Or the influence of having been "forced" to eat their grandmother's special peanut butter cookies when they were six. My favorite excuse was to tell everyone that my parents always made me join the "Clean Plate Club." I used to think of myself as a charter member.

At my grandfather's house I was always reminded about not wasting food because of the "starving children in Armenia." (I would have gladly shared my brussels sprouts with them!) Then, in the Marine Corps I used to hear the phrase "take all you want, but eat all you take." Cafeteria lines have always been tough for me! Sorry to disappoint you, but heredity isn't the problem; it's the excess calories.

How many people have an overweight friend who has a metabolism problem? Frank has told you that's probably not so. Metabolic problems related to obesity amount to only about 2 or 3 percent of the cases. The basic problem most of our patients have is eating too many calories and not doing enough activity.

Half the obese people say they overeat because they're depressed; the other half say they overeat because they're anxious. If depression and anxiety caused obesity, there wouldn't be any thin people because we all have these feelings. People have always had these feelings, but they weren't obese.

We haven't changed as a people, but certain things in our environment and culture have changed. If we choose to be thin in this modern and complicated society, we must acquire the skills to achieve that goal. The purpose of this book is to help you learn these skills.

CHAPTER XV

THE DISMAL FAILURE OF MOST DIET PLANS

Look at the bookcases in the homes of your friends and you will most likely see the sign of the times. Diet books. Not one or two, more like 10 or 12. They're the annual editions of past holiday resolutions in every color, shape and size, just like the people who write and read them. You see, we're just like the books, all different, and that's why it's difficult to find a single diet or plan that can be universally applied to every person. Most people fail in their attempts to follow another person's diet because dieting is a very individual matter.

Diet and weight loss programs have a pretty dismal record when it comes to long-term success. In fact, more than 90% of all persons who lose weight on any kind of diet program put on at least as much as they lost within a year or two. The main fact is that fewer than 50% of all people who try to diet can lose even 10 pounds.

When the published studies are looked at, it gets even more depressing. The average reported weight loss in the literature is about 11 pounds, and the average time the subjects remained on the various diets was 14 days. Moreover, only about 5 percent of all enrolled in weight loss programs lose 40 or more pounds. Even worse, only about 5-10 percent of *the population who want to lose weight actually lose that weight and then keep it off a minimum of one year.* That kind of data is tough to digest when you see a weight loss clinic on every corner.

Even the one million or so people who participate each week in the fine self-help weight reduction programs like Weight Watchers and Take Off Pounds Sensibly (TOPS) have a difficult time. These programs are usually most successful with helping people who have less than thirty pounds to lose. They tend to have a very high attrition rate, usually between 30% and 70% within three to six months. In addition, more than half of the participants in these self-help groups had previously joined and dropped out of the same group an average of three times. These programs often fail because most people with a weight problem discriminate only between overeating and dieting. They are able to discipline themselves for short periods of time in order to adhere to a diet. They can actually lose weight, but after the diet is over, they return to their "normal" eating habits and behaviors, and they regain the weight they had lost. The diet did not *teach* them anything about *balanced eating* and *learning the procedures* that control and balance periods of overeating with specific undereating and exercise strategies.

Our research seems to have uncovered some important facts while we worked with obese patients using a protocol of five days fasting and two days eating at maintenance calories: first, patients were able to follow the diet for periods of four weeks or longer, and second, they were able to establish a history of successful maintenance eating along with calorie problem solving and record keeping during the weekend eating. Basically, they were able to adhere to a weekday diet plan with planned sensible maintenance eating on weekends for periods of time that were much longer than the average 14 day periods reported in most weight loss programs. They also lost significant weight.

Traditional diets are very rigid and do not allow for individual differences related to lifestyle, occupation and individual strengths and weaknesses. We intend to teach you how to identify your own successful eating and exercise behaviors. We will also suggest how you can add new strategies to help replace behaviors that have caused problems in the past, such as binging, problem foods, holiday weight gains, and unplanned eating. Remember: long-term permanent weight control is only possible by making some changes in your eating and exercise behavior.

The nice thing about this program is that it doesn't really attack your lifestyle. It gives you the tools to make the choices that let you lose the weight and—more importantly—keep it off.

CHAPTER XVI

WHY OUR PROGRAM SUCCEEDS

Since 1978, the *Journal of American Medical Association* (JAMA) has noted the protein sparing modified fast as the state of the art treatment for obesity. Fasting has long been used as a means of cleansing the body and soul, but long-term fasting for weight loss has only been available since Dr. Vertes began his research in the late 1960's.

After looking at the accumulated data from thousands of fasting patients we got smarter on how to treat obesity in a safe, effective way. But as Frank has pointed out, the tremendous success of the fast did not serve as a *cure* for obesity. We started seeing people who had lost 50, 100, 150 pounds coming back six months or a year later with that amount and more put back on. Some were angry; some were depressed, but all who returned seemed determined to find a way to keep the weight off.

Consequently, in 1981, we implemented a long-term behavioral program to assist people with long-term weight maintenance. We saw promising results from this program. We felt hindered, however, because our eighteen-month maintenance program seemed to have such limited applicability for reaching the thousands of obese people who could not afford to participate in our medically-supervised fasting program.

We surveyed hundreds of patients who had fasted to goal weight, and looked at the changes that they had been able to make in their life styles that help them maintain their weight loss. We isolated the behavior that helped them accomplish long-term weight maintenance. This behavior turned out to be self-management skills resulting in successful weight maintenance.

Why not write a book teaching these simple skills? With these skills, along with a safe diet supplement, we could open the door to a world of fast weight loss *plus* long-term weight maintenance to everyone who needed it! And here it is.

The next few chapters will describe these skills. Read them. Think about them. Chapter XXV—Procedures for Success—is the "how to" chapter. It puts all the self-management skills together and gives you the simple tools you'll need to make it all work for you.

The Self Management Skills:
1. Confrontation and record keeping
2. Avoidance of failure
3. Breaking the anxiety cycle
4. Environmental management
5. Problem solving portion size and food choices
6. Knowing nutrition
7. Calories count—in
8. Exercise calories—out
9. Procedures for success

One final word before we get into the skills. That word is COMMITMENT. Commitment is the key that unlocks the door to success for both fasting and long-term weight maintenance. You must be committed to making a conscious daily effort to stay on the fast. While fasting during each week, you must commit yourself to learn the calorie values of the various food groups, to measure portion sizes, and be able to implement certain procedures that will insure your success on weekends and after you reach goal weight. In other words, you must be willing to make this entire program—fasting and maintenance—*priority one* in your life!

When you do commit, a new world of comfort, attractiveness, sexuality, health, longer life, confidence, pride, and sense of personal achievement will be yours.

CHAPTER XVII

CONFRONTATION AND RECORDKEEPING

One of our successful maintenance people said the word *confrontation* was the real key to his success. Confrontation means coming face to face with the problem. If you want to be thin, you will have to learn to confront your weight, not each holiday season, or on your birthday, but each and every day of the week.

Confrontation is a word that most obese people attempt to avoid. For some people, success will be helped along immeasurably by simply being able to confront the word *confrontation*. To succeed in weight maintenance, your most valuable tools will be your bathroom scale and your records. For some people it might also be looking in a mirror, or fitting into a pair of pants or a favorite new dress. Each time you learn to face your weight problem, it will lead to higher levels of confrontation.

Confrontation must be combined with some simple record keeping. Simple, yes, but absolutely essential. *Record keeping is the link that ties all the areas together.* Getting on the scale and recording your weight each day will be your own guarantee for success.

The use of the Calorie Tally Sheet and food records (Appendices 4 & 5) allows you to shift your attention to manageable tasks. By recording your weight, food, and exercise totals each day you eat you begin to hold yourself accountable. No judgments. "Even though I ate the pound of candy during the past week I kept accurate food records. I increased my exercise and I was able to lose a pound." You will be able to measure your own success. Daily.

By keeping food records you will learn calorie values, but you will also learn to problem solve and estimate portion sizes. Food records help you learn by doing, the most effective kind of learning. You give yourself instant feedback as you figure the calories, portion sizes, and weights of your food.

Moreover, you'll confront the types of food that you eat. It's difficult to ignore the calories for the six cups of ice cream if it's written down immediately. Without record keeping the ice cream might never have been remembered or remembered as a small dish. Tomorrow morning you might question whether you only dreamed about ice cream. That's called food amnesia. By recording the totals for food and exercise on the same sheet you will be able to see how the two totals can be used to "balance the book."

Remember, the bottom line is calories *in* versus calories *out*. For example, a 6,000-calorie surplus, earned by deficiting and by exercising, can help when you attend your cousin's wedding next week. Conversely, an excess of food calories for the week can be steadily reduced by small increases in daily exercise.

The use of food records also allows you to confront the calories. There truly are no "good" or "bad" foods—only calorie totals. No forbidden foods. No need for excuses like "the devil made me do it!" You are a part of a system that works. Overeating is not failure. Each week your records will lead to increased awareness that eventually leads to long-term calorie balancing. Use these tools to promote long-term planning and to assess your progress each day. A ten-pound weight gain can be translated into objective terms—calories—not into depressing emotions.

You will also be able to face the constant water fluctuations that cause varied but temporary weight shifts. The types of foods that cause these shifts are identified in this book. With knowledge, you will be better prepared to understand and control future fluctuations.

The great part of this program is that a backslide can now be looked at as only temporary and need not lead you into failure. Because you will be able to confront the problem, take action and move on toward your goal; you will not have to feel guilty.

Most importantly, these daily confrontations with the scale, the food calories and exercise totals will be cumulative. The more you confront, the more skilled you will become in self management of weight loss.

CHAPTER XVIII

FAILURE AND THE AVOIDANCE OF IT

For years obese people have learned to build up whole systems of avoidance responses for their failure. "I have a different metabolism," or "my parents made me clean my plate."

You cannot fail on this program because the standards and procedures you select for yourself will be yours alone—they will *work* for you. You will no longer have to use the excuses and rationalizations of the past. "I'll start my diet tomorrow"; "I'll wait until I'm over 200, or 300, or 400 pounds"; "I'll wait until after the holidays."

In this program, ten ounces of fudge becomes 1,150 calories. With a few undereating strategies during the week and an extra effort on the morning walk, you can soon see how the number 1,150 can become 1,000, then 900, then 600. Decreasing steadily until you have balanced the excess. As soon as the food items are turned into a number, you can begin to realize why this system has worked for so many people. Numbers are real. They are not emotional. Fudge causes anxiety; whereas the number 1,150 triggers a rational response followed by successful compensating strategies.

By setting some realistic goals you will be programming yourself for success. Remember, *this is a long-term intensive self-management program* and your own success depends greatly upon your willingness to use the tools that have worked for others. In order to succeed, you will have to develop your own individual style, one that will easily fit into your current life style. What does this mean? Once on maintenance, each episode of overeating or binging must be looked upon as a challenge to learn to find realistic ways to overcome its effects.

You will have to learn to set specific goals for achieving your success. Then you will need to define the exact procedures that you will use to reach your goal. For example, "I will not eat donuts" is *not* a procedure; driving home by a route that doesn't take you by the donut shop is. "I will lose the extra ten pounds before Thanksgiving" is *not* a procedure; undereating an extra day each week to save 1,000 calories *is*. "I'll work out at the spa tomorrow" is not a procedure; adding a mile to your walking route is a procedure. *Procedures* allow you to deficit excess calories.

If anything is wrong with the fasting method of weight loss, it is you lose the weight so fast you are tempted not to get serious about learning how to keep the weight off. Practicing the procedures for success help you develop the program that is right for you. Whenever someone tells me they have "cheated" and feel like a failure I know they have confronted the situation, and they are now one step closer to succeeding. If this program were easy, there would not have been any reason for us to write this book. If you falter a bit either during the fasting phase or on maintenance, reread this chapter and figure out which tool you are going to use to get back on the road to success.

CHAPTER XIX

THE ANXIETY CYCLE AND HOW TO BREAK IT

Most obese people have experienced years of failure in controlling their eating behavior. Consequently, they expect to fail when they diet. Anxiety related to feelings of failure tends to drive them further and further from success. Even worse, feelings of failure might then lead to overeating. By becoming aware of these overeating situations, and then converting them into numbers of calories, we can translate them into a workable and easily defined system in which excessive calories can be balanced out.

Record keeping, for example, will lower your anxiety by turning the emotional issues of weight fluctuations into the objective, rational terms of numbers and calories. It becomes a learned skill.

For people who have fought the battle of the bulge for years even normal eating situations can trigger feelings of anxiety and failure. Various food cues such as eating at a birthday celebration, or rewarding yourself for receiving a promotion at work can lead the formerly obese person back to old patterns of uncontrolled eating or binging behavior. Failure to learn new strategies for dealing with these events can lead to increased anxiety when they are present. We call it the anxiety cycle.

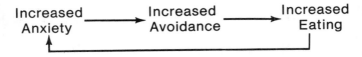

Increased Anxiety → Increased Avoidance → Increased Eating

Any increased anxiety about food triggers more anxiety which in turn leads to all of the old short term avoidance behaviors.

How long can you avoid the cookies in your cupboard you are saving in case the grandchildren drop in? (They probably live in another state!) Or the leftovers you saved for the dog you're going to get next Christmas? Avoidance is strictly short term and it always leads to eating, which then creates more anxiety, starting the cycle all over again. The rule is, if the food is in the house or car or bag, it will be eaten. No exceptions.

To break the cycle, we have to identify when overeating happens. This is where the tools of confrontation through record keeping become important aids to intervention. As you walk into a donut shop to "look around," you will decrease your anxiety by saying to yourself, "I'll only buy one or two things," or "I'll buy a dozen, since I'll get the discount, and then I'll give the extras to my neighbor." If the "extras" end up on your food records, it will not indicate a failure, but rather an opportunity to use some other self-management tools like writing the food calories down within fifteen minutes, and learning to manage your environment more effectively.

The key to learning and understanding how to break this cycle is to replace it with the long-term procedures of problem solving and calorie balancing. *You will overeat*, but now you can devise strategies that allow you to accept and deal with the overeating. Now, weight gains can be short-term gains that can and will be balanced out over a long period of time. Just as you had a lifetime to put on the weight, you will now learn to take the attitude that you have a long time to practice weight maintenance.

Increased awareness helps to break up the situations and circumstances that led to your overeating in the past. Now, you have a system that works. As you become proficient in practicing your own maintenance program, as you see it work for you, you will gain control over the anxiety cycle. Experience and confidence will turn anxiety and failure into success.

Frequently I heard people say, "I'm into failure." When I ask, "What are you going to do about it?", they dig into their box of tools and use the ones that have previously worked for them and for countless others who have learned to turn their anxiety into confident and demonstrated success.

CHAPTER XX

CALORIES COUNT AND HOW
TO PROBLEM SOLVE THEM

The techniques of problem solving are relatively simple. Basically, we have condensed the 300-page United States Department of Agriculture, *Nutritive Value of American Foods, Handbook* #456 into nine pages of calorie charts, a fairly efficient coup, Appendix 2.

Each chart covers a specific type of food such as meat, vegetables, fruits, or grains. It is not our intent to provide a "listing" of every food available to the consumer. Instead, we would like to provide a series of calorie guidelines that can be used to problem solve food items in a way that can be adapted easily to the varied life styles of the general public. We don't want to change your individual eating styles; we do want to teach you proven strategies that you will adapt to your own lifestyle.

You will not find lists of forbidden foods. Those have been left in Eden. There are no "good" or "bad" foods, no pages of "low calorie" recipes that seem to pad the typical diet book. Each one of these procedures has been instrumental in helping thousands of people implement their own long-term weight maintenance program. Which ones will you use? One to start. More as you become comfortable with your own program.

You must study the calorie charts found in Appendix 2. Each chart is set up in the same manner with lowest calorie foods listed on the bottom left of the page, higher calorie foods on the top right. As the food items move from left to right and bottom to top, they are gradually increasing in calories, usually because of an increase in fat or sugar content.

Note the unit of measure that is used for each page. The meat, grain, fruit, vegetable and dairy pages are measured in *ounces*. The condiment page is measured by level *tablespoons*. Beverages are measured by the *eight ounce cup*. Alcoholic beverages are listed by the *fluid ounce*. A prepared recipe page has been provided with a varied sampling of food items measured by the *eight ounce volume cup*.

Each page has the range of calories noted along the bottom of the chart and some of the charts have amplifying notes to explain any exceptions to the rules.

MEAT PAGE

On the meat page, a few points might require additional explanation. Any meat listed that has a dot under it can generally be considered as possessing very little variation in calorie content. However, if the meat has a dot with a line through it, it may be assumed that there is a significant calorie range for that meat, again, mostly due to higher fat content. Chicken, for example, has a range of about 35 to 65 calories per ounce. That can be interpreted as running from light meat without skin at 35 to dark meat with skin at 65. Likewise, hamburger has a range of about 75 to 100 calories per ounce for very lean meat at 75 to the less expensive ground meat with a higher fat content at 100. The general rule seems to be the darker the meat, the higher the calories, or the more slippery it looks, the more calories it has.

All meats are figured at raw weight, except for bacon which is 175 calories raw but for convenience is listed at about 90 calories per ounce, cooked crisp, unless you want a tapeworm for a partner! You might want to do a little experimenting by measuring various portions at 2, 4 or 6 ounce raw weights. Then cook them so you can see the finished product as it might appear on your plate in a restaurant or at your neighbor's home—situations where weighing your food would be inconvenient or rude to say the least!

A rule of thumb is that swimming meat has about 25 calories per ounce, flying meat has about 50 calories per ounce and walking meat has about 100 calories per ounce. The biggest problem with meat is that a multiplication factor must be figured into your calorie calculations if you deep fat fry any of the meats. The factors that you need to use are 4 for fish, 3 for poultry and 2 for red meat. The difference is based on the density of the meat as well as the existing fat content in it. Fish is a porous meat with very little fat and when you submerge it in 350 degree boiling oil, it acts like a sponge. Therefore, with fish you need to multiply by a large factor (X4) than a more dense and fat laden piece of beef (X2). Poultry is multiplied by 3.

Size of raw product versus cooked product.

107

The significance of this multiplication factor becomes very apparent when you compare the following servings of meats:

1	2
6 oz. Fried shrimp 600	6 oz. Boiled shrimp 150

```
    25         150              25
 ×   6 oz.  ×    4 (factor)  ×   6 oz.
   ─────      ─────            ─────
    150       600 calories     150 calories
```

1	2
6 oz. Fried chicken 900	6 oz. Broiled chicken 300

```
    50         300              50
 ×   6 oz.  ×    3 (factor)  ×   6 oz.
   ─────      ─────            ─────
    300       900 calories     300 calories
```

1	2
6 oz. Beef fondue 1200	6 oz. Broiled steak 600

```
   100         600             100
 ×   6 oz.  ×    2 (factor)  ×   6 oz.
   ─────      ─────            ─────
    600       1200 calories    600 calories
```

You can see that the broiling, boiling and baking (on a rack) methods of cooking preparation

6 ounces fried shrimp at 600 calories versus 6 ounces broiled shrimp at 150 calories.

6 ounces fried chicken at 900 calories versus 6 ounces broiled chicken at 300 calories.

110

6 ounces beef fondue at 1200 calories versus 6 ounces broiled steak at 600 calories.

offer the weight conscious person the best opportunity for eliminating *added* fat from the diet. Remember, the only thing that changed in the previous examples beside the calories was the method of preparation. The portion sizes of each meat remained at a constant 6 ounces. No extra food, only extra fat and calories.

Once you master the portion sizes by using your kitchen scale to weigh different shapes and cuts of meat, you will find it relatively easy to differentiate a 4 ounce portion from an 8 ounce portion. Practice really helps and must be continued until you develop a consistent proficiency of plus or minus 1 or 2 ounces. If you get that good, you won't have any problems maintaining your weight.

GRAIN CHART

The chart dealing with grain products has a range of 75 to 150 calories and can be easily mastered by using a simple format of checkpoints at 75, 100, and 125 calories. Anything made with flour and water has about 75 calories per ounce. Adding oil to the flour and water raises the calories to 100. Adding sugar to the flour, water and oil raises the calories to 125 calories per ounce.

An example at 75 would be flour and water in bread. Add some oil and you have pancakes or unfrosted cake at 100. With sugar added, you find yourself among the cookies, frosted cakes and donuts at 125. You will note that a few items like croissants or baklava have extremely high fat (oil) content and are listed at 150 calories per ounce. Chocolate is also listed at 150 calories an ounce, and believe me, my body never misses a chip. Every one gets counted!

Packaging is a real problem with items made with flour. Because the shelf life is so short, most manufacturers will increase the weight of their product, sometimes by as much as 50%! To illustrate, we have found English muffins that stated a 12 ounce package weight for 6 muffins. They actually weighed 18 to 21 ounces! Or a prepared garlic bread with a label weight of 7 ounces, weighing in at 12 ounces. The package might not count the extra calories, but your body will.

In one of our food labs, we looked up bran muffins in six different "calorie" books that people had brought in from their personal diet libraries. We found listings of "average," "medium," "regular" and "normal" bran muffins listed at calorie counts of between 107 and 175 calories each. On that day I had stopped by one of the local bakeries, strictly in the name of scientific research, and purchased a "regular" bran muffin.

When we weighed the muffin, it tipped the scale at a weight of 3.5 ounces. Now, using good problem solving techniques, you would look at the muffin and say it basically has flour, water, oil and sugar in it. Thus, at 125 calories per ounce, the little gem contains about 435 calories.

Now, for the woman who would like to maintain her weight at 120 pounds, we have an interesting finding with regard to why she may have had a difficult time in the past. Using the formula to figure her daily calorie needs, the following computations may help illustrate a point:

```
 120 pound maintenance weight
X  11 woman's multiplier
─────
1320 daily calories maintenance level
−435 bran muffin
─────
```

885 calories remaining for day to maintain weight

3.5 ounce bran muffin at 435 calories.

Now, if she had gone to her trusty little calorie book as she no doubt has done in the past after she has dieted down to her goal weight, she might have seen "107" or "175" listed for the "average" bran muffin. And at that "price" she might have had *two*!

Even if she had counted the muffins at 175 each for a total of 350 calories, her body had counted them at 435 each or 870 calories and now look what happens:

1320 daily calories
−870 bran muffins
_____
450 calories remaining for the day to maintain her weight

And what about butter? Or coffee with cream and sugar? Or lunch, or dinner? Do you see why she never could maintain her weight after dieting in the past?

To succeed, you must polish your problem solving skills so you can be more accurate than the box or the label or the calorie book. Practice and some dedicated commitment to succeed will go a long way toward insuring your future success at maintaining your weight.

The charts for fruits and vegetables are pretty straightforward. All items are measured in ounces and the ranges are stated along the bottom of the chart.

FRUIT PAGE

Fruits have a range of about 3 to 20 calories per ounce. Some are listed twice and represent calories with and without refuse. This seems to help simplify the problem solving process since some fruits are easier to figure with the refuse on them. Half of a cantaloupe that weighs 16 ounces would be figured at 5 calories per ounce since you would probably only eat about 9 ounces and throw the rind, about 7 ounces, away.

If you are the kind of person who takes the extra time to scoop out the edible portion and discard the refuse before you serve the food, like with grapefruit, pineapple, or mangoes, then you will have to figure at the higher calories per ounce listings. In any event, fruit is an excellent bargain.

I like to think of four common fruits as checkpoints and then problem solve others based on the sweetness (fructose) and density of the fruits.

If you figure plum at 20, apples at 15, citrus at 10 and melon at 5 you have a fairly good guideline.

Fruit	Calories/Ounce
Plum	20
Apple	15
Citrus	10
Melon	5

VEGETABLE PAGE

Vegetables are another bargain when it comes to good nutrition and quantities of food at a low caloric expenditure. The range for the page is from about 4 to 50 calories per ounce. Most of the listed items, however, are between 5 and 20 calories per ounce.

I have always attempted to simplify the problem solving of vegetables also by teaching my people to learn three vegetables and then to problem solve around those key checkpoints.

If you figure lettuce at 5, onions at 10 and potatoes at 20, all other vegetables seem to fall in place.

Vegetables	Calories/ounce
Potato	20
Onion	10
Lettuce	5

Considering the density of each of these items, it is easy to figure a green bean less than an onion, but more than lettuce. A value of 7 or 8 will put you in the ballpark. A carrot seems likely to be more than an onion, but less than a potato, and a sweet potato must be more than a regular potato.

You might find, as I did, that you will get to know the caloric value of a few items on each page because you or your family eat a lot of that item. You can either use the charts or make a close "guess-ti-mate" when the other items are eaten.

One further thing that seems to help in figuring specialty vegetables that are deep fried or sauteed in butter or oil (potatoes, onion rings, artichoke hearts, mushrooms, or zucchini) is to forget whatever the calorie count is for the actual item, and plan to figure them at 80-100 calories per ounce after they are prepared. The reason is simple. Most vegetables are comprised of mostly water (zero calories per ounce). During frying, the water evaporates and is replaced by—guess what?—oil at 250 calories per ounce. You can be assured that the oil will actually be responsible for most of the weight. The choice will be yours, but the following examples may convince you to consider the alternatives:

1	2	
8 oz. French fried potatoes	8 oz. Baked potato	160
	1 T. Butter	100
80 calories per ounce	2 T. Sour cream	60
× 8 oz.	Calories	320
640 calories		

117

French fries at 640 calories versus baked potato, butter & sour cream at 320 calories.

You could have two large baked potatoes, *with* butter *and* sour cream for about what one order of french fries costs in calories.

Or how about, a before dinner appetizer:

1	*2*	
8 oz. Deep fried breaded Zucchini	4 oz. Shrimp	100
	4 T. Cocktail sauce	60
100	Calories	160
X 8 oz.		
800 calories		

You could have *four* shrimp cocktails and still have calories left over!

DAIRY PAGE

The dairy page has a significant impact on the weight maintenance program for many people. A few things need to be looked at in terms of choices. Items are listed by the ounce, although many of them can be found on other charts listed under other measurements. Milk is also found on the beverage page by the 8 ounce cup and butter and margarine can be found on the condiment page measured by tablespoon.

Since many of the items on this page find their way into recipes and other prepared food items, the measured ounce has helped greatly in being able to problem solve the end products. One further thing you might consider when looking at the dairy products is the cholesterol levels that plague some people. By making a few better choices, cholesterol intake levels can be greatly reduced.

Butter and margarine have the same calories, but most margarine has zero cholesterol. Making a

8 ounces deep fried breaded zucchini at 800 calories versus 4 ounces shrimp and sauce at 160 calories.

switch from whole milk to 2% or skim milk is a matter of choice, but if the fat levels and cholesterol levels seem to be creating a problem, some people do choose to make the switch. Because egg yolks are very high in cholesterol, many people simply cut back in this area. Again, a matter of choice.

One of the problem solving tasks that we have practiced in food labs is to try to measure one ounce portions of cheese in different shapes and consistencies: melted, cubed, sliced, grated, pulverized, and wedged.

The theory of size conservation is very evident when you do this and it will help you when you find yourself at a party snack tray or when you are trying to problem solve a sandwich or figure out how much cheese is on the top of your french onion soup or covering your cauliflower.

CONDIMENT PAGE

The condiment page, *has proven to be the most important page* for people who want to successfully cut down on the fat content in their food. These are the items that we sprinkle, pour, spread or mix over, under, around and through our food that only add calories and do nothing to increase either the volume of food or the nutritional value of the food.

Concentrate on this page. I don't feel that you have to eliminate the items from your life, but you are going to have to make some better choices in what or how much of each you choose to use.

This is also the page where you can see the most frequent uses of "diet" substitutes that many diet conscious people decide to add to their lives. I neither advocate nor dissuade people from using

the low calorie mayonaise, salad dressings, imita-
tion butters, and salt, sugar, or cream substitutes,
but I have seen many people choose to use low
calorie substitutes and they seem to survive without any extreme feelings of deprivation.

Believe me, I want you to become intimate with
this page. Learn it cold. If you do, your own maintenance will progress with relative ease. Ignore it
and you will usually have noticeable problems in
attempting to cut back on your calories for undereating days.

BEVERAGE PAGE

The beverage page is also important. Beverages
are measured by the 8 ounce cup and you could
help your own program immensely if you do a little
measuring of the cups, glasses, and bowls that you
use on a daily basis at home.

The bowl that you use for breakfast cereal may
hold 2 to 3 ounces of cereal and a cup to two cups
of milk. This can make a big difference if you are
counting the cereal as a "normal" 1 ounce serving
with ½ cup milk that the label on the cereal box lists
as the regular serving size.

Your juice glass may only hold six ounces and
you may be counting it as a full cup. Experiment
with your measuring cups by filling them with water
and then measuring how much each holds.

ALCOHOL PAGE

The alcoholic beverage page is important for a
couple of reasons (friend's of Bill W. don't need to
learn it!). It is measured by the fluid ounce and has a
range of about 10 to 125 calories per ounce.

First, alcoholic beverages have lots of calories,
but very little, if any nutrients. I have yet to see a
beer or wine "fortified" with all the essential

vitamins and minerals to build strong bodies 12 ways. So the calories that you are getting are "empty" calories and, therefore, really don't do you a whole lot of good.

Secondly, people who have lost significant weight on the fast, 40 to 200 pounds, say they can't drink the same way at their new body weight. That's a fact. The tape that plays in their head about a couple of martinis before dinner, some wine with the meal, and a cordial for dessert being o.k. just isn't true anymore. In reality, you are a "cheap" drunk. It will only take a fraction of the alcohol to get you buzzed and at the calorie counts of alcoholic beverages, you might not want to spend your calories on wine or beer. Believe me, many people who have problems staying at their maintenance weight have to rethink their drinking habits. It may not be easy, but you'll save calories and money. Might live longer, too!

PREPARED RECIPE PAGE

One final calorie chart is provided so that you can add to or delete from the items that you eat. This one is the prepared recipe page that uses the eight-ounce cup as a means of measurement. Every recipe is not on it, but as you practice problem solving in your own home you can make up your own recipe page. We tend to be creatures of habit and most of the people in our program really enjoy finding ways to lower the calories in their favorite meals.

Perhaps a specific problem solving example would help to stimulate your interest. I want to convince you that it is both challenging and fun. One of the local pizza shops advertises a five item large pizza with cheese, Italian sausage, ground meat, pepperoni, onions, and mushrooms. It is guaranteed to weigh five pounds. Now using some simple problem solving techniques in conjunction with the calorie charts, you will see that the task is relatively simple.

1. List the estimated portion size.
2. List the ingredients.
3. Estimate the weight of each ingredient.
4. Estimate the calories of each ingredient.

Now, using the pizza example:

1. Convert five pounds to ounces ($5 \times 16 = 80$) and note that there are ten slices of pizza. Each slice is approximately 8 ounces (80 divided by 10 = 8).

2. Next, figure out what food items make up each slice of pizza.

Table 1

List of food

Crust
Cheese
Italian sausage
Ground meat
Pepperoni
Onions
Mushrooms
Sauce
Spices
Oil

3. Now figure an approximate weight for each item on a single 8 oz. piece of pizza.

Table 2

List of food	Estimated weight
Crust	3 oz.
Cheese	1 oz.
Italian sausage	.5 oz.
Ground meat	.5 oz.
Pepperoni	.5 oz.
Mushrooms/onions	.5 oz.
Sauce	1.5 oz. (= 3 T.)
Spices	—
Oil	.5 oz. (liquid oil)

4. Now, using the calorie charts and the estimated weights above figure the total caloric value of each food item.

Table 3

a. Crust—figured as flour, water and some oil or at 80 calories/ounce ($3 \times 80 = 240$)
b. Cheese—figured at 100 calories/ounce ($1 \times 100 = 100$)
c. Italian sausage—figured as a fatty, oily red meat at 125 calories/ounce ($.5 \times 125 = 62$)
d. Ground meat—figured as a lean red meat at 75 calories/ounce ($.5 \times 75 = 37$)
e. Pepperoni—figured as an oily red meat at 125 calories/ounce ($.5 \times 125 = 62$)
f. Mushrooms/onions—figured at about 9 calories/ounce ($.5 \times 9 = 4.5$)
g. Sauce—figured at 1.5 ounces which must be converted to tablespoons 1.5 ounces = 3 T. ($3 \times 15 = 45$)
h. Spices—zilch

i. Oil—this pizza shop adds olive oil to the sauce and it was figured at 250 calories per ounce (.5 × 250 = 125)

Total ---------------- 675 calories/slice

How do those 675 calories per slice figure in your total calorie balancing requirements? Have you ever only eaten *one* piece of pizza? Now can you see why understanding calories is so important? You are going to eat pizza, but now you can determine the calorie cost of each piece.

Now, look at each page and note the items that you know you have eaten in the past. These same foods will usually find their way back into your life once you are at your goal weight. Studying and understanding the calorie content of the foods you eat will gradually increase your awareness of the relationship between the kinds of food you eat and the consequences that each might have on your weight.

Problem solving takes time and effort, but it will be worth every minute you can devote to it. When you combine your calorie knowledge with some basic recordkeeping and increased physical activity you will be headed in the right direction. Practice may not make you perfect immediately, but it will surely increase your confidence and give you the opportunity to balance your caloric intake with your maintenance calories. That's what is needed to succeed in this program.

Success also means you will be eating some high calorie foods. However, you probably will be less likely to waste calories because you will now make decisions based on whether the food or calories are worth it. You now understand the caloric consequences and you will make new *choices* as a result.

Also, increasing your use of the calorie charts will make you less dependent upon them and more accurate with your problem solving. When problem solving becomes second nature, any natural or fresh food item becomes a challenge that you can compute as a caloric value. Remember, calories consumed in excess of those needed are the reasons people gain weight. Problem solving, not magic, is the way to successful weight maintenance.

CHAPTER XXI

CHOICES

The most important word you'll learn—and use—in *maintaining* your goal weight is CHOICES. You'll be amazed at how many great foods you already eat, that you'll be able to fill up on—at home and in restaurants—simply by being able to make the proper food CHOICES. And it's just not that hard to do with the unique tools that follow.

You must learn to make food choices that enable you to maintain your weight without feeling deprived. People who fail on diets counteract feelings of deprivation by overeating. Although they are able to maintain their weight for a short time by consciously undereating, this maintenance is only short term. They soon return to their previous eating habits.

To insure your own success, you must learn to make food choices that work for you and allow you to eat at maintenance calories.

Staying thin is going to be a matter of choice. It takes practice and experimentation while you are in the fasting phase and later as you enter the maintenance phase. You must practice to become aware of the value of estimating portion sizes and of making good food choices.

If you were to observe the following two meals side by side on a table would you know which one had the fewest calories? The first meal consists of an apple fritter donut and a cup of coffee with artificial sweetner. The other one has six pieces of whole wheat toast with 1½ teaspoons of raspberry jam on each one, one pound of cantaloupe, a bowl of cereal with ten large strawberries, a cup of whole milk for the cereal, a small glass of grapefruit juice and two cups of coffee with cream and sugar. Most people would not guess that the second meal had thirty fewer calories than the donut and coffee. Did you? Despite all of the other food, the second meal is very low in fat. Therefore, you get more food to eat for the same calories.

1		2	
Apple fritter		6W/W Toast—6 oz.	390
Donut (10 oz.)	1,250	Jam (3 T.)	150
Coffee	—	Melon—16 oz.	80
		Cereal—2 oz.	220
Calories	1,250	Strawberries—5 oz.	50
		Milk—8 oz.	160
		Juice—6 oz.	90
		Coffee	—
		Cream—2 T.	50
		Sugar—2t.	30
		Calories	1,220

How about a lunch with three pieces of fried chicken, fried potatoes and an iced tea, as compared to three pieces of broiled chicken, a baked potato with sour cream, iced tea and six 1.45-ounce chocolate bars. About the same calories People don't know that. Now no one says you have to eat all of the chocolate bars, but you could,

1250 calorie donut versus 1220 calorie breakfast.

and that's a lot more food than the first meal, and maybe more pleasure, too!

	1		2
(3) Fried Chicken— 8 oz.	1,200	(3) Broiled Chicken—8 oz.	400
Fried Potatoes— 8 oz.	640	Baked Potato— 8 oz.	160
Iced Tea—8 oz.	—	Sour Cream—1 T.	30
		Iced Tea—8 oz.	—
Calories	1,840	Calories	590
		(6) Choc. Bars— 8.7 oz.	1,305
		Calories	1,895

Three pieces of whole wheat toast with raspberry jam can be more satisfying than a donut, and the calories you "save" can be eaten at lunch, dinner, or whenever.

	1		2
Donut—4 oz.	500	(3) W/W Toast— 3 oz.	195
		Jam—1 T.	50
Calories	500	Calories	245

A two-pound cantaloupe might provide more bulk than a 1.45 ounce candy bar.

	1		2
Candy Bar— 1.45 oz.	220	Cantaloupe— 32 oz.	160
Calories	220	Calories	160

131

1840 calories of fried chicken versus 1895 calories of broiled chicken including 6 candy bars.

One 500 calorie donut versus 3 slices of toast with jam at 245 calories.

One 220 calorie chocolate bar versus 32 ounces of cantaloupe at 160 calories.

Three turkey sandwiches could provide more enjoyment than *one* California roast beef sandwich.

1		2	
3 Turkey Sandwiches		*1* Roast Beef Sandwich	
(6) W/W Bread—		(1) Sourdough	
6 oz.	390	Roll—3 oz.	225
Turkey—6 oz.	300	Beef—4 oz.	400
Lettuce—4 oz.	15	Cheese—1.5 oz.	150
Tomato—6 oz.	35	Mayo—2 T.	200
Mustard—1 T.	15	Calories	975
Calories	755		

What would you think if you saw a person eating a steak and a cup of black coffee? "Must be on a diet." Well, if the person at the next table eating a broiled fish dinner was eating *fewer calories* than the person eating the steak dinner, the "dieter" might choose to exchange meals.

1		2	
10 oz. Steak	1,000	10 oz. Filet	
Cup of coffee	—	of Sole	250
		Lemon Wedge	—
		Green Beans—	
		4 oz.	32
		Carrots—4 oz.	48
		2 Baked potatoes—	
		8 oz. ea.	320
		Sour cream—2 T.	60
		Roll—1 oz.	75
		Butter—1½ t.	50
		Salad	50
Calories	1,000	Calories	885

One roast beef sandwich at 975 calories versus 3 turkey sandwiches at 755 calories.

One steak at 1000 calories versus an entire fish dinner at 885 calories.

My maintenance group once problem solved my daily maintenance calories in fruit. I ended up with over twenty baggies filled with more than ten pounds of delicious and filling fruit, which took me about four days to consume!

		Calories
Watermelon—	16 oz.	48
Cantaloupe—	16 oz.	80
Grapefruit—	12 oz.	72
Honeydew Melon—	12 oz.	72
Peach (2)—	12 oz.	108
Orange—	8 oz.	80
Strawberries—	10 oz.	100
Tangerines—	12 oz.	120
Apricots (4)—	8 oz.	112
Mango—	12 oz.	168
Apple—	8 oz.	120
Pear (2)—	12 oz.	192
Banana—	10 oz.	160
Nectarine (2)—	10 oz.	160
Plums (4)—	8 oz.	152
Grapes—	12 oz.	228
	178 oz.	1,972

(10¾ pounds)

A calorie is a calorie. A three hundred calorie potato is the same as three hundred calories of beef, three hundred calories of fish or a three hundred calorie dish of ice cream. The lower the calorie content in the food, the larger the portion of food you can eat. Our most successful people are the ones who get the most food for the least calories.

10¾ pounds of fruit at 1972 calories.

139

We don't want you to eat a little bit of food and be thin. We want you to eat a lot of food, if that's what you want, and still be thin. Some of you may actually eat more food at your maintenance weight than you ate when you were overweight. By learning about calories, you will see that by eating a lot less fatty food, you can actually eat more and still weigh less.

We want to convince you that you must become a calorie expert if you want to maintain your weight. Calories count, but only if you know how to count them. Most people, whether obese or thin, don't know anything about figuring calories. With the problem solving techniques in this book, you will learn a system of figuring calories that will make you more of an expert about calories than your doctor, dietitian, neighbor, or local health food store guru. Our goal is to teach you balanced calorie eating.

Most dieters rely upon a calorie book or a list of foods with varied caloric values. They use these values to compute their daily caloric intake. How accurate are these books or lists? As you will see, not very accurate at all. The data supports the fact that more than 90% of people who lose weight on any diet fail to maintain their weight loss. Something must be wrong with these caloric computations, as you will see in a few minutes.

When most of these calorie books and manufacturer labels or lists are compared with the United States Department of Agriculture, *Nutritive Value of American Foods, Handbook #456,* it becomes apparent that there are indeed gross discrepancies in the calorie totals listed for common foods.

The majority of the foods listed in calorie books and on labels are figured at caloric levels that place them 25 to 50% below the totals for the same foods listed in the USDA publication. How could this be, you ask? Who are the authors and publishers of these Fantasy Island calorie books? The vast majority are written and distributed by the food industry public relations departments. How can they get away with publishing inaccurate information? They get away with it because there are no laws against this practice, and because inaccuracies sell more food.

In fact, the criteria used for truth in advertising and promotion requires that there be "at least the amount of food listed on the label," but it says nothing about providing inaccurate or erroneous information. Suing the food industry does not seem to be the way to insure a slim body. Learning about calories will. What you can do is learn to be smarter than the label on the box or can.

Why do other diet programs fail and what do we do differently? Most diet programs attempt to change your eating style. You eat at night; that's your problem. You snack; that's your problem. You binge; that's your problem. Have you ever met a reformed snacker? Or an ex-binger? If you eat in front of the T.V. now, you'll eat in front of the T.V. later. Our program tends to be one of reeducation, not rebirth.

The difference will be in the calories. One of the things you'll learn is that you don't have to give up snacking. You do have to make some changes in food *choices*, or cooking methods, but not ones that will greatly alter your own lifestyle.

A turkey sandwich with lettuce, tomato and spiced mustard may come out to be 250 calories. A pastrami and cheddar sandwich may be 1,000 calories. You may still choose to eat a sandwich as a midnight snack. If you start eating large 250-calorie sandwiches instead of small 1,000-calorie sandwiches, you can weigh a lot less and learn to keep your weight off.

Forty cups of lightly salted air popped popcorn equals one cup of peanuts. So if you ate only twenty cups of popcorn instead of one cup of peanuts, you could save half the calories, but you would still be snacking or eating at night. You're not going to give up your individuality. That's impossible; it just doesn't work. What you're going to do is change your choice of food and perhaps increase your physical activity so that your own program begins to make sense to you, and you can learn that you can balance your calories and successfully keep the weight off.

For example, a favorite meal that we like to serve when we entertain and want minimum fuss is oven-fried chicken, potatoes, fresh mixed vegetables, and salad. Now, the way we prepared this meal for years was to shake the chicken in a bag with flour and seasoning, put it on an oven tray and place a pat of butter on each piece so that it would brown. The pan drippings were used later to make gravy for the mashed potatoes, made with butter and milk. The vegetables were covered with a rich butter, flour and cheese sauce and the salad was tossed with fresh blue cheese dressing. How can we cut calories from this meal without changing the main ingredients? By making a few calculated choices. Compare the old way to the new way.

Pastrami cheddar sandwich at 1000 calories versus turkey sandwich at 250 calories.

Same number of calories—1 cup peanuts versus 40 cups of air blown popcorn.

Estimated Calories

	Portion Size	Old Way Estimated Calories
Baked Chicken	8 oz.	400
w/ flour & butter		50
and butter		100
Mashed Potatoes	8 oz.	160
w/ butter		100
and milk		40
Pan Gravy	8 T.	400
Steamed Vegetables	12 oz.	
(below)		
Broccoli	3 oz.	27
Cauliflower	3 oz.	24
Carrots	3 oz.	36
Pearl Onions	2 oz.	22
Mushrooms	1 oz.	8
Cheese Sauce	8 T.	400
(Cheese, flour, butter)		
Tossed Salad	1 c.	50
Blue Cheese Dressing	4 T.	300
		2,117

	Portion Size	New Way Estimated Calories
Baked Chicken (On rack) w/ flour	8 oz.	400 50
Baked Potato w/ butter & sour cream	12 oz. 1 T. 1 T.	240 100 30
Steamed Vegetables (below)	12 oz.	
Broccoli	3 oz.	27
Cauliflower	3 oz.	24
Carrots	3 oz.	36
Pearl Onions	2 oz.	22
Mushrooms	1 oz.	8
Parmesan	½ oz.	50
Tossed Salad	1 c.	50
Low Calorie Dressing	4 T.	44
		————
		1,081

Old Way   2,117
New Way   1,081
            ————
            1,036 Calorie Savings

Same quantity of food but the dinner on the right has 1000 fewer calories.

With a few simple adjustments, over 1,000 calories were saved. The new version of the old meal actually has the greater amount of food for less calories! By placing the chicken on a rack on the tray, eliminating the butter on top of each piece of chicken (350° in an oven for an hour will "brown" the chicken very nicely!), substituting baked potatoes for mashed, sending the pan drippings down the garbage disposal instead of down your stomach, sprinkling pulverized cheese over the vegetables instead of pouring the heavy cheese sauce on them, and switching to any of the excellent low calorie salad dressings versus the fat laden cream dressing you can save 1,000 calories per serving! These choices can begin to help you learn how to eat thin. Where could you begin to modify some of your favorite meals? Attack the fat?

What made the difference? We cut out the fat. We took the butter off the chicken, the gravy off the potatoes, and made different choices for the sauce and dressing that covered our vegetables and salad. Small changes, but big calorie savings. Remember how important I said the condiment page was going to be?

What if you don't have control of the kitchen? Recently, while attending a medical conference I was presented with the following menu at the banquet lunch:

	Estimated Portion Size	Estimated Calories
½ Rock Cornish Hen with Mushroom Sauce	6 oz. 2 T.	300 100

Boiled Potatoes	4 oz.	80
with butter and parsley		50
Broccoli	3 oz.	27
with cheese sauce	4 T.	200
Baked Stuffed Tomato	3 oz.	18
with bread crumb filling	2 oz.	200
Dinner Salad	1 c.	30
with oil and vinegar	3 T.	225
dressing		
Roll	1 oz.	75
and butter	1 t.	33
Coffee		-0-
Carrot Cake	5 oz.	625
		1,963

That one meal could have provided my total daily maintenance calories. However, knowing there would be a dinner reception later that night, I used my fork and knife to remove some of the sauces from the meat and vegetables and to pick through the salad leaving most of the dressing in the bowl. I chose to eat the bread dressing and a dinner roll with a pat of butter, but I eliminated 625 calories by saying "No, thank you" when the dessert cart came along! A savings of over 1000 calories!

All of the portion sizes were estimated. All of the calorie values were figured using problem solving techniques. No calorie charts or scales were used, but the preliminary work that allowed me to feel confident enough to do the figuring was accomplished during many practice sessions in my own kitchen. Practice will make perfect eventually, and practice is one of the keys to your success.

A typical business luncheon—1963 calories.

150

Learning to estimate portion sizes will be critical to your success. More calorie errors are made by misjudging the size of the portion than by misfiguring the calories for the type of food. To succeed, you must purchase and *use* the tools that can help you learn this skill.

1. Kitchen scale
2. Measuring spoons
3. Measuring cups

A small kitchen scale can be inexpensively purchased from any department or health food store. It should measure in ounces, weigh items up to at least two pounds and be adjustable to "zero out" if a plate or cup is used to hold the food item.

Food should be weighed raw and after it is prepared so you can learn to "eyeball" what two ounces of raw pasta or rice look like after they are cooked. This work is essential to your success. A few minutes each day while you are fasting will begin to build a wealth of knowledge that you will be able to carry with you wherever you go. Knowing how much *every* slice of bread weighs isn't as important as knowing how much *one* slice weighs.

If you always buy a certain size box of eggs, weigh one to see how much it weighs. This game of learning portion sizes is like throwing horse shoes or hand grenades; you only have to be close. Measuring a portion of breakfast cereal can show you whether your favorite bowl holds the "one ounce serving" listed on the box or the three-ounce portion that most cereal bowls hold.

The measuring spoons can also add valuable knowledge to your store house. A tablespoon of butter turns out to be much more than you find yourself putting on a single piece of toast. This is

Only necessary tools—scale, measuring cups & spoons.

important since I once had a patient who recorded 100 calories each time she used any butter. By measuring, she found she actually was using only about a teaspoonful—much less than a tablespoon. Now she knows she could eat a peach for each of the 60 calories of butter that she was recording but not eating.

How do you make tuna salad? Do you measure the mayonnaise by the tablespoon or by the cup, or do you just add the mayonnaise until the tuna salad looks right? Next time, try adding the mayonnaise a tablespoon at a time and watch how the consistency changes. Once you have done this a few times you will begin to get a feel for how much mayonnaise is in the next deli tuna sub that you purchase. Many people admit they used to order the "Diet Tuna Sandwich" when they were watching their weight. We problem solved the following deli-purchased tuna sub sandwich:

4 oz.	6" roll	300
	Tuna salad	
6 oz.	Tuna	240
8 T.	Mayonnaise	800
1 oz.	Onion	11
1 oz.	Celery	4
1 oz.	Lettuce	4
2 oz.	Tomato	12
2 T.	Mayonnaise (on bread to paste lettuce & tomato to bread)	200
		1,571

A 1,500-calorie sandwich would have a tough time making it on my diet menu! One of my patients chooses the following lunch on days that she wants to undereat at the deli:

	Estimated Portion Size	Estimated Calories
Whole wheat bread (2 slices)	2 oz.	130
Deli-sliced turkey (6 slices)	3 oz.	150
Dijon mustard	1 T.	15
Lettuce	1 oz.	4
Tomato	2 oz.	12
		311

Of course, if she wasn't concerned about her weight, she could always order four or five sandwiches like this and still be eating fewer calories than the person who orders the "diet" tuna submarine sandwich! Being thin—it's a matter of choice, not chance. The difference in the two sandwiches is in the amount of fat in the mayonnaise. Now, there are good diet mayonnaise products on the market that can save calories, but again switching brands is a matter of choice.

One patient confided that she used to use a soup mug to measure her vegetables when her doctor had put her on a restricted calorie diet. Her diet called for "a cup" of vegetables at each meal. She brought the mug to a food lab one day and we found that it held *two* cups by volume! Maybe she didn't count the calories, but her body did!

One tuna sandwich at 1571 calories versus 5 turkey sandwiches at 1555 calories.

Another patient made two zucchini breads. One was made with half the shortening and half the sugar of the original recipe. The other was a standard recipe. Both were delicious. Tasted side by side, it was apparent which one had the normal levels of oil and sugar, but the new recipe was almost half the calories and tasted like . . . zucchini bread! It will be your choice which one you allow into your life.

CHAPTER XXII

ENVIRONMENTAL MANAGEMENT

Environmental management means:

1. Keeping food out of the places where you can get your hands on it!

2. Substituting low-calorie food choices in place of high calorie food choices—popcorn for peanuts, turkey for pastrami, mustard for mayonnaise.

Environmental management is a critical aspect of both the fasting and the long-term maintenance program. It must be individualized to meet your needs, and it must be realistic. I like to hear about bringing new or different things into an environment rather than hearing people talk about all the things they are going to have to give up, or all of the things they must now do differently. These negative changes are not realistic.

It is a well documented fact that obese people are more influenced by external cues while thin people are more oriented toward internal cues. The old adage "out-of-sight, out-of-mind" is a great rule to abide by when possible.

I choose not to have chocolate in my home. I can eat chocolate and I do, but I refuse to allow it in my home. Why? Because I eat it. All of it. And I choose not to have it available so I don't have to deal with the calories. If I want some chocolate, I'll go down to the store and buy some. If my children want some chocolate, they can go buy some, but please keep it out of my house. I tried hiding it, but I always found it. I tried freezing it, but then I found that I loved frozen chocolate. I froze it in large containers of water to make it less accessible, but then I bought a microwave and found that 25 seconds on Defrost works very nicely to create slush, allowing the chocolate bar to be recovered. Keeping chocolate out of the house works for me. You might have to do something differently.

Your problem may be peanut butter, or peanuts, or cheese, or leftovers. You will have to see what shows up on your food records that perhaps requires some attention to environmental management.

If you find you have to have peanut butter in the house in case the grandchildren stop by, but the peanut butter turns up on your food records, perhaps you could send the jar home with the kids.

One person I know who has a tough time with leftovers cleans all the plates off with a spray bottle of window cleaner. That way she knows she'll stay out of the garbage can at night. Yes, she admits to sneaking down at night in the past and eating from the trash can!

Another person took a new route home from work when donuts began showing up on his food records. He was habitually going through a drive-thru donut shop on his way home. Now, he plans to have some fruit in the car and a route home that by-passes the donut shop.

We have to learn that we don't go into bakery shops "just to look around." Remember the rule: "If it's in the house, it will be eaten." That also applies to food in the car, office, bag, or pocket. Having other food choices at hand often helps us to observe this rule.

Intervention at the earliest possible time is important to stop unwanted behavior.

Store   Cabinet
  or   or
Restaurant → Bag → Car → Refrigerator → Eating

We must attempt to cut this chain as early as possible. Lots of things that were unpacked from bags in my kitchen never made it to the cabinet or refrigerator. Some items got into my car but never made it into the house. The "broken" cookie bag, or the aromatic french fry, and many other items never even got into my car before they got into me! We must make the decision as soon as possible to prevent the calories from going places where they are either unwanted or unneeded.

One woman who loved butter and sugar sandwiches found that she couldn't have granulated sugar in the house. When her boyfriend demanded that she have sugar for his coffee, she bought sugar cubes. Every now and again there she was wrapping the sugar cubes in a paper towel and smashing them with a mallet! She says it's not the same, however, because the broken sugar cubes are too lumpy on the buttered bread. She finally got rid of the boyfriend and is doing fine!

Your goal of controlling your environment must not be to continue struggling to overcome weakness, but rather to plan for your success. *Confronting* and *planning* both tend to allow us to lower anxiety levels and to learn good self-management skills.

CHAPTER XXIII

EXERCISE

This is a tremendously important chapter. It has been our experience that the people who increase their physical activity while on the fast have a much better chance of reaching their goal weight. They are also better able to maintain that weight once they are off the fast.

Since the bottom line is calories in (*eating*) versus calories out (*exercising*), it should not come as much of a surprise that exercise and physical activity are very important for total calorie balancing.

The reality of the importance of exercise occurred to me when I was discharged from the service to enter graduate school. I gained about 35 pounds in six months. I had always been active; sports in high school, a physical education major in college, and my years as a Marine Jet Pilot. All of the activity had helped me keep my weight under some control. Once the activity stopped, so did my weight control. Trading an A-4 for a shrinks couch didn't help one bit!

With today's attitude of "why walk if I can ride," people have allowed themselves to slip into a life of non-activity. We must fight to find places to fit the activity into our lives. I once went for a walk with my children to get some ice cream, and we got lost trying to walk out of our housing tract. After living in our tract for over two years I had never walked out of it! Sound silly? It's reality.

Regular physical activity is much preferred over periodic or occasional super human efforts, since the body cannot store the benefits of exercise. All physical activity burns calories, but it is true that vigorous exercise is better for the heart and lungs. In order to achieve and maintain an acceptable level of fitness, it is important to exercise long and vigorously enough (usually 20-30 minutes) in order to increase the heart rate and raise the body temperature.

Evidence reports you will actually burn calories in a resting state for a period of up to six hours after vigorous exercise, like running for 30 minutes. If you walk for two hours the body will burn calories at a higher rate for about two hours. Either type of exercise, vigorous, or mild to moderate, is beneficial. Most importantly, if you can work only 30 minutes of exercise and physical activity into your daily routine, you will be able to either lose 10 to 20 pounds in a year, or you can choose to eat the 35,000 to 70,000 calories that you burned while you exercised.

If a 150-pound woman begins walking and works up to only two miles each night, she will deficit 200 calories each day (100 calories per mile) which equates to 1,400 calories each week (7 days × 200 calories per day). In four weeks that same 150-pound female will have deficited 5,600 calories. Since we must deficit about 3,500 calories to lose one pound, that means that this woman would have lost an extra 1.6 pounds (5,600 divided by 3,500) in four weeks, just by walking two miles each night!

```
  200 calories for walking 2 miles
× 7 days
──────
1400 calories expended during week
× 4 weeks
──────
5600
```

divided by 3500 calories in one pound of fat
  = 1.6 pounds exercised out of your body

  While you are in the fasting phase it is usually best to wait until the second week to begin some mild activity. This gives your body time to adjust to the changes in fluid levels and body chemistry. If you have been leading a rather sedentary life style, an easy way to begin exercising is to buy an inexpensive pedometer and start keeping track of how much walking you do each day. We had a nurse who walked up to seven miles in one eight-hour shift! Begin walking late in the afternoon or early evening with another person. This will make it even more enjoyable for you. If the type of activity you choose is not fun or enjoyable you probably won't do it for very long. Most people don't know that. Use the charts in Appendix 3 which list the caloric expenditures for common forms of exercise and physical activity to total up the calories that you burn for each of your activities. Remember, do not go crazy with the exercise. Begin slowly, and let your body be your guide. When it says "enough already," stop. Walking one mile burns up just as many calories as jogging one mile. Your jogging friends won't want to hear that!

  Aside from the fact that many wonderful things will happen to you if you begin to exercise, two things have become very apparent with regard to exercise:

1. People who increase their activity level are much more likely to complete the fasting phase and reach goal weight.

2. People who exercise are much more likely to maintain their weight loss.

Also, exercise is one of the surest methods that a person has to gain control of the total calorie balancing system. This is important since changed eating habits are not the easiest things to find in any weight maintenance program. Research indicates all weight maintenance programs that report minimal success have effected some changes in the levels of exercise and physical activity of their patients.

A fasting person once asked why most exercise charts only feature things that children do. We have endeavored to compile an "adult" chart that should give you a rough estimate of calories used per minute at various body weights. It should be used as a guide and exact computations will be assessed based upon your own progress in maintaining your weight or in the recording of increased food calories that you are able to eat.

Exercise must be used as a tool for balancing calories. By recording the total amounts of exercise calories on the calorie tally sheet you can get instant feedback that tends to be very reinforcing when it is then converted into the total calories that can be eaten. Remember 1500 to 2000 is a *minimum* number of weekly exercise calories that you should attempt to add to your life. This truly is one of the best tools for effective, long-term weight maintenance. To tell you it is anything but essential to your continued success would be neither fair nor beneficial for you. Some people even say it makes weight maintenance *easy!* If calorie balancing is not going well exercise is one tool that you could use to tighten up your program.

It will also serve as the best means for tightening up some of the sagging parts of your new body!

Try to add the activity into your life by sneaking it in. Park your car in the outer edges of parking lots. No one else parks there and your car doors won't get dinged! You get the extra calories for walking the extra distance. Walk up the stairs the next time you're in a building with an elevator. Walk to the store the next time you think about it. Saves gas and wear and tear on the car, too! A recent study demonstrated that bike riding versus using your car added only five additional minutes to total travel time for distances within a five mile radius of your home.

I like to see people diversify the types of physical activity that they choose. People who walk might also use a rowing machine as an alternate form of activity for those rainy days in April. Swimming can be a year-round activity in California, but if you live in a colder climate joining the Polar Bear Club might not be your style! Many people use the small jogger trampolines, while they watch the evening news, some jog, and others have really enjoyed the new video aerobic workout tapes. My mother crochets while she peddles her stationary bike. If you can make the time you spend doing physical activity fun, you will most likely continue with the activity. Take a dance class with your husband. Walk with a friend. Roller skate with your children. Most importantly, have fun.

One further word. Before you go out and join a health spa with an expensive lifetime membership, look around for the 60-day or 6-month specials. Don't join until you know that you will use the facility. Try it. You may like it.

CHAPTER XXIV

KNOWING NUTRITION

To be successful in long-term weight maintenance you must reduce your consumption of refined sugars and fat.

In 1977 Senator George McGovern, Chairman of the Senate Select Committee on Nutrition and Human Needs, published a new set of nutritional guidelines for the American public. The purpose of the study was to find a nutritional solution that would help slow down or stop many of the killer diseases and medical problems that have plagued Americans increasingly during this century—high blood pressure, heart attack, stroke, diabetes, cancers of the colon and breast, arteriosclerosis, cirrhosis of the liver and, of course, obesity. Every one of these medical problems is linked to the American diet.

Senator McGovern's committee determined the dietary composition of the current American diet and then recommended a new composition that might help slow down, and, in some cases, stop the medical maladies caused by our high fat, low complex carbohydrate diet.

This chart depicts the findings and recommendations of the committee:

PERCENT OF CALORIES FROM DIFFERENT NUTRIENTS

Current Diet		Recommended Diet	
12% Protein	Meat and vegetable	12% Protein	Meat and vegetable
46% Carbo-hydrates	28% Complex Carbohydrates and "Naturally Occurring" Sugars	58% Carbo-hydrates	48% Complex Carbohydrates and "Naturally Occurring" Sugars
	18% Refined and Processed Sugars		10% Refined and Processed Sugars
42% Fat	16% Saturated	30% Fat	10% Saturated
	19% Mono-unsaturated		10% Mono-unsaturated
	7% Poly-unsaturated		10% Poly-unsaturated

Source: Dietary Goals for the United States, 1977; prepared by the Senate Select Committee on Nutrition and Human Needs.

When nutrition is looked at in terms of the Senate Select Committee's Dietary Goals for the United States which were updated in 1978, seven specific changes in the current American diet were called for. The revised goals are:

1. Increase the consumption of complex carbohydrates and naturally occurring sugars from 28 to 48% of total caloric intake.

2. Reduce overall fat consumption from approximately 40 to 30% of caloric intake.

3. Reduce saturated fat consumption to account for about 10% of the total caloric intake; and balance that with 10% poly-unsaturated and 10% mono-unsaturated fats.

4. Reduce cholesterol consumption to about 300 milligrams a day.

5. Reduce the consumption of refined sugars by about 45% to account for about 10% of total caloric intake.

6. Reduce sodium consumption to no more than 5.0 grams each day.

7. To avoid obesity, consume only as many calories as you expend. If you are obese, decrease caloric intake and increase energy expenditures.

It becomes obvious that the medical problems stem from the high fat and low complex carbohydrate content of the American diet. People who are concerned about improving their diets are going to have to learn about food so that they can identify the types of foods that contain fats and complex carbohydrates and to avoid one and increase the intake of the other.

These might be considered as the nutritional goals for the general population, but specifically they are directed toward the person who has had problems maintaining an acceptable body weight.

By implementing these goals on an individual basis you will be able to regain control over an area of your life that has been badly out of control for years or your entire lifetime.

Doing some "man-in-the-street" type of research has proven to be very enlightening when we look at the base of knowledge of the general public regarding food and energy sources. Most people identify candy bars as instant energy carbohydrate food. In fact they can contain as much as 52% fat. A hamburger is usually identified as a source of protein, but many fast food burgers, regardless of method of preparation, contain as much as 55% fat. Instead of asking "where's the beef?", we should ask "why so much fat?" The average person, with or without a weight problem, doesn't know what's in any of the foods that he eats. Taste, appearance, and ease of preparation seem to be the deciding factors that motivate the consumer.

The two most over used additives that are used to enhance the taste of a product are salt and sugar. Neither enhances nutrition. Americans consume more than a hundred pounds of sugar and sweetners each year, adding virtually nothing but calories and chemicals to our diet. These simple carbohydrates supply no protein, no fat, no vitamins, no dietary fiber, and practically no minerals. They are *empty calories*. What they do is replace more nutritious sources of calories and greatly contribute countless extra calories to our diet, that are stored by our bodies as fat. Moreover, they are also the source of tooth decay. (Appendix 6 has a listing of the sugar content of various common foods.)

Salt and other forms of sodium used in food preparation and food processing also create problems for a large segment of the American public. To be sure, the body needs salt. It helps maintain needed levels of water in the body. However, when we consume too much salt our kidneys, in order to maintain the lower salinity of the blood, hold on to as much water as possible. This increases the amount of fluid in our veins and arteries which, in turn, increases the blood pressure. Most estimates of daily salt requirements range from 0.5 to 5 grams each day. The average American consumes approximately 12-14 grams of salt each day. Americans are among the leaders in the world in two categories, salt intake and the prevalence of high blood pressure. Actually, Japan has a higher prevalence of high blood pressure than the United States. Guess what else the Japanese beat the Americans at? That's right. Their daily consumption of salt. Various studies have concluded that 75% of *all* high blood pressure could be controlled simply by lowering salt intake.

There are two basic ways to lower salt in our diet. The first is to avoid processed foods that are high in salt, such as pickles, canned soups, and lunch meats. I am not an advocate of long laundry lists of foods, but Appendix 7 does provide a listing of the salt levels in various common foods. The list is provided to inform, not reform, the interested reader about sodium levels.

As you will discover, it is possible to obtain a one-month supply of salt simply by eating one large deli pickle!

A second way to reduce salt is to attempt to keep your hand off of the salt shaker. That, for most of us, is easier said than done. For these people another alternative might be to add a salt substitute to their diet. Willpower aside, salt in excess can be a killer and if high blood pressure is a problem for you, some control will be necessary.

Two additional items need to be addressed that add either calories or chemicals to our daily intake. They are alcohol and caffeine-containing beverages. Alcohol consumption levels have not changed very much in the past eighty years. We have seen with our fasting patients that they are not able to drink at the same levels that they did prior to the fast. Besides the obvious problem with blood alcohol levels, the other thing that must be considered is the absence of nutrients in alcohol as we outlined earlier. Just as refined sugars provided calories without nutrients, alcohol also has many empty calories.

Caffeine seems to cause more health-related problems than previously recognized. As a stimulant that is present in coffee, tea, some soft drinks and candy, caffeine has been linked, in some studies, to adverse effects in reproduction. Other studies link caffeine to cancer of the pancreas and heart rhythm problems as well as to headaches and circulatory problems. While in a fasting state, it is recommended that caffeine be limited because of its diuretic effects as well as being a source of appetite stimulations in some people.

One further thought on a way to obtain control over our weight is to look at dietary fiber. Appendix 8 has a listing of food sources that are high in this non-caloric food item. It used to be called "roughage" and was commonly prescribed to improve or regulate bowel movements. Basically, fiber is the nondigestible part of grain products like rye, whole wheat bread, and cereals, as well as most fruits and vegetables. It provides bulk and serves to draw water into the digestive tract thereby aiding digestion as well as elimination.

The term "gut transit time" applies to the time that it takes for food to be processed through the digestive system. In underdeveloped nations with diets high in fiber researchers have discovered the amount of time it takes for food to be processed through the digestive system can be literally cut in half compared to the gut transit times of nations like ours with diets low in fiber and high in protein and fats. In fact, while the gut transit time in high fiber populations proves to be around 36 hours, the amount of time for food to be processed and eliminated in low fiber diet populations is about twice that amount of time, or 72 hours. Also, the amount of feces eliminated by the high fiber populations weighs four times as much as the feces of the low fiber populations. Furthermore, with the addition of fiber to our diets, the amount of time that it takes for food to pass through the system is decreased ("gut transit time") and the food spends less time in the body. Finally, people on relatively high fiber diets have a lesser incidence of cancer of the gut or colon than their counterparts on a low fiber diet.

When we look at the direction that our patients have taken with their food choices when they finish the fasting phase, two things become apparent. The first is that there is a tendency for people to begin eating more fresh food as opposed to processed food, fresh fruits and vegetables (literally natural vitamin stores), rather than canned or frozen, and fresh and frozen meats versus canned or smoked varieties, with a dramatic salt/sodium reduction!

Secondly, they tend to lower their fat intake by becoming more aware of the methods of food preparation and by watching the types of oil laden condiments that we tend to place *over* food. Both increase the caloric value without increasing the amount of food we consume. The calorie chart that seems to get the most use during the initial stages of weight maintenance is . . . the one that deals with condiments, the gravies, sauces, salad dressings, butter, oil and sugar that we shake, pour, sprinkle and spread over our food. Food preparation becomes important when you consider that meat, vegetables and other food items act like sponges for calories when they are deep fat fried rather than boiled, broiled or baked.

CHAPTER XXV

PROCEDURES FOR SUCCESS

This chapter provides the building blocks for your individual program. Your commitment to succeed will be the most important ingredient. The only way you can fail is not to try.

Where do we start? With a few basics about weight maintenance. The body is the perfect calorie counter so we first must understand how many calories will be required for our own weight maintenance. This daily calorie requirement is known as the Basal Metabolic Rate (BMR). It is the minimum calories required to operate or "fuel" the body. As previously stated, men burn about 12 calories per pound each day and women burn about 11 calories per pound each day. That's all there is to it. That is a critical point. We have monitored thousands of dieters and the numbers still come out as 12 and 11. *Most* current fad diet guides and even some medical models suggest multipliers that are much higher, even 16 to 18 times body weight! DON'T BELIEVE THEM. For example, a man who weighs 165 pounds: 12 × 165 = 1,980. A woman who weighs 125 pounds: 11 × 125 = 1,375 calories. Appendix 1 has been provided to help you see at a glance the various recommended caloric intakes for men and women according to the desired maintenance weight.

Now, man does not live by BMR alone. This caloric total is the bare minimum required to fuel the body. Everything else that we do in the form of physical exercise or activity increases the body's need for calories. The more exercise people do, the more likely they are to succeed in this program. Why? It's very simple. People who exercise say they feel healthier and they like it. They feel more in control. In reality, the main reason they exercise is so they can eat more.

Once you understand what your daily caloric requirement is, you can figure your weekly caloric needs simply by multiplying by seven.

Male

```
        165 Maintenance weight
       ×12 BMR
      ──────
      1,980 Daily calories
         ×7 Days
      ──────
     13,860 Weekly calories
```

Female

```
        125 Maintenance weight
       ×11 BMR
      ──────
      1,375 Daily calories
         ×7 Days
      ──────
      9,625 Weekly calories
```

See Appendix 1 for average calories for men and women at the various maintenance weights. As most people who have tried to eat at a specific daily calorie total know, it is very difficult and after a few weeks becomes boring and nearly impossible.

By keeping a simple chart of your own eating behavior you will be able to make observations regarding problem days and thereby be able to plan undereating strategies that will be discussed later.

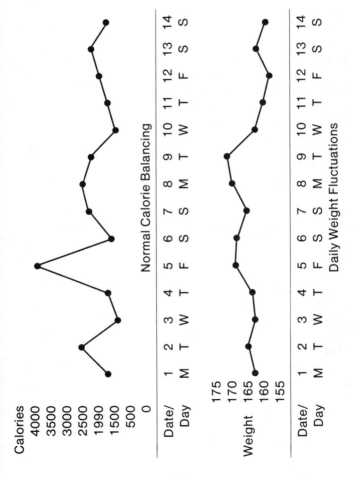

This brings us to the real key to success. Confrontation through record keeping is the number one predictor of success in our program. You must keep daily records of weight, calories, exercise and deficit/surplus totals for the week. The following chart illustrates an example of a typical calorie tally sheet. (P. 177)

Although we recommend that people only weigh once each week during the fasting phase, weighing daily after maintenance weight is reached is essential. There is sound basis for this requirement. While fasting, weight tends to fluctuate daily because of the large amounts of water and other liquids consumed. Four things grossly effect water retention:

1. Carbohydrate intake
2. Salt intake
3. Changes in physical activity
4. Hormonal changes

With experience, each of you will develop your own style concerning maintenance weight. However, successful people share two common practices: record keeping (CTS Sheet), and exercising. Some people have joined formal exercise programs whereas others simply take a two-mile relaxing stroll with a friend each evening. Also, these people have made a ritual of weighing themselves each day to monitor their progress. Daily weighing also reminds them that they have a problem. Your scale now becomes your ally rather than your enemy, in a conscious effort to manage your maintenance program.

One of the most important skills that you will have to master is the use and implementation of the calorie charts found in Appendix 2. These are basic to your success. The more familiar you are

Date Day Weight		Food Calories	Activity Calories	Net Calories	Computations
3/26 M	168	850	250	600	165 X 12 X 7 = MAINT. CAL.: 13,860
T	166	1340	150	1190	E.C./P.A. CAL. + 2,100
					15,960
W	167	1900	400	1500	FOOD CAL. MINUS 14,140
					1,820
TH	167	2110	200	1910	(DEFICIT)
F	166	2250	—	2250	
S	166	3650	1100	2550	
S	167	2040	—	2040	
4/2 M					
T					
W					

177

with them the easier your progress will become. You will need the measuring spoons, measuring cups, and the adjustable kitchen scale. You will also need a reliable bathroom scale. Digital scales are fine as long as the batteries are good.

Problem solving food items is one of the real keys to learning calories and understanding your daily needs. After people have kept records for a short time, they can begin to understand their eating behavior and begin to make the choices that help in the ultimate goal of calorie balancing.

Daily food records should be kept in a single unit, like a steno pad, a small notebook, or even a calendar book. You will discover a system convenient for you. See Appendix 5 for a sample food record.

Here are the basics that should allow you to use the information to your best advantage once you start keeping records:

Date Day Time Cue Type Amount Calories C/F . . . .E.C./P.A.

1. Date/Day—self explanatory.

2. Time—approximate time. Can help isolate "problem" times during the day.

3. Cue—this has allowed many people to get in touch with the reasons they eat (e.g., "lunch hour," "saw food on table," "T.V. commercial" or "hunger").

4. Type—this can include the method of preparation as well as the kind of food (e.g., broiled chicken or whole wheat toast).

5. Amount—listed according to estimated ounces, tablespoons or cups that correspond with the measurements on the calorie charts.

6. Calories—figured from charts in Appendix 2.

7. C/F (Cumulative frequency)—this column represents the running total of calories for the day. This is a very important factor if you are going to eat at maintenance calories or are planning an under-eating day. Don't forget that overeating days are not planned, but they happen. So write them down.

8. E.C./P.A.—records the exercise or physical activity calories completed for the day.

A typical food record would look like the chart on page 180.

The commitment to *do* the food records and to transfer the information onto the Calorie Tally Sheet (CTS) is very important, but the ability to *use* the records is the reason why they work.

For example, a person who has regained seven pounds must first convert that gain into a number. Seven pounds = 24,500 calories (7 × 3500). That is a workable number. The way that number can be lowered is by working out a series of undereating strategies that can begin to chip away at the total excess. Many people figure their CTS like they do their check book. They determine whether they have any deficit calories in the "bank" or if they are "overdrawn" and need to begin a period of "pay back" that will once again balance the overall total.

Now if the person, who is trying to maintain a weight of 165 pounds, uses his CTS to help him work on the excess 24,500 calories this might be the plan: 1. Undereat 500 calories two days during the week; 2. Eat at maintenance calories during other days; 3. Increase exercise by 100 calories

Date	Day	Time	Cue	Type	Amount	Calories	C/F	E.C./P.A.
2	Mon.	6 AM						1.5 walk 250
		7 AM	Time	W/W Toast	2 oz.	130	130	
				Rasp. Jam	1 T.	50	180	
				Wh. Chex	2 oz.	220	400	
				2% Milk	8 oz.	140	540	
				Sanka	10 oz.	—	540	
		11 AM	Break	Orange	6 oz.	60	600	
				Grapes	5 oz.	100	700	
		2 PM	Lunch Mtg.	Fr. Onion Sp.	8 oz.	50	750	
				W/W Bread	2.5 oz.	160	910	
				Turkey	3 oz.	150	1060	
				Mustard	1 t.	5	1065	
				L & T	—	15	1080	
				Iced Tea	10 oz.	—	1080	
		9 PM	Hunger	Baked Pot (2)	16 oz.	320	1400	
				Cot. Cheese	6 T.	150	1550	
				Melon	16 oz.	80	1630	
				Diet Soda	12 oz.	—	1630	
		10 PM	T.V.	Popcorn (Air)	10 c.	230	1860	

each day. The resulting CTS might look like this at the end of a week:

Date	Day	Weight	Food Calories	Activity Calories
1	M	172	1700	300
	T	171	2500	400
	W	172	1200	400
	TH	173	1700	500
	F	170	3500	500
	S	170	1200	300
	S	171	2200	400
	Weekly Totals		14000	2800

Computations

165 × 12 (Male)	1980
	× 7 Days
Maintenance Calories	13860
+ Activity Calories	2800
Total Calories *Out*	= 16660
Food Calories *In*	14000
Total	− 2660

$$\frac{2660}{3500} = -.76 \text{ pounds}$$

(I lost ¾ pound)

Although the math portion rarely comes out exactly the same as the figures on the scale it does tend to be close. Being able to use the CTS as a tool to confront the excess or deficit total is important. Some people simply choose to go back to the fasting phase for a day or two until they learn more about problem solving.

181

CHAPTER XXVI

AFTER THE FAST

Remember that after the fasting phase your body will be sensitive to increased carbohydrates and sodium. Therefore, expect your weight to vary from the water fluctuations until you have stabilized. This usually occurs within 3-4 weeks.

Since you will be starting to eat at maintenance calories soon, start thinking about implementing your plans for that time. Avoid alcohol, raw vegetables, fatty and highly spiced foods, as they may make you ill. Use your knowledge of measuring portion sizes and calories.

Eating is a learned behavior that is not easily forgotten. There were periods in most people's lives when they didn't smoke or drink, but eating from hand to mouth has been a part of daily living since we were weaned from the bottle. We have never had a case of someone not being able to begin normal eating after the fast, but if you do, consult your doctor!

Often a mild anxiety precedes this phase of the program. By practicing the program fundamentals of problem solving, record keeping, exercise, nutrition, environmental management, and confrontation of both avoidance and failures while you are doing the fasting phase, you will be able to make an easy transition to the maintenance phase.

It is our hope that you will be able to remain in the fasting phase until you reach your goal weight. However, there are a few reasons that might require you to refeed prior to that time.

1. You develop individual medical problems, either related to or unrelated to the fast.

2. You lose significant weight and decide to go off the fasting phase prior to attaining your goal weight.

During the first week you should steer clear of fatty or highly spiced foods. This helps the digestive system readjust to increased amounts of food in a gradual and less gaseous manner. Raw vegetables and high fiber foods should also be avoided in the beginning, allowing the lower intestine to refill with minimal abrasiveness. Alcohol should also be avoided until the digestive tract has stabilized.

Sticking with easily digested foods like low fat broiled fish and poultry, cooked vegetables, low fat soups, and soft fruits will make the process a snap.

You can gradually add more calories to your daily intake until you have reached your maintenance levels. Now, you are ready for beginning your self-management program. It is extremely important to continue with your food records and Calorie Tally Sheet for a minimum of two months. It will take at least that amount of time to develop and practice the calorie balancing system that is going to work for you. I have not worked with anyone who succeeded in long term weight maintenance who failed to keep records.

CHAPTER XXVII

WHAT DO YOU DO
WITH THE NEW YOU?

Losing a significant amount of weight can be almost the same as being born again into a new body. Many people in our program report experiences that are similar to those occurring during adolescence: high energy levels, increased self-confidence, band wagon sex lives, pride in their appearance, and improved mental outlook.

Professional people in the psychological field call these feelings "latency." Really, what it boils down to is either the reexperience or the initial experience of things that others who have never had to live with a weight problem call "normal" living. Coping with some of these latency feelings can be difficult and even a bit frightening.

When a young girl in her early twenties is asked out on a date for the first time; that's exciting. A young man proudly wears his first pair of designer blue jeans at age 23, with a wall-to-wall smile. A divorced person attends a singles dance after years of solitude. A woman finds flowers on her desk at work with a card from a secret admirer.

We've seen marriages and pregnancies occur when perhaps a year previous they were not even part of the person's wildest dreams or desires. Unfortunately, we've also seen a few divorces.

Most people are able to adjust rapidly to their new body image, but it takes many months for the mind's eye to readjust to what the new body actually looks like. Sometimes it seems that we have a lot of people living at their maintenance weights of 120 or 160 pounds but contending with a brain that still thinks it inhabits a 200- or 250-pound body.

Over the period of the first 12-18 months of living at your maintenance weight you should gradually gain the skills and confidence to begin readjusting your own mental image to conform to the new total you. Patience and persistence are important during this period. Also, consulting a professional therapist might be a wise choice if things really get too confusing.

Expect good things to happen and I am sure they will. Plan for good things to happen and I *know* they will. Enjoy your new you and don't forget to share yourself with others.

APPENDIX 1

GUIDELINE FOR GOAL WEIGHTS
AND MAINTENANCE CALORIES

WOMEN

Height	Ideal Weight	Weight Range	Ideal Weight Maint Calories Daily/Weekly
4'10"	96	86-115	1056/7392
4'11"	100	90-120	1100/7700
5'0"	103	93-124	1133/7931
5'1"	107	97-128	1177/8239
5'2"	110	100-132	1210/8470
5'3"	114	104-137	1254/8778
5'4"	117	107-140	1287/9009
5'5"	121	111-145	1331/9317
5'6"	124	114-149	1364/9548
5'7"	128	118-154	1408/9856
5'8"	131	121-157	1441/10,087
5'9"	135	125-162	1485/10,395
5'10"	138	128-166	1518/10,626
5'11"	142	132-170	1562/10,934
6'0"	145	135-174	1595/11,165
6'1"	149	139-178	1639/11,473
6'2"	152	142-182	1672/11,704

MEN

Height	Ideal Weight	Weight Range	Ideal Weight Maint Calories Daily/Weekly
5'2"	120	111-145	1440/10,080
5'3"	125	115-150	1500/10,500
5'4"	129	119-155	1548/10,836
5'5"	133	123-160	1596/11,172
5'6"	137	127-164	1644/11,508
5'7"	141	131-169	1692/11,844
5'8"	145	135-174	1740/12,180
5'9"	149	139-179	1788/12,516
5'10"	153	143-184	1836/12,852
5'11"	157	147-188	1884/13,188
6'0"	161	151-193	1932/13,524
6'1"	165	155-198	1980/13,860
6'2"	169	159-203	2028/14,196
6'3"	173	163-208	2076/14,532
6'4"	177	167-212	2124/14,868
6'5"	181	171-217	2172/15,204
6'6"	185	175-222	2220/15,540

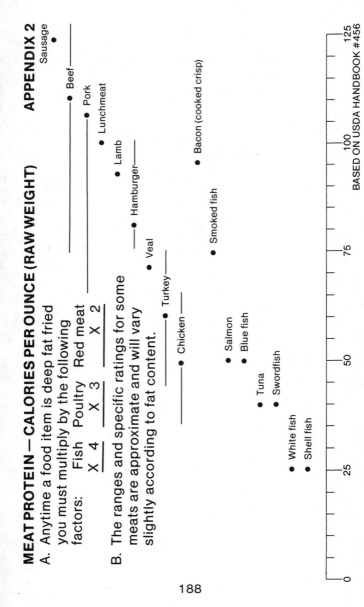

MEAT PROTEIN — CALORIES PER OUNCE (RAW WEIGHT)

APPENDIX 2

A. Anytime a food item is deep fat fried you must multiply by the following factors:

Fish	Poultry	Red meat
X 4	X 3	X 2

B. The ranges and specific ratings for some meats are approximate and will vary slightly according to fat content.

BASED ON USDA HANDBOOK #456

- Sausage
- Beef
- Pork
- Lunchmeat
- Lamb
- Hamburger
- Bacon (cooked crisp)
- Veal
- Turkey
- Smoked fish
- Chicken
- Salmon
- Blue fish
- Tuna
- Swordfish
- White fish
- Shell fish

Scale: 0 — 25 — 50 — 75 — 100 — 125

188

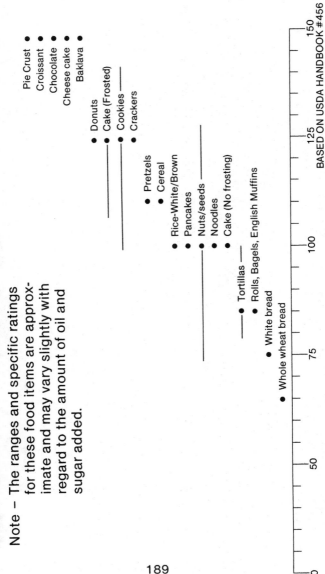

GRAIN PRODUCTS — CALORIES PER OUNCE

Note – The ranges and specific ratings for these food items are approximate and may vary slightly with regard to the amount of oil and sugar added.

Pie Crust
Croissant
Chocolate
Cheese cake
Baklava

Donuts
Cake (Frosted)
Cookies
Crackers

Pretzels
Cereal
Rice-White/Brown
Pancakes
Nuts/seeds
Noodles
Cake (No frosting)

Tortillas
Rolls, Bagels, English Muffins

White bread

Whole wheat bread

50   75   100   125   150

BASED ON USDA HANDBOOK #456

0

189

FRUITS — CALORIES PER OUNCE (RAW WEIGHT)

Note – Asterisk(s) indicate how fruit
should be weighed.
*With refuse (skin, seeds, etc)
**Edible portion only

BASED ON USDA HANDBOOK #456

- Watermelon*
- Cantaloupe*
- Lemon*
- Grapefruit*
- Honeydew Melon*
- Lime
- Papaya
- Watermelon**
- Cantaloupe**
- Peach**
- Orange*
- Strawberries**
- Tangerines**
- Grapefruit**
- Apricot**
- Mango*
- Apple*
- Pineapple**
- Pear*
- Banana*
- Raspberry**
- Bosenberry**
- Nectarine*
- Plum*
- Mango**
- Grapes
- Cherries**
- Banana**

190

VEGETABLES — CALORIES PER OUNCE (RAW WEIGHT)

- Avocado
- Sweet Potato
- Corn
- Winter Squash
- Peas
- Potatoes
- Corn on the cob
- Brussel sprouts
- Carrots
- Onions
- Bean sprouts
- Turnips
- Green beans
- Broccoli
- Mushrooms
- Cauliflower
- Spinach
- Cabbage
- Asparagus
- Bell peppers
- Tomato
- Zucchinni
- Celery
- Lettuce
- Cucumber

0   5   10   15   20   25   30   50

BASED ON USDA HANDBOOK #456

191

DAIRY — CALORIES PER OUNCE

Butter/Margarine •

• Cheese

• Cream (heavy)

• Sour cream

• Cream (light)

• Eggs

• Eggnog

• Chocolate milk

• Cottage cheese

• Yogurt

• Whole milk

• 2% Milk

• Skim milk/buttermilk

0   25   50   75   100   200

BASED ON USDA HANDBOOK #456

192

CONDIMENTS — CALORIES PER TABLESPOON

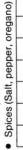

- Liquid oil
- Peanut butter
- Mayonnaise
- Butter/margarine

- Salad dressing
- Maple syrup
- Honey
- Hot fudge
- Whipped cream
- Gravy
- Jam/jelly
- Sugar
- Cream sauce
- Mayonnaise (diet)
- Sour cream
- Flour/corn starch
- Gravy (skimmed)
- Mustard
- Catsup
- Soy sauce
- Horseradish
- Vinegar
- Spices (Salt, pepper, oregano)

0   25   50   75   100   125

BASED ON USDA HANDBOOK #456

193

BEVERAGES — CALORIES PER 8 OUNCE CUP

- Tomato juice
- Buttermilk
- Skim milk
- Soft drinks
- Beer
- Lemonade
- Grapefruit juice
- Orange juice
- Apple juice
- 2% milk
- Whole milk
- White wine
- Cranberry juice
- Grape juice
- Red wine
- Chocolate milk
- Eggnog
- Evaporated milk
- Light cream
- Heavy cream

0   100   200   300   400   800

BASED ON USDA HANDBOOK #456

194

ALCOHOLIC BEVERAGES — CALORIES PER OUNCE

- Beer
- White wine
- Red wine
- Sherry
- 80 Proof liquor
- 90 Proof liquor
- 100 Proof liquor
- 150 Proof Liquor
- Liqueurs

0   25   50   75   100   125

BASED ON USDA HANDBOOK #456

195

PREPARED RECIPES – CALORIES PER 8 OUNCE CUP

Note – Calories are approximate and may vary depending upon the types and amounts of ingredients added.

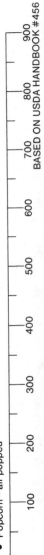

- Nuts
- Gravy
- Sugar
- Ice cream-cream based
- Fruit-dried
- Cheese-noodle
- Meat-beans
- Flour
- Rice-fried
- Pudding
- Soup-cream based
- Meat-noodle casserole
- Beans
- Fruits-canned with sugar
- Rice-white/brown
- Coleslaw
- Pasta
- Ice cream-milk based
- Soup-tomato based
- Soup-water based
- Popcorn – air popped

0   100   200   300   400   500   600   700   800   900

BASED ON USDA HANDBOOK #456

196

Calorie Value Per Minute for Various Physical Activities   APPENDIX 3

Body Weight

Physical Activity	110	120	130	140	150	160	170	180	190	200	210	220	230	240	250	260	270
Archery	3.8	4.1	4.4	4.7	5.0	5.3	5.6	5.9	6.2	6.5	6.8	7.1	7.4	7.7	8.0	8.3	8.6
Badminton, Rec.	4.8	5.1	5.4	5.7	6.0	6.3	6.6	6.9	7.2	7.5	7.8	8.1	8.4	8.7	9.0	9.3	9.6
Baseball	3.8	4.1	4.4	4.7	5.0	5.3	5.6	5.9	6.2	6.5	6.8	7.1	7.4	7.7	8.0	8.3	8.6
Basketball	8.8	9.1	9.4	9.7	10.0	10.3	10.6	10.9	11.2	11.5	11.8	12.1	12.4	12.7	13.0	13.3	13.6
Bicycling, 5 MPH	3.8	4.1	4.4	4.7	5.0	5.3	5.6	5.9	6.2	6.5	6.8	7.1	7.4	7.7	8.0	8.3	8.6
Bicycling, 10 MPH	8.6	9.2	9.8	10.4	11.0	11.6	12.2	12.8	13.4	14.0	14.6	15.2	15.8	16.4	17.0	17.6	18.2
Billiards	1.6	1.7	1.8	1.9	2.0	2.1	2.2	2.3	2.4	2.5	2.6	2.7	2.8	2.9	3.0	3.1	3.2
Bowling, Rec.	2.6	2.7	2.8	2.9	3.0	3.2	3.4	3.5	3.6	3.7	3.8	3.9	4.0	4.1	4.2	4.3	4.4
Bowling, Compet.	4.8	5.1	5.4	5.7	6.0	6.3	6.6	6.9	7.2	7.5	7.8	8.1	8.4	8.7	9.0	9.3	9.6
Calisthenics, Warm-up	2.1	2.2	2.3	2.4	2.5	2.6	2.7	2.8	2.9	3.0	3.1	3.2	3.3	3.4	3.5	3.6	3.7
Calisthenics, Vigorous	3.8	4.1	4.4	4.7	5.0	5.3	5.6	5.9	6.2	6.5	6.8	7.1	7.4	7.7	8.0	8.3	8.6
Canoeing, 4 MPH	5.4	5.8	6.2	6.6	7.0	7.4	7.8	8.2	8.6	9.0	9.4	9.8	10.2	10.6	11.0	11.4	11.8

Body Weight

Physical Activity	110	120	130	140	150	160	170	180	190	200	210	220	230	240	250	260	270
Chopping Wood	4.8	5.1	5.4	5.7	6.0	6.3	6.6	6.9	7.2	7.5	7.8	8.1	8.4	8.7	9.0	9.3	9.6
Dance, Slow	1.6	1.7	1.8	1.9	2.0	2.1	2.2	2.3	2.4	2.5	2.6	2.7	2.8	2.9	3.0	3.1	3.2
Dance, Vigorous	4.8	5.1	5.4	5.7	6.0	6.3	6.6	6.9	7.2	7.5	7.8	8.1	8.4	8.7	9.0	9.3	9.6
Digging	4.8	5.1	5.4	5.7	6.0	6.3	6.6	6.9	7.2	7.5	7.8	8.1	8.4	8.7	9.0	9.3	9.6
Driving, Auto	1.6	1.7	1.8	1.9	2.0	2.1	2.2	2.3	2.4	2.5	2.6	2.7	2.8	2.9	3.0	3.1	3.2
Driving, Truck	2.1	2.2	2.3	2.4	2.5	2.6	2.7	2.8	2.9	3.0	3.1	3.2	3.3	3.4	3.5	3.6	3.7
Dishwashing	1.6	1.7	1.8	1.9	2.0	2.1	2.2	2.3	2.4	2.5	2.6	2.7	2.8	2.9	3.0	3.1	3.2
Football, Rec.	3.8	4.1	4.4	4.7	5.0	5.3	5.6	5.9	6.2	6.5	6.8	7.1	7.4	7.7	8.0	8.3	8.6
Gardening	2.1	2.2	2.3	2.4	2.5	2.6	2.7	2.8	2.9	3.0	3.1	3.2	3.3	3.4	3.5	3.6	3.7
Golf, 4 some	2.7	2.9	3.1	3.3	3.5	3.7	3.9	4.1	4.3	4.5	4.7	4.9	5.1	5.3	5.5	5.7	5.9
Golf, 2 some	3.3	3.6	3.9	4.2	4.5	4.8	5.2	5.5	5.8	6.1	6.4	6.7	7.0	7.3	7.6	7.9	8.2
Horseback Riding, Walk	2.6	2.7	2.8	2.9	3.0	3.1	3.2	3.3	3.4	3.5	3.6	3.7	3.8	3.9	4.0	4.1	4.2
Horseback Riding, Trot	3.9	4.1	4.4	4.7	5.0	5.3	5.6	5.9	6.2	6.5	6.8	7.1	7.4	7.7	8.0	8.3	8.6
Jazzercise, Warm-up	2.1	2.2	2.3	2.4	2.5	2.6	2.7	2.8	2.9	3.0	3.1	3.2	3.3	3.4	3.5	3.6	3.7

Body Weight

Physical Activity	110	120	130	140	150	160	170	180	190	200	210	220	230	240	250	260	270
Jazzercise, Vigorous	4.8	5.1	5.4	5.7	6.0	6.3	6.6	6.9	7.2	7.5	7.8	8.1	8.4	8.7	9.0	9.3	9.6
Kitchen Work	1.6	1.7	1.8	1.9	2.0	2.1	2.2	2.3	2.4	2.5	2.6	2.7	2.8	2.9	3.0	3.1	3.2
Karate	9.6	10.2	10.8	11.4	12.0	12.6	13.2	13.8	14.4	15.0	15.6	16.2	16.8	17.4	18.0	18.6	19.2
Love Making, Warm-up	2.1	2.2	2.3	2.4	2.5	2.6	2.7	2.8	2.9	3.0	3.1	3.2	3.3	3.4	3.5	3.6	3.7
Love Making, Vigorous	3.8	4.1	4.4	4.7	5.0	5.3	5.6	5.9	6.2	6.5	6.8	7.1	7.4	7.7	8.0	8.3	8.6
Making Beds	2.6	2.7	2.8	2.9	3.0	3.1	3.2	3.3	3.4	3.5	3.6	3.7	3.8	3.9	4.0	4.1	4.2
Mountain Climbing	8.0	8.5	9.0	9.5	10.0	10.5	11.0	11.5	12.0	12.5	13.0	13.5	14.0	14.5	15.0	15.5	16.0
Racquetball	7.5	8.0	8.5	9.0	9.5	10.0	10.5	11.0	11.5	12.0	12.5	13.0	13.5	14.0	14.5	15.0	15.5
Rowing, Machine	10.2	10.9	11.6	12.3	13.0	13.7	14.4	15.1	15.8	16.5	17.2	17.9	18.6	19.3	20.0	20.7	21.4
Running, In place 120 steps/min	9.6	10.2	10.8	11.4	12.0	12.6	13.2	13.8	14.4	15.0	15.6	16.2	16.9	17.4	18.0	18.6	19.2
Running, Jog 5 MPH	6.4	6.8	7.2	7.6	8.0	8.4	8.8	9.2	9.6	10.0	10.4	10.8	11.2	11.6	12.0	12.4	12.8
Running, Fast 7 MPH	11.2	11.9	12.6	13.3	14.0	14.7	15.4	16.1	16.8	17.5	18.2	18.9	19.6	20.3	21.0	21.7	22.4
Rope Jumping, 120 RPH	8.0	8.5	9.0	9.5	10.0	10.5	11.0	11.5	12.0	12.5	13.0	13.5	14.0	14.5	15.0	15.5	16.0
Sailing	1.6	1.7	1.8	1.9	2.0	2.1	2.2	2.3	2.4	2.5	2.6	2.7	2.8	2.9	3.0	3.1	3.2

Body Weight

Physical Activity	110	120	130	140	150	160	170	180	190	200	210	220	230	240	250	260	270
Sewing, Machine	2.1	2.2	2.3	2.4	2.5	2.6	2.7	2.8	2.9	3.0	3.1	3.2	3.3	3.4	3.5	3.6	3.7
Shopping	1.6	1.7	1.8	1.9	2.0	2.1	2.2	2.3	2.4	2.5	2.6	2.7	2.8	2.9	3.0	3.1	3.2
Skating	3.8	4.1	4.4	4.7	5.0	5.3	5.6	5.9	6.2	6.5	6.8	7.1	7.4	7.7	8.0	8.3	8.6
Skiing, Downhill	8.0	8.5	9.0	9.5	10.0	10.5	11.0	11.5	12.0	12.5	13.0	13.5	14.0	14.5	15.0	15.5	16.0
Skiing, Cross Country	9.6	10.2	10.8	11.4	12.0	12.6	13.2	13.8	14.4	15.0	15.6	16.2	16.8	17.4	18.0	18.6	19.2
Soccer	7.0	7.5	8.0	8.5	9.0	9.5	10.0	10.5	11.0	11.5	12.0	12.5	13.0	13.5	14.0	14.5	15.0
Stair Climbing	14.0	15.0	16.0	17.0	18.0	19.0	20.0	21.0	22.0	23.0	24.0	25.0	26.0	27.0	28.0	29.0	30.0
Swimming, Back 20 yds/min	3.2	3.4	3.6	3.8	4.0	4.2	4.4	4.6	4.8	5.0	5.2	5.4	5.6	5.8	6.0	6.2	6.4
Swimming, Breast 20 yds/min	3.8	4.1	4.4	4.7	5.0	5.3	5.6	5.9	6.2	6.5	6.8	7.1	7.4	7.7	8.0	8.3	8.6
Swimming, Crawl 20 yds/min	3.8	4.1	4.4	4.7	5.0	5.3	5.6	5.9	6.2	6.5	6.8	7.1	7.4	7.7	8.0	8.3	8.6
Tennis, Rec.	5.4	5.8	6.2	6.6	7.0	7.4	7.8	8.2	8.6	9.0	9.4	9.8	10.2	10.6	11.0	11.4	11.8
Tennis, Compet.	8.0	8.5	9.0	9.5	10.0	10.5	11.0	11.5	12.0	12.5	13.0	13.5	14.0	14.5	15.0	15.5	16.0
Trampoline	6.4	6.8	7.2	7.6	8.0	8.4	8.8	9.2	9.6	10.0	10.4	10.8	11.2	11.6	12.0	12.4	12.8
T.V. Computer Game	0.3	0.3	0.4	0.4	0.5	0.5	0.6	0.6	0.7	0.7	0.8	0.8	0.9	1.0	1.0	1.1	1.1

Body Weight

Physical Activity	110	120	130	140	150	160	170	180	190	200	210	220	230	240	250	260	270
Vollyball, Rec.	3.2	3.4	3.6	3.8	4.0	4.2	4.4	4.6	4.8	5.0	5.2	5.4	5.6	5.8	6.0	6.2	6.4
Vollyball, Compet.	5.4	5.8	6.2	6.6	7.0	7.4	7.8	8.2	8.6	9.0	9.4	9.8	10.2	10.6	11.0	11.4	11.8
Walking, 2 MPH	2.7	2.9	3.1	3.3	3.5	3.7	3.9	4.1	4.3	4.5	4.7	4.9	5.1	5.3	5.5	5.7	5.9
Walking, 3 MPH	3.8	4.1	4.4	4.7	5.0	5.3	5.6	5.9	6.2	6.5	6.8	7.1	7.4	7.7	8.0	8.3	8.6
Walking, 4 MPH	4.9	5.3	5.7	6.1	6.5	6.9	7.3	7.7	8.1	8.5	8.9	9.3	9.7	10.1	10.5	10.9	11.3
Waterskiing	5.9	6.3	6.7	7.1	7.5	7.9	8.3	8.7	9.1	9.5	9.9	10.3	10.7	11.1	11.5	11.9	12.3
Weight Training	6.4	6.8	7.2	7.6	8.0	8.4	8.8	9.2	9.6	10.0	10.4	10.8	11.2	11.6	12.0	12.4	12.8
Yoga	2.6	2.7	2.8	2.9	3.0	3.1	3.2	3.3	3.4	3.5	3.6	3.7	3.8	3.9	4.0	4.1	4.2

DATE	DAY	WT	FOOD CALS	ACT CALS	Computations
	M				
	T				
	W				
	T				
	F				
	S				
	S				
	M				
	T				
	W				
	T				
	F				
	S				
	S				
	M				
	T				
	W				
	T				
	F				
	S				
	S				
	M				
	T				
	W				
	T				
	F				
	S				
	S				

DATE	DAY	WT	FOOD CALS	ACT CALS	Computations
	M				
	T				
	W				
	T				
	F				
	S				
	S				
	M				
	T				
	W				
	T				
	F				
	S				
	S				
	M				
	T				
	W				
	T				
	F				
	S				
	S				
	M				
	T				
	W				
	T				
	F				
	S				
	S				

DATE	DAY	WT	FOOD CALS	ACT CALS	Computations
	M				
	T				
	W				
	T				
	F				
	S				
	S				
	M				
	T				
	W				
	T				
	F				
	S				
	S				
	M				
	T				
	W				
	T				
	F				
	S				
	S				
	M				
	T				
	W				
	T				
	F				
	S				
	S				

							P.A./
DATE	DAY	TIME	CUE	TYPE	AMOUNT	CALORIES	C/F	E.C.

TOTAL FOOD CALORIES _____

TOTAL PHYSICAL ACTIVITY _____

APPENDIX 6

SUGAR CONTENT OF POPULAR FOODS

The approximate sugar content of popular foods in tea-spoonsful of granulated sugar was compiled from current publications of food values:

Candy runs from 75% to 85% sugar. Popular candy bars are likely to weigh one to five ounces, and may contain five to twenty teaspoons sugar.

T = Tablespoon   t = teaspoon

CANDIES

Hershey candy	1 bar	7	t sugar
Chewing gum	1 stick	½	t sugar
Chocolate cream	1 piece	2	t sugar
Butterscotch chew	1 piece	1	t sugar
Chocolate mints	1 piece	2-3	t sugar
Fudge	1 oz. square	4½	t sugar
Life Savers	1	⅓	t sugar
Peanut brittle	1 oz.	3½	t sugar

CAKES AND COOKIES

Angel food	1 (4 oz. piece)	7	t sugar
Cheese cake	1 (4 oz. piece)	2	t sugar
Chocolate cake (iced)	1 (4 oz. piece)	15	t sugar
Cup cake (iced)	1	6	t sugar
Strawberry shortcake	1 serving	4	t sugar
Brownie (unfrosted)	1 (¾ oz.)	3	t sugar
Gingersnaps	1	1-3	t sugar

Macaroons	1	3-6	t sugar
Chocolate eclair	1	7	t sugar
Cream puff (iced)	1	2-5	t sugar
Donut (plain)	1	3-4	t sugar
Donut (glazed)	1	6	t sugar

DAIRY PRODUCTS

Ice cream bar	1	1-7	t sugar
Chocolate sundae	1 dish	14	t sugar
Ice cream soda	1	5	t sugar
Malted Milk shake	1 (10 oz. glass)	7-10	t sugar
Chocolate milk	1 glass	6	t sugar
Eggnog	1 glass	4½	t sugar
Cocoa	1 glass	5	t sugar
Ice cream	⅛ quart	2-3	t sugar

JAMS AND JELLIES

Jelly	1 T	4-6	t sugar
Orange marmalade	1 T	4-6	t sugar
Strawberry jam	1 T	3-4	t sugar

DESSERTS, MISCELLANEOUS

Blueberry cobbler	½ cup	3	t sugar
Custard	½ cup	2-4	t sugar
Apple Pie	1 sl. (1/6 pie)	12	t sugar
Berry Pie	1 slice	10	t sugar
Butterscotch pie	1 slice	4	t sugar
Cherry pie	1 slice	10-14	t sugar
Lemon pie	1 slice	7	t sugar
Pumpkin pie	1 slice(1/6 pie)	5-10	t sugar
Chocolate pudding	½ cup	4	t sugar
Berry tart	½ cup	10	t sugar
Sherbet	½ cup	4-6	t sugar
Gelatin (sweetened)	½ cup	4	t sugar

SYRUPS, SUGARS & ICINGS

Brown Sugar	1 T	3	t sugar
Chocolate icing	1 oz.	5	t sugar
Honey	1 T	3	t sugar

Maple syrup	1 T	2½-5	t sugar
White icing	1 oz.	5	t sugar
Chocolate sauce	1 T	4½	t sugar

BEVERAGES

Soft Drinks	1 bottle (12 oz.)	9	t sugar
Gingerale	6 oz. glass	3⅓	t sugar
Sweet Cider	6 oz. glass	4½	t sugar

CANNED FRUITS AND JUICES

Canned fruit juice (sweet)	½ cup	3-4	t sugar
Canned peaches	2 halves & 1 T syrup	3½	t sugar
Pineapple juice	½ cup (unsweetened)	2½	t sugar
Grapefruit juice	½ cup (unsweetened)	2	t sugar
Grape juice	½ cup (commercial)	3&⅔	t sugar

DRY FRUITS

Apricots, dried	4 to 6 halves	4	t sugar
Prunes, dried	3 to 4 medium	4	t sugar
Dates, dried	3 to 4 pitted	4½	t sugar
Figs, dried	1½ to 2 small	4	t sugar
Raisins	½ cup	4	t sugar

BREAD AND CEREAL

White bread	1 slice	3	t sugar
Hamburger bun	1 whole bun	3	t sugar
Hot Dog bun	1 whole bun	3	t sugar
Corn flakes	1 bowl & ½ tsp. sugar	3-4	t sugar
Cheerios	1 bowl & ½ tsp. sugar	3-4	t sugar
Wheaties	1 bowl & ½ tsp. sugar	3-4	t sugar

HOW SWEET IS BREAKFAST?
THE SUGAR CONTENT OF READY-TO-EAT CEREALS

Product	Manufacturer	Total Sugar (% dry weight)
Sugar Smacks	Kellogg	56.0
Apple Jacks	Kellogg	54.6
Froot Loops	Kellogg	48.0
Sugar Corn Pops	Kellogg	46.0
Super Sugar Crisp	General Foods	46.0
Crazy Cow (chocolate)	General Mills	45.6
Corny Snaps	Kellogg	45.5
Frosted Rice Krinkles	General Foods	44.0
Frankenberry	General Mills	43.7
Cookie-Crisp, Vanilla	Ralston-Purina	43.5
Cap'n Crunch's Crunch Berries	Quaker Oats	43.3
Cocoa Krispies	Kellogg	43.0
Cocoa Pebbles	General Foods	42.6
Fruity Pebbles	General Foods	42.5
Lucky Charms	General Mills	42.2
Cookie-Crisp, Chocolate	Ralston-Purina	41.0
Sugar Frosted Flakes	Kellogg	41.0
Quisp	Quaker Oats	40.7
Crazy Cow (strawberry)	General Mills	40.1
Cookie-Crisp, Oatmeal	Ralston-Purina	40.1
Cap'n Crunch	Quaker Oats	40.0
Count Chocula	General Mills	39.5
Alpha-Bits	General Foods	38.0
Honey Comb	General Foods	37.2
Frosted Rice	Kellogg	37.0
Trix	General Mills	35.9
Cocoa Puffs	General Mills	33.3
Cap'n Crunch, Peanut butter	Quaker Oats	32.2
Post Rasin Bran	General Foods	30.4
Golden Grahams	General Mills	30.0

Cracklin' Bran	Kellogg	29.0
Raisin Bran	Kellogg	29.0
C.W. Post, Rasin	General Foods	29.0
C.W. Post	General Foods	28.7
Frosted Mini-Wheats	Kellogg	26.0
Country Crisp	General Foods	22.0
Life, Cinnamon Flavor	Quaker Oats	21.0
100% Bran	Nabisco	21.0
All-Bran	Kellogg	19.0
Fortified Oat Flakes	General Foods	18.5
Life	Quaker Oats	16.0
Team	Nabisco	14.1
Grape-Nuts Flakes	General Foods	13.3
40% Bran Flakes	General Foods	13.0
Buc Wheat	General Mills	12.2
Product 19	Kellogg	9.9
Concentrate	Kellogg	9.3
Total	General Mills	8.3
Wheaties	General Mills	8.2
Rice Krispies	Kellogg	7.8
Grape-Nuts	General Foods	7.0
Special K	Kellogg	5.4
Corn Flakes	Kellogg	5.3
Post Toasties	General Foods	5.0
Kix	General Mills	4.8
Rice Chex	Ralston-Purina	4.4
Corn Chex	Ralston-Purina	4.0
Wheat Chex	Ralston-Purina	3.5
Cheerios	General Mills	3.0
Shredded Wheat	Nabisco	0.6
Puffed Wheat	Quaker Oats	0.5
Puffed Rice	Quaker Oats	0.1

Source: Based on an analysis published in 1979 by the U.S. Department of Agriculture of cereals that account for 90 percent of those purchased by Americans.
Note: For a more reasonable balance of nutrients, concentrate on those cereals that contain less than 10 percent sugar. Note that most of these are the brands you grew up with, in contrast to the sugar-laden brands introduced during recent decades. If additional sweetening is desired, garnish your cereal with fresh fruit.

FOODS LOW IN SODIUM
(less than 100 mg per serving)
Emphasize These

Spices, Sauces & Condiments

Unsalted seasonings:

Basil	Oregano	Parsley
Bayleaf	Paprika	Tabasco sauce
Cinnamon	Pepper	Tomato (fresh or paste)
Cloves	Thyme	Vanilla
Curry	Bitters	Vinegar
Dill	Garlic (fresh or powdered)	
Dry mustard	Mint	Most salt substitutes
	Onion (fresh or powdered)	(check with your doctor)

Grains & Cereals

Unsalted grain products:	Noodles	Whole grains
Low-sodium breads and	Puffed rice or wheat	
crackers	Rice	Baked products made
Flour	Shredded Wheat	without salt, baking
Hot cereals (except instant)	Corn tortillas	powder or baking soda
Matzoh	Unsalted popcorn	

Emphasize These (con't.)

Vegetables & Fruits

Fruits
Fruit juices

Unsalted vegetables (except as noted)

Fish, Poultry, Meat & Other Main Dishes

Fresh meat prepared without salt:
Beef & veal
Fish
Lamb

Poultry
Pork
Dried beans cooked without salt or salt pork
Eggs

Unsalted nuts

To control fat, choose lean meats, poultry, fish & beans.

Dairy Products

Cream cheese
Gruyere cheese
Ricotta cheese
Swiss cheese

Unsalted cheese
Cream
Unsalted butter or margarine

Sherbet

To control fat, choose low-fat dairy products; limit butter, margarine & cream.

Use In Moderation

100-400 mg per serving
Lightly salted seasonings:

Gravies

Prepared salad dressings

Use In Moderation (con't.)

Barbecue sauces
Catsup
Chili sauce

Mayonnaise
Mustard
Monosodium Glutamate (MSG)

Steak sauce
Tomato puree or sauce
Worcestershire sauce

Grain products made with small amounts of salt, baking powder, or baking soda:
Breads & rolls
Dry cereals
Biscuits & muffins

Cakes
Cookies
Pastries
Pies
Doughnuts
Pancakes & waffles

Baking soda and baking powder contain sodium. Avoid using large amounts. Baked products using yeast are good alternatives.

Beet greens
Celery
Chard

Lightly salted vegetables:
Canned vegetables
Frozen lima beans

Frozen peas

Fresh shellfish

Salted nuts

Salted peanut butter

Milk
Buttermilk
Cheese (except as noted)

Custard
Ice Cream
Pudding

Salted butter & margarine
Yogurt

211

Beware of These

(over 400 mg per serving)
Salt
Highly salted seasonings:
Bouillon
Lemon-pepper marinade

Salted meat tenderizers
Salt-salt substitute mixtures
Salted spices (garlic salt,
onion salt, seasoned salt)
Soy sauce
Teriyaki sauce

Salted crackers & chips
Salted popcorn

Higly salted grain products:
Commercially prepared
spaghetti & pasta dishes

Instant hot cereal
Pretzels

Highly salted vegetables:
All pickled vegetables
Olives and pickles

Sauerkraut
Vegetable juices

Vegetables with seasoned
sauces

Smoked, cured or pickled
products:
Bacon
Corned beef
Dried meat or fish

Ham
Luncheon meats
Sausages & frankfurters
Fish or meat canned with salt

Frozen dinners
Most commercially
prepared entrees
Packaged or canned
soups

Beware of These (con't.)

American cheese
Blue cheese

Cottage cheese
Parmesan cheese

Roquefort cheese
Processed cheese products

APPENDIX 8

FOODS HIGH IN FIBER

Grains	Portion Size	Calories	Fiber
Rye bread	1 oz.	65	2.0
Whole wheat bread	1 oz.	65	2.4
White bread	1 oz.	75	.5
Graham crackers	1 oz.	110	3.0
Rye crackers	1 oz.	110	3.5

Cereals			
All-Bran	2 oz.	220	18.4
Bulgar	2 oz.	200	6.2
Grape Nuts	2 oz.	220	6.2
Grits, dry	2 oz.	205	6.0
Rolled Oats, dry	2 oz.	250	5.0
Shredded Wheat	2 oz.	200	6.8

Vegetables	Portion Size	Calories	Fiber
Broccoli, cooked	4 oz.	36	2.4
Cabbage, cooked	4 oz. (raw)	28	2.3
Cabbage, raw	4 oz.	28	3.1
Carrots, cooked	4 oz. (raw)	48	2.2
Carrots, raw	4 oz.	48	3.9
Cauliflower, cooked	4 oz. (raw)	32	1.3

Cauliflower, raw	4 oz.	32	1.9
Celery, cooked	4 oz. (raw)	20	2.5
Celery, raw	4 oz.	20	3.2
Corn, cooked	4 oz.	108	4.3
Cucumber	4 oz.	16	1.6
Green beans, cooked	4 oz.	36	2.6
Kidney beans, cooked	4 oz.	200	5.3
Lentils, cooked	4 oz.	200	4.2
Lettuce	4 oz.	16	1.8
Parsnips, cooked	4 oz.	36	5.4
Peas, cooked	4 oz.	96	7.2
Potatoes, cooked	4 oz.	80	3.8
Rice, brown, cooked	4 oz.	100	1.9
Rice, white, cooked	4 oz.	100	.7
Spinach	4 oz.	28	4.0
Squash	4 oz.	100	2.3

Fruits

Apple	4 oz.	60	3.9
Banana	4 oz.	68	2.0
Cantaloupe	4 oz.	16	1.3
Cherries	4 oz.	72	1.3
Grapefruit	4 oz.	20	1.5
Grapes	4 oz.	68	.7
Orange	4 oz.	60	2.2
Peach	4 oz.	40	1.4
Pear	4 oz.	64	2.6
Plum	4 oz.	60	2.0
Strawberries	4 oz.	40	2.3